Silent Messages:

Implicit Communication
of Emotions and Attitudes
Second Edition

Albert Mehrabian

University of California, Los Angeles

Wadsworth Publishing Company
Belmont, California
A Division of Wadsworth, Inc.

Senior Editor: Rebecca Hayden

Production Editor: Pamela Evans

Designer: Cynthia Bassett

Copy Editor: Carol Dondrea

Cartoonist: David Broad

Technical Illustrator: Virginia Mickelson

Silent Messages: Implicit Communciation of Emotions and Attitudes was previously published under the title *Silent Messages.*

Mehrabian, Albert.
    Silent messages.
    Bibliography: p.
    Includes index.
    1. Nonverbal communication (Psychology)
I.   Title.
BF637.C45M44   1981   153.6   80-19662
ISBN 0-534-00910-7

Preface

Our speech-oriented culture is beginning to take note of the profound and overlooked contribution of nonverbal and implicit verbal behavior to the processes of communication. This contribution of our actions and ways of saying things, rather than our words, is especially important since it is inseparable from the feelings that we knowingly or inadvertently project in our everyday social interaction, and since it determines the effectiveness and well-being of our intimate, social, and working relationships. Indeed, in the realm of feelings, our facial and vocal expressions, postures, movements, and gestures are so important that when our words contradict the messages contained within them, others mistrust what we say—they rely almost completely on what we do.

People who have a greater awareness of the communicative significance of actions not only can ensure accurate communication of their own feelings but also can be more successful in their intimate relationships, in artistic endeavors such as acting, or in work that involves the persuasion, teaching, leadership, and organization of others. There are also those who somehow are constantly misunderstood, and others whose social style discourages friendships and causes them to live lonely and isolated lives. Most can benefit considerably from a greater awareness of their social style: the effect it has on casual and brief interactions with others, or its more general effect on their social life.

Politicians on the campaign trail can obtain dramatically different results depending not so much on what they say but on how they say it and on the medium through which they elect to say it. Of two people who are given the same script of a television or radio commerical, one may produce a far more effective message because of a highly arousing and undomineering manner, whereas the other may fail because of a bland vocal or facial expression.

People must select media for delivering messages to the masses according to their idiosyncracies. A politician who relies more heavily on gestures and facial expressions than on tone of voice may make a good showing on television but be less effective on radio.

Distinctly different styles are apparent not only in politics or advertising but also in everyday situations. We may observe strangers conversing socially in a distant group and, without being able to hear their words, can sometimes decide whom we like or dislike or form definite feelings and judgments as to the kinds of people they are. Thus, appearance, and especially nonverbal and speech mannerisms, can contribute significantly to the impression we make.

Our physical surroundings—the props that we almost inadvertently select as the background for our interactions with others—often help foster our particular effective or ineffective manner in relating to others. The furniture arrangement of a professional's office, the architecture of a person's house, or the design of a living room can enhance an already effective way of relating to people, or it can hamper that style or, worse yet, make things even more difficult for someone who has trouble relating to others.

Where do we sit if we enter a lounge and notice a stranger we'd like to get to know? The answer to this simple problem raises a lot of additional questions, some of which will be taken up in Chapter 7 where we examine the environment's contribution to the regulation of implicit messages.

Our discussion will frequently turn to the distinctive roles of implicit behaviors and speech in communication, and point to the more restricted denotative scope of actions relative to words. This narrower scope of implicit behavior is more than adequately offset by its transcultural quality. Consensus among different nationals as to which actions reflect what kind of feeling is far greater than the correspondence of the words they use for the same feeling. It follows that actions are more suitable than words or other abstract symbols for the attempt to develop a limited international language—an enormous task we are only now beginning to undertake.

The present approach to the description of implicit messages is one answer to "How is it possible to have consensus within and sometimes between cultures in using and understanding nonverbal and vocal signals when, unlike language, such matters are hardly ever explicitly discussed or taught?" Only a very few basic dimensions of human emotions are conveyed implicitly. These are variations in pleasure-displeasure, arousal-nonarousal, and dominance-submissiveness. Each of these qualities is in turn related to a basic metaphor that provides the necessary link between the feeling, such as arousal, and the behaviors that can reflect that feeling, such as level of physical actitivy. The shared metaphors (for example, people approach and like pleasant things and avoid and dislike unpleasant things) make it possible to attain consensus in interpreting feelings along each of these three dimensions. In addition, various combinations of these three dimensions allow us to express even the most subtle nuances of feeling.

The first of the three primary feeling dimensions, pleasure-displeasure, requires little definition. Arousal-nonarousal refers to the extent of physical activity and/or mental alertness. Alternatively, it reflects how much someone else, whether for good or bad reasons, is important or in the foreground for us. Nonarousal or low arousal is seen in the withdrawn depressive patient who is oblivious to the people around him. This is contrasted with the high arousal of a very emotional and manic person who readily expresses joy, surprise, or anger.

Dominance-submissiveness refers to a controlling and influential attitude versus a controlled and dependent one. Extreme examples are the dignified postures and movements of a monarch and those of a snob who exudes aloofness; in contrast is the shrinking posture of a weak and submissive person, which almost connotes, "Don't hurt me, please!"

Many people have contributed to make this book possible. I am most grateful to my colleagues and graduate students who worked with me on the experiments that were essential to this effort. I am thankful to Professors Ralph V. Exline, the late John P. Garrison, Robert G. Harper, Ralph B. Hupka, and Young Y. Kim for their very helpful comments and suggestions during the preparation of the second edition of this manuscript, and am especially thankful to Lena Chow who very patiently worked along on the many versions of the first edition.

A. M.

Beverly Hills, California

Contents

Chapter 1

Theoretical Framework*

Defining the Field of Study

This book is about the many implicit, in contrast to verbal and explicit, ways in which people communicate. The designation "nonverbal behavior" will be avoided for our subject of study because, in its narrow and more accurate sense, "nonverbal behavior" refers to actions as distinct from speech, and includes only such phenomena as facial expressions, hand and arm gestures, postures, positions, and various movements of the body or the legs and feet.

The designation "nonverbal behavior," however, has traditionally also referred to a variety of subtle aspects of speech. Examples of such paralinguistic or vocal phenomena are the expressive quality of the voice, including speech errors or pauses, rate, duration, volume, inflection, and pitch [142; 238; 377]. These aspects of speech are not dictated by correct grammar but are rather expressions of feelings and attitudes above and beyond the contents conveyed by speech. We refer to these vocal phenomena as "implicit" aspects of speech.

The field of "nonverbal communication" has also included complex communication phenomena such as sarcasm, where inconsistent combinations of verbal and nonverbal messages take on special significance in subtly conveying feelings.

Additional topics studied under this rubric have included clothing and hair styles; uses of cosmetics and jewelry; style of talking, listening, sitting, walking (as in the case of a person's general social style of interaction); body type (obese, lean, muscular); olfactory and thermal cues, which become important when individuals assume close positions; touching; degree of synchronization of speech and movement, or accenting of speech with gesture; choice of communication media; and environmental props (decor, home style, equipment) with which people surround themselves [64; 161].

It is thus more the subtlety of a communication form than its verbal versus nonverbal quality that determines its consideration within the "nonverbal" literature. Nonverbal behaviors per se form the backbone of this literature. Their subtlety can be attributed to the lack of explicit coding rules for these behaviors in most cultures.

---

*Parts of this chapter have been taken from Mehrabian's *Basic Dimensions for a General Psychological Theory*. Copyright © 1980 by Oelgeschlager, Gunn & Hain, Publishers, Inc. Reproduced by permission.

Verbal cues are definable by an explicit dictionary and by rules of syntax, but there are only vague and informal explanations of the significance of various nonverbal behaviors. There are also no explicit rules for encoding or decoding paralinguistic (or vocal) phenomena, or the more complex combinations of verbal and nonverbal behavior in which the nonverbal elements contribute heavily to the significance of a message.

Both within and between cultures, however, there is some degree of consistency in the use of subtle behaviors to convey a certain state, relation, or feeling (encoding), and in the ability to infer another's state, relation, or attitude from such behaviors (decoding). Although the exact degree of this consistency cannot be established readily because it differs for different people, situations, and types of behaviors, it is nevertheless legitimate to consider such behaviors *communicative*.

The explicit-implicit dichotomy seems quite suited for distinguishing these subtle communication phenomena from verbal-linguistic cues. Usually, an idea or feeling is made explicit with words and remains implicit when the speaker refrains from talking, or says the words in a voice that conveys a subtle or even contradictory shade of meaning. The explicit-implicit dichotomy also reminds us of the idea that the coding rules for verbal-linguistic phenomena are explicit and that the coding rules for subtle communication phenomena are implicit.

This book and the theory it outlines deal with implicit and subtle communications, and we prefer the designation "implicit communication" to the commonly used misnomer, "nonverbal communication," in referring to our subject.

Our Theory

Although there are instances in which implicit behaviors have clearly defined cultural significance, which puts them on a par with words in language (such as the handshake, waving goodbye, thumbing one's nose at someone, or pointing), such occurrences are unusual. It is our thesis that people rarely transmit implicitly the kinds of complex information that they can convey with words; rather, implicit communication deals primarily with the transmission of information about feelings and like-dislike or attitudes. The *referents* of implicit behaviors, in other words, are emotions and attitudes or like-dislike.

Nevertheless, we should place these most important aspects of implicit communication within the broader set of categories noted by various investigators [87; 90; 96; 229; 366]. A case in point is the occurrence of *uh-huh* or head nods in conversations. Along with some investigators [208; 238] we shall focus primarily on how such behaviors convey respect toward, and agreement with, a listener; that is, how they serve as social reinforcers. However, these cues also may be used to regulate another's speech—suggest that the speaker continue, or prompt the listener to take over when the speaker stops talking.

Five major categories of implicit behavior that illustrate some of these other functions have been proposed [96]. The first category, *emblem*, refers to the small class of nonverbal acts that can be accurately translated into words (for example, a handshake, shaking a fist at someone, a smile, a frown). The second category, *illustrator*, is very much a part of speech and serves the function of emphasis. Examples are head and hand movements that occur more frequently with primary-stressed words [83], pointing gestures, or other movements that redundantly draw a picture of the linguistic referent. Included in this category are movements that seem to add punctuation or emphasis, such as pointing with the hand or with a turn of the head, or tracing the contour of an object or person referred to verbally.

The third major category, *affect display*, deals with the function we shall be discussing most. However, instead of focusing on so-called primary affects (happiness, anger, surprise, fear, disgust, sadness, and interest), we shall use a three-dimensional scheme that subsumes these "primary affects," their combinations, and many other affects or emotions. The fourth category, *regulator*, refers to acts that help to initiate and terminate the speech of participants in a social situation [87; 350]. These regulators might suggest to a speaker that he keep talking, that he clarify, or that he hurry up and finish. The last category, *adaptor*, refers to acts that are related to the satisfaction of bodily needs, such as moving into a more comfortable position, or scratching.

Coding Rules

Within the broad framework of communication theory, any communication act involves, on the one hand, a group of symbols and, on the other hand, the referents (objects, events, or relationships) designated by those symbols. Coding rules are used to infer referents from symbols (decoding) and to convey referents through the use of symbols (encoding). Analogously, within the field of implicit communication, the implicit behaviors are the symbols of communication, and the referents are our emotional states and our attitudes, likes-dislikes, or preferences. Coding rules are revealed by studies that, for example, show speech errors increasing in frequency when people become anxious [160, Table 2-3; 231] or when they are uncomfortable because they are lying [267], or show that people stand closer to those they like than to those they dislike [259; 395].

The Three Emotional Response Dimensions

If we were to rest our case with the statement that the referents of implicit communication are feelings and attitudes, likes-dislikes, and preferences, we would hardly have created a useful theoretical base. Even an incomplete list of the various feelings humans are capable of experiencing runs into the hundreds, and there are, in addition, numerous variations in attitudes and preferences. Fortunately, a considerable accumulation of evidence from various fields of psychology points to a very elegant conceptualization of human emotions, attitudes, likes-dislikes, and preferences. Very simply, all emotional states can be described adequately in terms of the three independent dimensions of pleasure-displeasure, arousal-nonarousal, and dominance-submissiveness [275; 280; 301; 325; 354; 355; 358]. These three dimensions, which are both necessary and sufficient for the description of *any* emotional state, are independent of one another, that is, uncorrelated. Further, as we shall see, it is possible to relate a composite measure of attitudes, likes-dislikes, and preferences to these basic dimensions of emotion.

The pleasure-displeasure dimension is defined simply in terms of adjective pairs like happy-unhappy, pleased-annoyed, or satisfied-unsatisfied.

The dimension of arousal-nonarousal refers to a combination of *activity* and *alertness* [273, Chapter 3]. A high state of arousal is one in which the individual is both active and alert (for example, a tennis player who is actively moving about the field and simultaneously planning a strategy while trying to anticipate the opponent's moves). A moderately high state of arousal may involve high alertness but little activity (someone solving a complex mathematical problem) or high activity and low alertness (a jogger who is daydreaming). A very low state of arousal involves low alertness and low activity (such as someone who is comfortably asleep).

Although physiological psychologists have long been interested in the study of arousal [84; 218], they have failed to produce a coherent definition of this dimension or, for that matter, a composite measure for it. Arousal has been measured physiologically with (1) EEG desynchronization, that is, fast EEG activity and a concomitant decrease in alpha waves; (2) measures of the sympathetic nervous activation system—GSR, rise in blood pressure, pupillary dilation; and (3) measures of behavioral activity—respiratory activity, oxygen consumption, pulse rate, muscle tension, and skin temperature. Group (1) taps what we refer to as "alertness"; groups (2) and (3) tap what we refer to simply as "activity."

There has been considerable controversy among physiological psychologists regarding the definition of arousal. The basis of this controversy is that the various measures of arousal noted are either not correlated or exhibit low correlations. Of particular concern is the fact that different individuals habitually exhibit variations in arousal in terms of different clusters of physiological cues [210]: For some, high arousal is evidenced in greater muscle tension, whereas, for instance, others exhibit high arousal by high blood pressure. It has been tempting to hypothesize several (functionally independent) dimensions of arousal, but this solution detracts from the effort to develop a succinct or parsimonious theory and to develop a reliable and valid measure of arousal. Our approach employs a different resolution of the problem, a resolution shared by others in this field [31]. Arousal has been defined theoretically as "how wide awake the organism is, how ready it is to react" [30, p. 48]. More specifically, we define it as a composite of the organism's mental alertness and physical activity levels. This simple dimension has been extremely useful in a large variety of research contexts [280; 300].

The third basic dimension of emotion, dominance-submissiveness, is defined in terms of adjective pairs such as controlling-controlled, influential-influenced, or important-awed. This dimension assesses the degree to which a person feels in power or in control, or feels influential versus weak, controlled, or dominated.

Measures for the Three Emotional Response Dimensions

Since the three dimensions of pleasure-displeasure, arousal-nonarousal, and dominance-submissiveness are of central importance in our theory of implicit communication, it is helpful to consider one set of measures for them (see Table 1-1).

The instructions accompanying Table 1-1 indicate to subjects that each pair of words on a line describes a feeling dimension and that subjects should put a check mark somewhere along each line to show how they feel at the moment.

A numerical scale of +4 and −4 is used to score responses to the

Table 1-1: Verbal Report Measures of the Three Dimensions of Emotional State*

Pleasure

Happy	----:----:----:----:----:----:----:----	Unhappy
Pleased	----:----:----:----:----:----:----:----	Annoyed
Satisfied	----:----:----:----:----:----:----:----	Unsatisfied
Contented	----:----:----:----:----:----:----:----	Melancholic
Hopeful	----:----:----:----:----:----:----:----	Despairing
Relaxed	----:----:----:----:----:----:----:----	Bored

Arousal

Stimulated	----:----:----:----:----:----:----:----	Relaxed
Excited	----:----:----:----:----:----:----:----	Calm
Frenzied	----:----:----:----:----:----:----:----	Sluggish
Jittery	----:----:----:----:----:----:----:----	Dull
Wide-awake	----:----:----:----:----:----:----:----	Sleepy
Aroused	----:----:----:----:----:----:----:----	Unaroused

Dominance

Controlling	----:----:----:----:----:----:----:----	Controlled
Influential	----:----:----:----:----:----:----:----	Influenced
In control	----:----:----:----:----:----:----:----	Cared-for
Important	----:----:----:----:----:----:----:----	Awed
Dominant	----:----:----:----:----:----:----:----	Submissive
Autonomous	----:----:----:----:----:----:----:----	Guided

*For additional work on the measurement of the three emotional state dimensions, see [280, Chapter 4]. Requests for a complete set of scales, administration instructions, scoring procedures, and norms should be addressed in writing to Albert Mehrabian.

items. For the pleasure-displeasure dimension, check marks in the extreme left-hand spaces (that is, extremely happy, pleased, and so on) are assigned a score of +4; checks in the adjacent spaces, +3; those in the center spaces, 0; and so forth to the extreme right-hand spaces (extremely unhappy, annoyed, and so on), where check marks are assigned a score of -4. Similarly, for the arousal-non-arousal dimension; check marks in the extreme left-hand spaces receive a score of +4, and so on to the extreme right-hand spaces, which receive -4. Responses to the dominance-submissiveness items are similarly scored. A subject's responses are averaged across the six items in each category to obtain an overall pleasure score, an overall arousal score, and an overall dominance score.

In actually administering these measures, three items within each group are inverted to control for response bias, and the items from each of the three groups are alternated.

Using these measures, three studies were conducted in which subjects rated their emotional states in different situations [301]. Across the three studies, pleasure-displeasure correlated -.01 with arousal-nonarousal, and .16 with dominance-submissiveness; arousal-nonarousal correlated .12 with dominance-submissiveness. These small magnitudes of correlation among the three basic dimensions of emotion support our assumption that the dimensions are, in principle, independent of one another. In general, then, knowledge of a person's emotional state along any one of the three dimensions tells us very little or nothing about how he feels along the other two dimensions.

For a broad and heterogeneous set of situations [299, Appendix A], norms for subjects' pleasure, arousal, and dominance levels are given in Table 1-2.

The norms in Table 1-2 can be used to assess the significance of any particular set of scores obtained from a subject in a situation. For instance, a subject who reports a pleasure level of 3.81, arousal of −2.52, and dominance of zero, is showing extremely high pleasure (two standard deviations above the mean), extremely low arousal (two standard deviations below the mean), and an average level of dominance-submissiveness (no deviation from the mean).

The Semantic Differential

The measures of Table 1-1 evolved from an extensive research base provided by Charles Osgood and his colleagues [325; 326; 381]. In attempting to describe the most general aspects of meaning in language, these investigators found that about one-half the significance of any verbal concept is contained in the following three dimensions of the semantic differential: evaluation (good-bad, beautiful-ugly, pleasant-unpleasant), activity (active-passive, fast-slow), and potency (large-small, strong-weak, heavy-light). Various combinations of these three dimensions can be used to describe any specific concept. For instance, "earthquake" is very low on evaluation, very high on potency, and moderately high on activity (that is, it is unpleasant, powerful, and moderately active). "Baldness" is very low on all three dimensions, thus explaining extreme concerns with this situation. The feeling of "envy" is very low on evaluation but only slightly low

Table 1-2: Norms for the Three Measures of Emotional State*

	Mean	Standard Deviation
Pleasure-displeasure	.55	1.63
Arousal-nonarousal	.30	1.41
Dominance-submissiveness	−.01	1.46

*Note: These norms refer to −4 to +4 response scales for each measure.

on potency and activity. In other words, envy is judged as unpleasant but only slightly impotent and inactive. People, then, can readily characterize any concept in terms of these three basic dimensions, and when they do, about 50 percent of the meaning implied by the concept is conveyed.

Given our more recent findings on the description of emotional states [280, Chapters 2 and 3], we can now examine the Osgood et al. findings and suggest why the three semantic differential dimensions are so important for the characterization of concepts. These dimensions are the *common denominators* in our experience of things, events, and people; they refer to basic feelings. Evaluation permits us to make the crucial judgment of whether someone or something gives us pleasure or displeasure. Our judgment of someone or something as active rather than passive reflects how alive and aroused it is. Living things, especially people and animals, of course, are much more active and aroused in reaction to us than inanimate objects. We need to be more concerned in our everyday transactions with things that are changing and somehow reacting to us than with static entities. Thus, the greater activity of things that stimulate us and arouse us to respond is a very basic element of our reaction to the environment [300]. Finally, potency informs us about the power someone or something has and can exert over us, or vice versa, thereby providing a much needed clue for intelligent dealings. For instance, something that is evaluated negatively and as powerful is much more of a threat than one that is evaluated negatively and as weak.

In short, our judgments of objects, events, or people on the three dimensions of evaluation, activity, and potency are very basic, fundamental aspects of our cognitive functioning. Such cognitive decisions are for the most part automatic rather than deliberate, and may be viewed as emotional-connotative associations we have to various things and happenings in our lives [323, pp. 166–168]. Thus, our three dimensions of emotional reaction are simply the emotional response correlates of the three semantic differential dimensions. Pleasure-displeasure is the emotional counterpart of positive versus negative evaluation; an object that is evaluated positively gives us pleasure, and one that is evaluated negatively gives us displeasure. Arousal-nonarousal is the emotional counterpart of judging something as active versus passive; an object that is active makes us feel aroused; one that is passive or inactive elicits lower arousal [300]. Dominance-submissiveness is the emotional counterpart of judging something as potent versus impotent; an object that is potent makes us feel submissive; one that is impotent makes us feel dominant.

If the three dimensions of emotional reaction are necessary and sufficient for the characterization of all emotional states, then (1) we need all three dimensions, that is, all three are *necessary* for an adequate characterization of every conceivable emotional state; and (2) no more than these three dimensions are needed for an adequate characterization of any conceivable emotional state, that is, the three dimensions are *sufficient*.

Both of these assertions were tested in two studies [358]. In the first study, forty-two verbal-report measures of emotional state were explored as functions of the three dimensions of pleasure-displeasure, arousal-nonarousal, and dominance-submissiveness. The results showed that almost all of the reliable variance in the forty-two scales could be explained in terms of the three dimensions. Thus, the three basic dimensions of emotional response were sufficient for describing a wide sample of emotional states as measured by forty-two scales devised by investigators. A second study employed the scales given in Table 1-1 to obtain ratings of 151 emotion-denoting terms (which is tantamount to the definition of those terms) on the three emotional response factors. Subjects, for example, rated the meaning of "fear" by placing appropriate check marks on each of the eighteen items in Table 1-1.

Representative results of this second study showed that a combination of high pleasure and high arousal yields emotions such as elation or excitement; high pleasure and low arousal yields relaxation or contentment; low pleasure and high arousal yields anxiety or anger; low pleasure and low arousal yields boredom or depression. The combination of a dominant versus submissive feeling with each of these four broad categories of emotional state yields additional refinements. Thus, among the low pleasure and high arousal states, those associated with dominance represent anger and are distinguished from those associated with submissiveness, which represent anxiety or fear. Among the high pleasure and high arousal states, those associated with dominance are exemplified by feelings of vigor or power whereas those associated with submissiveness are exemplified by feelings of infatuation or surprise.

Table 1-3 provides some additional examples of the eight emotional state categories that result when each of the three emotional state dimensions is dichotomized and all possible combinations of high versus low pleasure, high versus low arousal, and high versus low dominance are considered.

We have examined this issue of the basic dimensions of emotional reaction in some depth because the experimental findings described help to simplify the study and description of implicit communication. The major theoretical assertions so far are that (1) the bulk of the referents of implicit communication are emotions and attitudes,

Table 1-3: Examples of the Eight Emotional State Categories That Result When Each of the Three Emotional State Dimensions is Dichotomized*

Arousal	High Pleasure		Arousal	Low Pleasure	
	Dominant	Submissive		Dominant	Submissive
High	bold	amazed	High	cruel	humiliated
	creative	infatuated		hateful	pained
	vigorous	surprised		scornful	puzzled
	powerful	impressed		disgusted	unsafe
	admired	loved		hostile	embarrassed
Low	unperturbed	consoled	Low	uninterested	lonely
	untroubled	sleepy		uncaring	unhappy
	& quiet				
	untroubled	tranquilized		unconcerned	bored
	relaxed	sheltered		blasé	sad
	leisurely	protected		uninterested	depressed
				& proud	

*Reprinted with permission of publisher from: Mehrabian, A. Effect of emotional state on alcohol consumption. *Psychological Reports*, 1979, *44*, 271–282.

likes-dislikes, or preferences, and (2) all emotional reactions can be described concisely in terms of various combinations of pleasure-displeasure, arousal-nonarousal, and dominance-submissiveness.

The Relation Between Emotional Reactions and Preferences

We can now describe what is meant by attitudes, likes-dislikes, and preferences, and examine the relations of these to various emotional states. Attitudes and preferences refer to the extent to which we like versus dislike a person, an object, or an event. Positive attitude and preference mean liking; negative attitude and lack of preference mean dislike. Henceforth in our discussion, we shall use the more generic term "liking" to refer to positive attitude, liking, and preference; and "dislike" to refer to negative attitude, dislike, and lack of preference. Justification for such a grouping is provided by experimental data [278; 299, p. 140].

Figure 1-1 summarizes part of the relationships between emotional reactions and liking. The relationships shown are a somewhat simplified version of findings reviewed and reported elsewhere [171; 273, Chapter 3; 280, Part II; 303; 356; 357; 359; 360]. Note that when an object or person elicits pleasure, there is a positive correlation between the arousing quality of that object or person and its liking—that is, the more arousing a pleasurable entity is, the more it is liked.

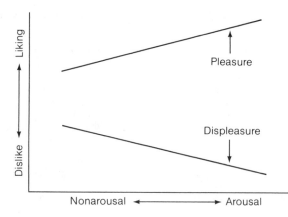

Figure 1-1: The Relations of Pleasure-Displeasure and Arousal-Nonarousal with Degree of Liking*

When an entity elicits displeasure, there is a negative correlation between the arousing quality of that entity and its liking—the more arousing an unpleasant entity is, the less it is liked.

Additional findings from studies of social interaction [302] show a third and more complicated relationship involving dominant-submissive feelings. The relationships shown in Figure 1-1 between pleasure-displeasure and arousal-nonarousal on the one hand, and liking on the other hand, are stronger or more pronounced when a person feels dominant than when he or she feels submissive (see Chapter 7). That is, when people feel dominant, they show more variability in liking of others, situations, and things than when they feel submissive. And when they feel extremely submissive, they show hardly any variation in liking despite large variations in pleasure, arousal, or both.

Numerous implications follow from Figure 1-1, and these will be discussed in later chapters. The main point here is that a simple set of relationships allows us to infer a person's liking of people and things by knowing her emotional reactions to those people and things; or, conversely, to infer the person's emotional reactions to different people and objects from the liking she exhibits.

A specific definition of implicit communication is now possible. It is an area of study that clarifies the relationships among implicit behaviors and their emotional and attitudinal referents. Major findings in this field can thus be formulated in terms of the relationships

---

*From A. Mehrabian, *Basic Dimensions for a General Psychological Theory*. Copyright ©1980 by Oelgeschlager, Gunn & Hain, Publishers, Inc. Reproduced by permission.

among (1) implicit behaviors and emotions (as defined by the dimensions pleasure-displeasure, arousal-nonarousal, dominance-submissiveness), and (2) implicit behaviors and attitudes (liking).

Metaphors Underlying Implicit Communication

From a very early age, children are taught language. Parents, relatives, and teachers take every opportunity to introduce them to new concepts and to help correct errors in their speech, reading, and writing. However, this is hardly ever the case with implicit communication. There is no systematic effort in this culture, or in most cultures, to try to teach a child how to express his feelings and his likes and dislikes implicitly. It is very puzzling, therefore, that any such thing as implicit communication exists. How is it possible that, despite the absence of any explicitly accepted standards as to what certain behaviors mean, people are still able to understand each other's implicit communication?

Since there are only four major referent dimensions in implicit communication (pleasure, arousal, dominance, and liking), it is conceivable that the codes used to translate these referents into behavior or to infer the referents from somebody else's behavior can be described in a simple and very basic way. Our thesis is that these codes are based on a few metaphors that are a common and important part of human life.

Approach Metaphor   The first of these metaphors is the approach or proxemic metaphor [425]. A basic and transcultural element of human life is that people approach and get more involved with things they like, things that appeal to them; and they avoid things that do not appeal to them or that induce pain and fear [217; 311]. Even an infant lying in her crib, incapable of locomotion, makes grasping movements and bodily reaches for certain things that interest her. These grasping movements subsequently develop into reaching to touch in the presence of another, which is one of the most elementary forms of denoting interest in something or someone else. Later this is freed from emotional connotations and evolves into pointing to underlie the demonstrative adjectives "this," "that," or "those" [269, Chapter 9; 420].

Due to its universal quality, the approach metaphor (that is, people approach liked and avoid disliked things) provides one important framework within which people can translate their actions and expressions into likes-dislikes or vice versa. The metaphor is so pervasive that it takes very little explicit instruction for even children to understand what is meant by certain behaviors or to communicate their own feelings using implicit cues.

There are also many subtle variations of approach-avoidance in speech [see Chapter 8]. For instance, I could say to a visitor, "I have been talking with Jane" or "I am talking with Jane." The second statement is temporally closer and implies greater liking of my activity. Or I could say, "I'm writing this paper for those people ...," versus, "I'm writing this paper for these people ..." Again, the closeness implied by "these" instead of "those" reflects a more positive feeling.

For the first of the three metaphors, then, behaviors relating to likes-dislikes are expressed and understood in terms of the approach metaphor. Approach or closeness in the interaction between two people includes greater physical proximity and/or more perceptual stimulation of the two by one another. Closeness between a person and an object involves greater perceptual availability of that object to the person. Approach indicates preference, positive evaluation, and liking, whereas avoidance indicates lack of preference, dislike, and, in extreme cases, fear. The approach metaphor helps to identify behaviors that are communicative and that relate to expressions of likes-dislikes. These include a closer position to another, touching, turning the head so it is face-to-face with the other person and allows mutual observation, and leaning forward toward another while seated.

Arousal-Activity Metaphor   Life, and the vitality and activity associated with it, provide the metaphor for the communication of the second primary feeling dimension, arousal. Living things, in contrast to inanimate objects, react and change in response to their environments. The reactive and changeable quality of living things is especially highlighted by the rapid changes in animals, as distinguished from slow growth changes shared with plants. These changeable qualities result from the awareness of the surroundings. This particular combination of greater awareness of the environment and the adaptive change associated with it is encompassed in the concept of arousal.

Arousal is probably the most basic way in which humans convey their feelings. It covers the gamut of behavior from sleeping to a manic state. Thus, arousal is the basic act of emotional reaction to one's environment and can be either positive or negative in quality.

In discussing Mythical thought, Ernst Cassirer [58] described the concept of *Mana*, which in many cultures distinguished unusual things and happenings involving strong emotional reactions of fear, surprise, or joy, from everyday and common entities and events. This dichotomy, which is almost universal in Mythical thought, supports our idea that arousal is indeed a basic aspect of human reaction to the world.

The environmental counterpart of high arousal is the interesting, changeable, unusual, and foreground rather than common and background quality of people or events in one's surroundings. We are aroused and change our activity patterns in reaction to unusual things of a pleasant nature or those of an unpleasant, repulsive, or threatening quality [30; 300]. According to Jean Piaget [336], it is this changing and reactive quality of animal life that defines intelligent and adaptive functioning.

In reacting to another person, we shift the direction of our look; our facial expression changes; and we converse, which in turn involves how fast we speak, our vocal expressiveness (fluctuations in the tone of voice), and our speech volume. So arousal is indexed in part by the amount of change in our facial and vocal expressions, the rate at which we speak (number of words per minute), and the volume of our speech. The combination of an expressive voice and face and rapid high-volume speech—high arousal—can be associated with feelings as diverse as anger and attempts at persuasiveness. In contrast, a person who is physically exhausted and who is incapable of any of these behaviors is in a low arousal state.

People are more aroused by and are more responsive to strange, novel, and changing things than they are to familiar and static entities [280, Chapter 8; 300]. Some experimenters have suggested that we tend to synchronize our movements and speech with those of people with whom we interact [65; 66; 196]; this implies that in synchronizing with an active speaker we tend to become aroused. Recent findings have disproven the general idea of interactional synchrony, however [243], and thus tend to rule out synchronization of speech and movements as the mechanism of arousal. Nevertheless, even without specific copying or imitation of another's speech or movement rhythms, we are still more aroused by more changeable and unexpected events and situations, including persons [300].

Power Metaphor   For the third dimension, dominance-submissiveness, the communication codes seem to be based on a power or fearlessness metaphor. Power coexists with large size (for example, strutting versus shuffling, expansive versus small and controlled postures and movements), height (for example, standing upright versus bowing). Fearlessness is also part of the power metaphor and is used in various cultures to convey a higher status. A person who is not afraid is more likely to turn her back on others. That is, she tends to be more relaxed and less vigilant in the presence of others who are weaker and have reason to fear her. The latter are more watchful, observant, and alert; they are less relaxed or more tense (for example, standing rather than sitting; erect rather than leaning or reclining).

More generally, any combination of postures and movements that implies power and strength can become part of some culture's accepted mode of the show of status. However, strength need be shown only occasionally to maintain status; so, persons of high status are simply more relaxed and less fearful most of the time. Even though the specific behaviors involved are different in different cultures, the underlying metaphor is the same—power. Detailed experimental findings on the various implicit manifestations of dominance-submissiveness and the consistency of these with the power metaphor are noted in Chapters 3 and 4.

Metaphors—Shared but Implicit   Metaphorical expressions of liking, arousal, and dominance are only sometimes formalized and explicitly taught in a culture. For example, in the Middle East, students are taught to stand up when a teacher enters a classroom or when they address him. In the Orient, we would have no trouble getting an explanation of the significance of bowing and its relation to status. In this culture, most people would agree that it is impolite to put one's feet on somebody else's office desk, particularly when that person is in a prestigious social position. Nevertheless, the coding rules for implicit behavior and the metaphors that underlie them are not systematically discussed or taught. We do not have a dictionary that defines our implicit behavior, and we certainly do not have a corresponding grammar. The metaphors that have been described can be viewed as a set of guidelines for discussing implicit behavior.

We can appreciate the important function of these metaphors when we consider that any behavior that is observable can serve as an outlet for feelings and is thus, in principle, communicative. Behaviors as diverse as the eye blink, crossing of legs while seated, postures, gestures, head nods, facial and vocal expressions, tension in the muscles, and twitches are all potentially significant in communication, although of course some are more communicative than others (for example, facial expressions compared to foot movements). One of the biggest stumbling blocks in the study of communication is precisely this fact; there are so many behaviors we can observe and study [75; 83; 94; 160; 365; 367] that it becomes difficult to know where to start, what to exclude, or how to order the priorities. In desperation, some investigators turned to a physical characterization of movements. Ray Birdwhistell [33; 34; 35] described movements of each body part in terms of their width, extent and velocity. In dance, where we would expect at least some reliance on feeling and intuition for describing movements, it is discouraging to find that the only comprehensive system of notation describes movements merely as motion, with no reference to what the movements signify [177]. Such reliance on physical description alone for implicit behavior is inadequate. It fails to take into account the similar significance of unlike movements that emanate from different body parts (for example, approval given with a head nod or a pat on the back). Even more importantly, it fails to provide a direction for identifying significant implicit behaviors.

Consideration of the underlying metaphors shows that descriptions of implicit behavior need not be physicalistic and arbitrary. Despite the absence of dictionaries and grammar for implicit behavior, there is a consensus among the people of one culture and even people of different cultures [6; 73; 92; 97; 98; 99; 353; 404; 405] as to how they translate their feelings into behaviors or infer other people's feelings from others' behaviors. This consensus supports our thesis that the codes are based on implicit and universal metaphors that are basic parts of human experience.

Types of Experimental Method Used in Studying Implicit Communication

Basically, there are two complementary avenues for experimentally studying implicit communication phenomena. In the first, *decoding*, subjects are presented with prepared stimuli (for example, photographs of different facial expressions or of different postures) and are instructed to infer feelings and likes-dislikes from those stimuli. Such a method is advantageous since it allows a comparison of the effects of a number of cues, singly or in combination, on the inferences made by subjects. For instance, photographs of various postures can be prepared that systematically combine three degrees of postural tension (tense, moderate, relaxed) with each of three degrees of bodily orientation toward the addressee or subject (facing the subject directly, facing away at a small angle, facing away at a large angle). The decoding method also allows the study and assessment of the relative effects of these cues or experimental factors for various communicator and addressee groups (for example, different sex or personality of individuals shown in the photographs or of the subjects viewing those photographs). Finally, possible confounding effects of other implicit cues that are not the subject of study (for example, verbalizations or gestures, when only postural tension and bodily orientation are of interest) are easily eliminated when the decoding method is used. The stimuli are recorded or prepared so that unwanted cues are excluded or extraneous cues maintained at a constant level. Thus, a decoding method yields considerable information because it makes possible the systematic variation and control of different sets of variables.

In the second method, *encoding*, subjects are placed in experimental situations that elicit different kinds of emotion- or liking-related behavior. Typical encoding methods employ role-playing, in which a subject is requested to assume a certain role toward his or her addressee. For instance, the subject is instructed to interact with a stranger and to posturally (but not verbally or facially) convey different degrees of liking or dislike to that stranger. Or, subjects may be requested to employ any or all of the implicit (but not verbal) cues at their disposal so as to make a stranger like or dislike them. Subjects may also be instructed to assume a stationary posture and position relative to a stranger (without speaking or moving) so as to convey a feeling of dominance or submissiveness to that stranger.

Occasionally studies take advantage of existing likes and dislikes or of known emotional responses of subjects to various others or situations (for example, how subjects position themselves and move about in the presence of a harmless versus a frightening animal). Alternatively, experimental procedures are used to induce likes-dislikes or specific emotional states in the subject and then record the implicit behaviors associated with various emotional state or like-dislike conditions. For instance, a confederate may provide subjects with bogus assessments of their personality based on questionnaires administered to the subjects. The confederate, who poses as an expert in the field of personality description, meets subjects individually a day or two after they have responded to the questionnaires and provides them with detailed and highly complimentary (versus highly derogatory) assessments of their personality. The implicit behaviors of subjects in interacting with this "expert" during a five-minute follow-up period are videorecorded and analyzed.

When an encoding method is used, subjects spontaneously produce a variety of implicit cues. Therefore, in contrast to the decoding method, implicit cues cannot be produced in a systematic and controlled fashion. Nevertheless, the encoding method is particularly valuable for producing a wealth of data, with the relative importance of various implicit cues being determined by the spontaneous behaviors of subjects. Thus, although the encoding method does not lend itself to precise manipulations of the implicit cues (for example, in terms of the factorial designs noted for decoding studies), it is extremely valuable in the beginning stages of implicit communication research.

Almost all research in implicit communication is based on decoding or encoding methods. A third method, which encompasses the major advantages of both these methods, can also be valuable. In one such method, stimuli are prepared as they would be with a decoding method. They are then presented to subjects, who are asked to indicate their *preferences* for using these stimuli in various social situations. There are several advantages to this method. First, if the experimenter prepares stimuli that are inappropriate for the communication of the particular referents being studied, subjects will characteristically show very low preferences for using those stimuli. This informs the experimenter how well suited the stimuli are for the communication of the particular referents—an inference that is not possible when the decoding method is used. Also, this third method allows a systematic control of the communication cues such that factorial designs can be used to study the independent and interactive effects of various cues in determining a referent. An early study [266] illustrates the use of this *encoding-decoding* method.

The encoding-decoding method does not require the experimenter to possess an advanced understanding of the phenomenon being explored. Extensive knowledge is, however, required to prepare an appropriate set of stimuli in using decoding methods. Thus, whereas encoding methods are appropriate in the beginning stages of implicit communication research, encoding-decoding methods are appropriate for intermediate stages, and decoding methods are appropriate during the highly developed phases of such research.

Summary

The field of implicit communication deals with subtle and less explicit expressions of emotions and attitudes. Within a broad communication model, the *symbols* used in implicit communication are nonverbal behaviors; vocal aspects of speech that are not affected by grammatical considerations; and complex combinations of verbal, vocal, and nonverbal behaviors. The bulk of the *referents* in implicit communication are emotions, attitudes, likes-dislikes, and preferences. A review of the available evidence reveals that these referents can be described in terms of pleasure-displeasure, arousal-nonarousal, dominance-submissiveness, and "like-dislike" (a superordinate concept that includes variations in positive-negative attitude, preference, and liking). We can infer a person's emotional reactions to things or persons with some degree of certainty by observing the liking he exhibits to those entities, or we can predict liking from a knowledge of emotional reactions. Within this framework, the field of implicit communication is defined as one where relationships among implicit behaviors (the symbols) and pleasure, arousal, dominance, and liking (the referents) are studied and described.

In relation to the conventions underlying language, those that underlie implicit communication are fewer in number and are more intuitively obvious. We referred to these conventions as the metaphors that allow us to convey varying degrees of pleasure, arousal, and dominance. Even though this seems extremely limited, it is not, since combinations of different degrees of pleasure, arousal, and dominance (and liking, which can be expressed in terms of those three) can result in innumerable shades of feeling and attitude.

Since the codes for understanding and using implicit behaviors are much simpler than those for verbal ones, it is not surprising to find that implicit messages are of paramount importance in the communications of children up to the age of about four [262; 307; 317; 318; 420].

Our analysis of communication in terms of metaphors illustrates their more general function in human thought. Metaphors draw upon the elementary and familiar aspects of sensory-perceptual experience whose rich connotations provide the basis for understanding the novel (as in science) and the unfamiliar (as in learning). Philosophers Ernst Cassirer [58] and Stephen Pepper [335] discussed the function of metaphors in human culture; I have illustrated the specific application of metaphors in social science [252]. Metaphors are also frequently used in art (for example, when the poet likens a human being to a tree) and in the altogether familiar realm of advertising (for example, naming a car "Jaguar" to capitalize on shared impressions of that animal's qualities or associating strength and wild qualities with a beer by giving it the logo of a bull).

Suggested Readings

A concise description of emotional reactions provides the key to the study of implicit communication. The early studies of Osgood and his colleagues [325; 326; 381] made a most significant contribution along these lines. Studies conducted in our laboratory [280, Chapters 2 and 3] drew upon this and related experimental literature and provide the empirical support for the proposed three-dimensional description of emotional reactions. Experimental evidence on the relationships among liking-preference and emotional reactions is given in [280, Part II]. The following sources contain classifications and discussions of implicit behaviors in relation to emotions: [124; 130; 145; 261; 270; 324; 372; 407].

Chapter 2

Liking and Approach

General Framework

An individual's degree of like-dislike for various people, events, or objects is one of the four major referents of implicit communication. The inference of liking from implicit behaviors is straightforward: People approach what they like and avoid what they don't like; that is, there is a positive correlation between various approach behaviors and level of liking [217; 311; 425]. This very general and well-supported hypothesis links two sets of phenomena. At one end, as we have seen, the generic concept of "like-dislike" as defined here subsumes variations in preference, positive-negative attitude, as well as like-dislike. At the other end, its positive correlate, "approach-avoidance," subsumes (1) physical approach versus avoidance, as when we move toward or away from a person or an object, (2) degree of attending to and exploration and examination of an entity, as when we pay attention to and explore the statements of another person in contrast to ignoring him or her, and (3) the degree of striving to get close to or away from an entity even though actual movements toward or away are socially inappropriate or unacceptable, as when a bored conference participant turns away from the speaker. Evidence has been provided showing that the various dimensions subsumed under liking and approach are positively correlated [278; 280, Chapter 9; 299, pp. 135–144]. Figure 2-1 summarizes these relationships.

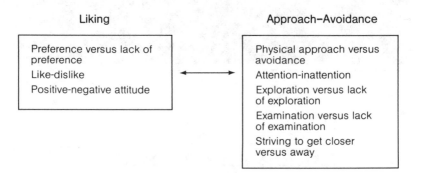

Liking	Approach–Avoidance
Preference versus lack of preference	Physical approach versus avoidance
Like-dislike	Attention-inattention
Positive-negative attitude	Exploration versus lack of exploration
	Examination versus lack of examination
	Striving to get closer versus away

Figure 2-1: The Hypothesized Direct Correlation Between Liking and Approach-Avoidance*

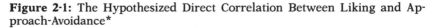

A primary example of the general liking-approach relationship is the well-established finding that people assume closer positions to those they like than to those they dislike. Also, closer positions are assumed to people who are liked more, such as friends versus strangers [2; 5; 53; 55; 85; 105; 150; 216; 219; 250; 254; 256; 259; 287; 331; 395; 398; 400; 430]. There is related evidence showing that psychologically disturbed and physically handicapped people (who generally are likely to have less positive or more negative interpersonal experiences [295]) are approached less and approach others less than normals [201; 202; 216; 417; 418].

When social interaction takes place in close proximity, the frequency or extent of touching can be used as an indicator of approach and therefore of liking. Experiments have revealed that liked others are touched more than disliked (or less liked) persons; also, more touching elicits greater liking and can act as a social reinforcer [36; 122; 167; 168; 188; 189; 190; 204; 315; 332; 379; 422]. The reinforcing effect of being touched by a stranger applies in the case of females, but not in the case of males [122; 421].

Looking at another and establishing eye contact with them is yet another aspect of approach. Although there are some important exceptions, which we will examine in Chapter 3, considerable evidence has been accumulated showing that more eye contact is associated with greater liking and more positive feelings among interactants [43; 63; 69; 89; 107; 108; 110; 113; 141; 143; 194; 195; 254; 256; 259; 287; 334; 352; 401; 406]. Thus, eye contact with, and looking at or observation of, another (which are important elements of abbreviated approach) have evidenced the expected positive correlations with preference, liking, positive affect, and positive attitude.

Implicit verbal behavior—specifically, amount of conversation with another—is also an important indicator of approach and involvement and has been shown to be positively correlated with liking of the individual one converses with. Thus, amount of conversation (measured in terms of number of simple sentences and independent clauses uttered) can be a reliable index of how much the speaker likes the person he or she is addressing [268; 283; 293].

Finally, we should note a somewhat subtle or indirect form of approach that is evidenced when people posturally, gesturally, or vocally imitate one another—that is, make themselves more like another. Generally, in social interaction (which is maintained through exchanges of pleasure and approach cues [294]) people have been shown to imitate each other's vocal behaviors. During interviews, for instance, interviewees tend to imitate the speech length, speech rate, loudness, pause length, and interruption rate of the interviewer. Such imitation of the generally higher status interviewer subtly conveys greater similarity and thus agreement and rapport [182; 237; 319; 416; 426]. Although movement mirroring or synchrony is assumed to occur when peers interact socially [196; 365], such findings have been questioned in recent research [243]. Thus, the implication in all these findings is that copying or imitation is more likely when the other is of higher status or is more influential (such as a therapist who is being imitated by a client). Further, such imitation implies greater liking of, or respect for, the individual imitated [72], and is more likely to occur when a positive or congenial feeling is present, as during periods of rapport in psychotherapy [60; 211; 212].

Some examples may help illustrate the many facets of the relationships incorporated in Figure 2-1. A baby is encouraged to raise its arm and move its fingers in a curling and grasping motion in greeting. Adults often raise an arm forward and up, more or less expansively, when greeting a friend at a distance. As we prepare to terminate a conversation, we may not indicate in words but simply change position by moving forward to a more upright, less relaxed position in a chair—a move in the direction of departure. These implicit messages signal to others a wish to leave, and when the messages are understood and accepted, the discussion draws to a close by mutual consent and without rancor.

An inexperienced gambler betrays too much for his own good at the poker table. Sometimes he places his chips in the middle of the pot; at other times, he places them close to himself, barely touching the pot. Sometimes he sits close to the table; at other times, he leans back and away. Sometimes he moves fast to place his bet; at other times, he moves slowly, with deliberation, and almost reluctantly. In the first of each pair of behaviors, the novice gambler shows a greater approach to the betting situation, thus signifying a greater liking for his hand. A shrewd observer could (and a good poker player does) use such variations to estimate when his opponent has a good hand and when he is less certain of its value (as when he places the chips more toward himself than the pot, when he leans back, and when he places his bet slowly). Expert gamblers, particularly the professionals, know that subtle actions can betray their feelings about the value of the cards they hold. Therefore, a good poker player not only maintains a "poker" face but also always assumes the same posture, always places the chips in the same location as he bets, and always moves at the same speed and with the same decision time. A uniform and neutral set of behaviors guarantees that minimal information is conveyed about feelings. In poker at least, this is wise, because it is difficult to manipulate implicit behaviors; there are too many ways in which information about feelings can be revealed [95; 267].

Of course, most often we do not (or cannot) physically approach things that we like or physically move away from things that we dislike. We do not snuggle up to someone while she is discussing a subject of interest, then stalk away when she turns to uninteresting topics. However, most of us reveal our reactions most of the time. Approach-avoidance behavior comes across in a number of *abbreviated* forms. An abbreviated approach can be expressed by attentive observation or mutual gaze. In response to a remark that appeals to us, we may "approach" by asking questions or leaning forward. In response to discussion we find uninteresting or objectionable, we may "avoid" by remaining silent and leaning back, farther away from the speaker. Whether we look at a speaker or look away while she talks is also a measure of our interest.

The curling and grasping of a baby's fingers in greeting illustrates an abbreviation of grasping, which of course is a form of approach since it indicates a desire to bring the other person closer and implies liking. The lift of a hand in the direction of someone greeted at a distance is not so much an abbreviated grasp, but rather an abbreviated reaching to touch [269, Chapter 9; 420]. Touching is a variant of approach—a very important one—and is indicative of positive attitudes and liking in most instances. This arm gesture that accompanies a called greeting conveys a warmer and more friendly feeling than words alone.

Edging forward in a chair or pushing the chair back when we want to end a conversation can be considered an abbreviated movement of departure. Such abbreviations should make words unnecessary. The change in bodily position alone should be sufficient to clue the other person that we would like to leave.

We also use abbreviated movements of departure in conversations while standing. We move around, away from, and back to the person we are talking with—especially if we are extremely anxious about getting away but feel that we can't say anything about it. The abbreviated walking away signals our desire to leave. More generally, walking about during conversation with another indicates distress, particularly when the facial expression is neutral or negative [268; 293].

We are sometimes forced to remain in a situation with people who are offensive and whose presence becomes nearly intolerable. We avoid their eyes and try not to look in their direction. We may turn to one side [250] and look at various objects in the room or through a window [283], or we may take refuge in meditative silence [294]. Here again, turning away and looking away are abbreviations of the movements associated with leaving; they show our dislike for the people we are with or our dislike for what they say. Physically, we may be confined for a long time with these insufferable people, but our unspoken messages tell of our desire to get away.

Abbreviated approach includes such behaviors as assuming a position close to someone, leaning toward him, touching, reaching out as though to touch (as in a raised hand during a greeting), abbreviated grasping gestures, bodily turning toward him, and looking into his eyes [197]. Also included is talking to someone instead of remaining silent, since when we talk, eye contact and involvement with the other person are increased, whereas when we are silent, we are less likely to have eye contact and are more likely to be preoccupied with other things [268; 347; 348].

Approach involves an increase in the sensory stimulation between two people. When we stand close to someone or talk to her, a great deal more stimulation and information are exchanged than if we were to stand farther away or remain silent.

Approach-avoidance reveals our feelings about things as well as people. In an art gallery, we tend to spend more time with a painting that interests us. We seek the best distance for viewing all of it, and we spend more time looking at it. There is often a temptation to touch sculptures we find appealing. On the other hand, we tend to walk past other exhibits, glancing only long enough to determine that they are of little or no interest. Generally then, we select positions that increase stimulation from objects we prefer or like and try to shut off stimulation from those that do not interest us. Important exceptions to this general positive correlation between approach-avoidance and like-dislike are considered in Chapter 3.

Approach behaviors can be indicative of both transitory feelings and more stable attitudes. By using this concept, we can gain a greater awareness of how we feel toward others and how others feel toward us.

Notice where you choose to sit at a party, at a meeting, in a classroom. When there is ample choice of seats, you probably select a seat close to the person you like best and where you can comfortably have eye contact with him. When you talk in a group, note that you tend to address the people whom you are trying to please, or those whom you like better. In corollary, you probably are more attentive toward these people when they talk [383].

Observe others as they join groups. Where do they choose to sit? If there is a choice of seats, do their selections reveal anything about their preferences among the people already seated? (If an acquaintance who has shared little mutual liking with you selects a seat close to you, watch out! He may be seeking an opportunity to ask a favor!) Can you determine by the way members of a group subtly approach and avoid each other who the socially likable or important people are?

In a conversation group, the person most frequently addressed directly and looked at by speakers is almost certainly the best liked (most preferred, admired, or respected member). In a social group of supposed peers, a person whom nobody addresses or even notices may well feel left out and lonely.

Notice where people look when they are talking and when they are allegedly listening. Notice their postures as they talk and as they listen. How much abbreviated approach and avoidance can you infer from eye contact and posture? How much like and dislike?

The liking-approach correlation has also been subtly, though probably unintentionally, applied in some social rules [337]. For example, the host customarily sits at the head of a long rectangular table. Should he sit at a longer side of the table, he could have eye contact only with the people across from him and could not easily look at those sitting on his side of the table. From the head position at the table, he can distribute his attention more evenly among the entire group. Such attention is of course conveyed in terms of his eye contact and his conversation. Since the people who are seated farthest away from him are less likely to be attended to even with this seating arrangement, the guest of honor, who rates extra courtesies and attention, usually is seated next to the host, customarily to his right.

Observe implicit behavior when you are among strangers at a large party. If you see someone interesting whom you want to meet, casually make your way to a spot within five feet of him (or her) and be alert for nonverbal cues. Eye contact—better yet, a smile—encourages more direct approach. Someone who approaches you, looking in your direction, and not avoiding eye contact, may be trying to find a suitable opening to introduce herself. If you welcome the approach, return her look, and smile at her. If you are not interested, look, or turn, away. Of course, some boors (who may also be bores) will fail to get the message.

Goodbyes and Handshakes

The important and prominent role of implicit messages in the communication of liking in social situations is also evident when people say goodbye to each other. Since departure is akin to avoidance, it usually is easy enough to assess people's likes-dislikes from their willingness to terminate an interaction. In a conversation group, one of the participants may begin to talk less, start looking around, or actually stand up and move about. These signs of restlessness constitute abbreviated departing movements. If a number of participants in the conversation start exhibiting these behaviors, for all practical purposes, the discussion is over.

At the conclusion of a social evening in a private home, the process of saying "goodnight" varies. I have noticed consistent differences among different friends in their handling of this last part of an evening, as hosts or as guests. Some guests repeatedly say, "I've really got to go," but remain seated and keep introducing new topics into the conversation. Others get up abruptly and leave. Some hosts act as though the parting is made with great reluctance. For others, the farewell is always brief, no matter whom they see to the door.

In more or less formal situations, social amenities sometimes make it more difficult to interpret implicit messages. In most unstructured situations, postponement of the actual moment of parting probably does signal genuine reluctance, whereas abrupt departure does indicate less liking of the situation at that point. The amenities dictate that guests in a home exhibit positive enjoyment of the hospitality and that hosts exhibit equally positive delight in the company of guests in the home. The guest who says he must go, then stays on, may be genuinely reluctant to lessen the contact with liked people; however, he may be reluctant only because his host might interpret early departure as an expression of dislike for the hospitality. A host who prolongs farewells may be genuinely reluctant to end the social encounter, or he may be (dishonestly) sending the "proper" signals dictated by the amenities.

While saying goodbye, as in saying "hello," the handshake can also signify different degrees of approach. In cultures in which a handshake is a must when people meet, it is difficult to detect feelings and attitudes from it. However, in the American culture and its many subcultures, customs involving the handshake vary, there being only a few generally accepted rules, such as the following two. The handshake is almost universally obligatory for men at time of introduction, but not at subsequent meetings. It is also the case that very few men or women would refuse to respond to a proffered hand. In situations in which it is not socially dictated, there is considerable variation from one person to another in the willingness to shake hands. Since a handshake involves bodily contact, it is a definite instance of approach to another. Thus an individual's general level of preference for handshakes reflects how positively he feels toward others. Some happy male extroverts gladhand their way through life, shaking hands at every opportunity. Many women reach out selectively—to increase contact with others and thus transmit an attitude of general liking for close, human interaction.

The style of handshake can also be very revealing. A firm handshake is more intense and is indicative of greater liking and warmer feelings, and politicians become quite adept at giving but (to protect their hands) not receiving such. A prolonged handshake involves more approach than a brief one, and in most situations is unacceptable—too intimate to be comfortable. We compensate for unavoidable excessive approach through other simultaneously occurring avoidance behaviors; for instance, when a stranger approaches to a close position, we tend to look away [16; 330]. There is little we can do to compensate for the prolonged handshake; however, we loosen our own grip, and if that cue is ignored, we withdraw our hand.

A loosely clasping hand—or worse, a cold and limp one—is usually interpreted as indicating aloofness and unwillingness to become involved; we tend to react to a shake from this kind of hand with a shuddering thought: "What a cold fish!" The limp handshake generally is interpreted as signaling an unaffectionate and unfriendly nature; we take it as an indication of unwillingness to get involved, emotionally or otherwise. This assumption of a pervasive style that includes explicit and implicit behaviors received support in some of the earliest research on nonverbal behavior [7].

Watch for handshakes as people meet. Are they all mutually spontaneous? If not, can you tell which person initiated the handshake? How do women, in general, differ from men in initiating and responding to handshakes? You may catch aborted handshakes, in which one person starts to offer his hand and withdraws the offer. Can you determine the implicit cues that caused him to withdraw? In what circum-

stances do you spontaneously shake hands, or are reluctant to initiate one? Notice your own reactions to handshakes. How do you think others react to the clasp of your hand?

Dance

It is difficult to describe exhaustively all the behaviors that can draw on the liking-approach relationship. Some examples from dance, however, illustrate the extensive scope of such applications.

In a typical pattern of movement in ballet, one dancer runs away from her partner, taking a position at the farthest corner of the stage with her head turned away from the partner. This pattern, which dramatically shows a desire not only to increase distance from the other but also to avoid any possibility of looking at him, portrays anger or hurt feelings.

Other movements toward or away from others in a dance are used to convey shades of liking that depend on the other qualities that accompany these movements. For example, a slow, lyrical movement toward another person shows warmth and love, whereas a faster and lighter rhythmic approach conveys a happy and more playful feeling. When a dancer playfully moves toward and away from her partner, she conveys the underlying ambivalence that is associated with teasing—the feelings that motivate teasing are a mixture of desire and apprehension.

In a group dance, smooth, flowing movements of the dancers as they come together can show a congenial and harmonious quality that is also associated with warmth. Dancers bunched together in a close group, making short, erratic, percussive movements of the arms, legs, and torsos outward, away from the group but always returning to it, communicate conflict and yet a desire to maintain their close relationship.

Self-disclosure

The tendency to position oneself closer to others and to reveal more of oneself is closely related to a greater tolerance of and preference for intense personal relationships. For instance, in initial psychotherapy interviews, if there is no desk between the therapist and a female patient, some women tug on their skirts in a determined effort to cover as much as possible [95]; and some patients are unable to sustain eye contact and frequently avoid it by looking at the floor. These expressions are blatant announcements to the therapist of a fact he already knows—few patients *want* to reveal themselves in an initial interview.

Our facial expressions, eyes, and postures, in addition to uncovered parts of our bodies, all communicate information about ourselves and tend to intensify interaction [86]. People in the same culture [187; 396], but especially those from different cultures or ethnic groups [14, p. 362; 27; 156, Chapter 11; 413], differ in terms of the amount of self-disclosure they characteristically allow. Some people carefully and consistently guard against such self-disclosure by physically keeping their distance and appearing uninvolved. When forced to be close to others, they look away and sometimes shrink physically from the very threat of contact, giving the impression of acute anxiety and discomfort. Their inability to reveal themselves to others or to seek information from others through eye contact and proximity is indicative of unfriendliness, coldness, and, in some extreme cases, fear or antisocial qualities.

Characteristic differences in levels of self-disclosure are also revealed by the ways in which people handle their physical environment. An office door may be generally left open or kept closed; the window coverings in a house or an apartment may be generally drawn or left open. Almost always, given free choice, the occupants of offices or dwelling units show a consistent preference for one arrangement or the other. Where there is no organizational policy about it, some people almost invariably leave the doors to their offices open, while others invariably keep theirs closed. Some apartment dwellers leave their curtains open, even with frequent passersby; others seldom if ever open their curtains.

Individuals and families usually exhibit characteristic levels of self-disclosure in terms of how they deal with nudity or use bathrooms [187; 396]. In some families, the door to the bathroom is left open even when in use; in others, it is never left open even when the bathroom is not in use. In some families, varying stages of undress including complete nudity are taken as a matter of course as family members move about within the house. In others, family members hasten to dress as soon as they return from the beach wearing swim suits. For these people, the near nudity acceptable on a beach seems inappropriate and uncomfortable in a home.

We can only speculate about the effects of family attitudes toward self-disclosure on children's attitudes and ideas about people in general. Does a child who grows up in a family where nudity is an everyday phenomenon also learn to be more open about her feelings? Is this child better able to have intimate relationships through a superior ability to express her fears, aspirations, likes, and dislikes?

Communication Media

Few of us enjoy bringing unwelcome (disliked) news to another. We do not like being disliked, even temporarily, and few people like the bearer of bad news. The news need not be of death or major tragedy. A parent may have to be informed of a child's failure in school. A worker may have to be laid off. A request may have to be denied.

The next time you have to bring unwelcome information to someone, note your eye contact, distance, and bodily orientation relative to him as you break the news. You will probably tend to avoid looking directly at him, and will stand at a distance, oriented to one side—all of which decrease your approach toward him.

Sometimes it is so difficult to be the bearer of bad news that we select an intermediary (if we can find one), in order to minimize the approach toward the person receiving the news. We may resort to the telephone, or preferably a letter, to avoid a face-to-face confrontation.

On the other hand, when we bring good news, most of us welcome approach; we are happy to present good tidings in face-to-face confrontation. If we cannot perform our function in person, we telephone; if we cannot phone, we write. To transmit good news, an intermediary is a last resort.

Thus, the degree of our liking for what we have to say can determine the degree of approach we use in saying it [253; 425]. The "Dear John" letter and the firing of an employee through an intermediary or a curt formal memo or letter instead of in a face-to-face confrontation illustrate the choice of a more distant medium when there is considerable discomfort about the message.

A written message from a friend who lives in the same city may be quite appropriate—it may be a formal invitation or a birthday card, for example. It may be necessary if you are never at home when your friend can phone. Or, a written message may indicate that your friend does not like (for example, feels uncomfortable about) the contents of the message and cannot bring himself or herself to say them to you on the telephone or in person.

In terms of the degree of approach they afford, media can be ordered as follows: face-to-face situation, picturephone, telephone, telegram, letter, direct intermediary, and most distant of all, a carefully leaked message that is transmitted through an intermediary. (This last technique is rapidly becoming U.S. presidents' method of expressing dissatisfaction with, or even hinting at a desire for the resignation of, their cabinet members.) If a letter and a telegram are the same length, the telegram involves greater approach because transmission is faster. Usually letters, although they take longer to transmit, can be more detailed; the choice between mail and telegraph and the significance of this choice therefore depends on the length of the essential part of the message.

In comparing degree of approach, it is important to distinguish situations in which a free exchange of information is possible from those in which long delays are interposed between one-way messages. When two different means of communication use the same medium, the one that allows faster feedback involves more approach. Surface mail is lower on approach than air mail; a televised communication is lower on approach than one on the picturephone in which an exchange is possible; an audiorecorded message rates lower than a conversation on the telephone.

The message leaked through an intermediary not only involves the least approach, but is also the least reliable—it may never reach the person it is intended for. Frequently there are good reasons for avoiding closer and more reliable means of transmission. Sometimes we do not want to be personally and directly involved with delivery of the message, or perhaps we cannot be directly involved without drawing unnecessary or unseemly attention to the message or to ourselves. In all cases, however, the use of the intermediary is motivated by dislike in conveying the particular message to a particular other. In one kind of situation we may leak a criticism of, or warning to, a friend or coworker. In another situation we may leak a compliment or praise that we are unwilling or unable to deliver more directly since it might be construed as ingratiating. Similarly, we may sometimes brag a bit, with the thought that our virtues may be brought to the attention of someone we want to impress. There are some good experimental methods available for testing the idea that, in trying to ingratiate ourselves by communicating our own good qualities to a higher status other, we prefer to use more distant channels of communication [186].

Similarly, unsuccessful applicants are usually notified by letter—if at all—even if they live in the same city. In contrast, the winner of an award or a successful applicant for a position is often notified by phone—perhaps coast to coast at person-to-person rates. Even in negotiations for positions on very high levels—presidencies of corporations and universities or high-level governmental posts—acceptance is generally communicated by phone, whereas rejection is transmitted by the more distant medium of a letter.

In many situations, responses to applications—for example, applications for admission to colleges or for employment in large organizations—are made by letter. The nature of the answer may be evident simply from the thickness of the letter or package sent to the applicant. A larger package, which includes a lengthier communication and involves more approach [257], is more likely to be the bearer of good news. A brief paragraph of response may start with "We regret. . . ."

A short letter of recommendation may well be a means of "damning with faint praise." A letter that says in effect, "I think Joe Doakes is very mature, intelligent, and diligent," without elaboration, reflects a lack of involvement and a desire to take care of the chore quickly. The writer feels she must say something positive about the person in question, for whom she has little liking [245].

Within a few years picturephones will become available for common use. Of course, some people will install picturephones in offices and homes as soon as they are available for prestige and status reasons; however, many in the vanguard of users will be people who prefer the greater approach that a picturephone affords in dealing with others at a distance. So, more affiliative people will purchase and use these phones earlier than those who are less gregarious.

As compared with a telephone, a picturephone not only intensifies contact but also improves the accuracy of communication [12; 296]. This is especially true for people who make liberal use of facial expressions and gestures in expressing themselves. In a telephone conversation, such visual cues are not available to the listener. Since facial expressions and gestures can be an important part of the effort to explain an idea or to convey a feeling, the received message is at best incomplete and may possibly even be misleading if they are absent [12; 296].

When a person knows that his facial expressions are not available to his listener, he still does not stop using them or automatically start to compensate for their absence by using other behaviors. In one of our studies, we asked the subjects to produce sarcastic messages that were to be audiorecorded [266]. Many subjects who tried to say something sarcastically consistently relied on their facial expressions; when we listened to the recordings from these subjects, we found them totally lacking in sarcasm. Even when this was pointed out, however, these persons still were unable to produce a sarcastic expression vocally—they continued to use their facial expressions.

In contrast, other subjects were very adept in producing sarcastic messages with negative vocal expressions (that is, tone of voice). One of the students, who was an actress, excelled in this and could also readily say unpleasant words such as "scram" or "don't" with positive vocal expressions to produce messages with overall pleasant impact. Most people cannot get this effect when the listener can only hear them, but considerably more can do so if they can be seen as well as heard.

Another study showed that our subjects differed considerably in their abilities to express pleasure or displeasure through their vocal or facial expressions [440]. The introduction of picturephones should be of value to people who are unable to use vocal cues and therefore rely heavily on facial expressions in their conversation.

A Politician's Image

In communication by television or picturephone, the portion of the speaker visible on the receiver set indicates different degrees of approach. For example, if during a televised address to the nation, the president of the United States sits beside his desk so that he is fully visible, the effect is greater approach and more implied liking for the public than when he sits behind his desk, with only his head and shoulders visible. In the latter case, the address seems more impersonal and more distant—more formal.

In face-to-face encounters with constituents who visit them in their offices, elected officials (like everyone who works in an office) can regulate approach by their arrangement of furniture. They can position their desks so visitors must sit away from them, on the opposite side. This kind of arrangement seems more impersonal than one in which the desk is placed against a wall and the people can sit facing, and fully visible to, each other. The latter arrangement not only allows people to sit closer but also increases the amount of sensory input that each receives from the other. Thus, most visitors tend to judge the host in such a situation as receptive and "open." When the desk is between the two, many visitors may become unfavorably aware of a covert stress on the difference in status.

In watching war movies, I have yet to see a German or Russian officer portrayed in his office with his desk placed against the wall so that he is fully exposed to visitors. On the contrary, the officer usually sits behind a huge desk; visitors stand in front. Perhaps this is only the artist's intuitive touch to bring out the stereotype of an authoritarian culture and to symbolize unconcerned and distant leadership.

The behavior of a candidate for political office when on the campaign trail is usually consistent with appearances on TV or the way in which he or she elects to have the office arranged. Many American voters viewed Adlai Stevenson as a distant and aloof intellectual. He was not the kind of candidate who could pretend to enjoy rubbing shoulders with mobs of potential voters, touching and being touched. The impression he gave to the electorate was largely due to his tendency to be less available and distant. In contrast, Lyndon Johnson's image as a candidate, senator, president, or a private person, was one of an exceptional degree of approach. On the campaign trail, he had a need, as he put it, to "press the flesh," to shake thousands of hands, to touch and be touched. His lapel-twisting tactics as Senate majority leader may have seemed excessive to some, but on the whole they proved effective in accomplishing his purposes. His use of the telephone aroused much comment, particularly in the early days of his presidency—there was no precedent for such frequent presidential use of telephone communications. Presidents usually use the more distant and formal medium of written communication.

The implicit style of a person in the political arena usually has little to do with her political ideology or intellect, but it can and does have a tremendous effect on the way she is received, how much she is liked, and especially the kinds of people she appeals to. Thus, as far as the electorate at large is concerned, the public image of an "intellectual" is determined more by manner of dress, the infrequency and quality of contacts with constituents, and aloof and distant mannerisms than by academic background or rational powers. On the other hand, the style of a politician who has considerable intellectual skill may be carefully cultivated to appeal to a constituency of antiintellectual types. Such a quality can be conveyed by informality of speech and by a greater willingness to come into frequent and close contact with the constituency, to assume close positions to people around him or her in meetings, to gesture more when talking, and to be more expressive with face and postures.

The Microenvironment

A friend tells me that on one occasion during her visit to Soviet Russia, she had to visit a People's Militia (police) Station. From the entrance to the office, a long red carpet extended to a giant desk at the other end of the room, behind which sat the officer in charge. A smaller desk was placed in front of this large one. A subordinate officer sat to one side, and the interpreter sat at the other side, slightly to the front of this smaller desk. Seated along the walls on chairs were members of the People's Council.

This microenvironment (that is, interior space of a building) dramatically shows the way in which people of differing statuses can use furniture arrangement to enforce varying degrees of avoidance in contacts with strangers, particularly possibly unpleasant contacts. The officer of highest status was least accessible; the lower-ranking officer and the interpreter who sat alongside the smaller desk, rather than behind it, were more accessible; finally, the People's Council who sat alongside the walls were most accessible, since a visitor occasionally sat with them while waiting for decisions to be made.

People of higher status show the greatest degree of avoidance when they experience displeasure and high arousal—much more so than people of lower status [302]. Thus, the ability to limit disliked interactions is one of the important prerogatives exercised by higher status individuals. Analogously, a person's ability to protect himself from intrusions into his privacy (that is, unwanted interpersonal approach) tells us something about his position on the status scale. Indeed, this relationship has become so much a part of our implicit inferences about status that sometimes a person will insist on privacy primarily to convey high status rather than to shield himself from troublesome (unpleasant and arousing) interpersonal contacts. The furniture arrangement in the People's Militia Station certainly accomplished this purpose by highlighting the status differences of those within it.

In a somewhat different context, a large office may strike us as cold and impersonal instead of friendly and casual, depending on its furniture arrangement. A bank may include many partitions to separate customers from officers and employees, and may have a regimented arrangement of furniture (side-by-side seating alongside a wall or rows of desks for employees who face each other's backs). This design minimizes approach behaviors between customers and employees, thereby creating an impersonal and formal atmosphere. My favorite bank is about half the size of most, and all the officers are seated in the open, with their desks in an irregular arrangement. Only the tellers are separated from the customers. Also, lounge chairs are placed around circular tables for the customers, and coffee is available. The accessibility of the employees, the small size, and the less formal arrangement of the furniture give this bank a very pleasant and comfortable quality.

Often the arrangement of furniture in a professional office is haphazard and left primarily to chance, and, in some situations, the result can have quite detrimental effects on professional effectiveness [273, Chapter 13; 282; 283; 384, Chapter 6]. For situations in which it is important to establish good rapport and a relationship of trust with clients or patients, a seating arrangement involving large distances and/or barriers may be quite a handicap. For example, a psychotherapist who deals with patients across a desk may be ineffective in helping those who cannot tolerate the large distances or who, even mistakenly, attribute the coldness of the office to the therapist.

Consider various offices you have visited—for example, those of school principals, professors, managers, doctors, lawyers. Was there any relation between the way the furniture was arranged and the general friendliness of the host?

The interior design of cafeterias, bars, restaurants, or discos not only influences the general atmosphere but also has a direct effect in encouraging or discouraging conversation among the people who patronize these places. If people can somehow be induced to assume positions close to one another and to orient themselves so they can have eye contact comfortably, then conversation is far more likely to occur than if they select seats that are far apart or are oriented so there is little possibility of eye contact [282; 283; 384].

To create a cozy and comfortable atmosphere in which people can relax and enjoy their food and company, an irregular arrangement of tables placed close together seems effective. Background music helps further by giving people the feeling that they can converse comfortably without being overheard by those at adjacent tables. This design promotes a feeling of greater intimacy and is considered cozy because of the smaller distances; but, since conversations remain private, customers do not feel self-conscious about being seated very close to strangers. From a managerial viewpoint, the effective and economical use of floor space yields more income per square foot. This intimate arrangement does have drawbacks, however—the noise level from the music and others' conversations can become intolerably high.

More generally, it is helpful to remember that furniture arrangement determines seating choice and therefore the quality of social interaction. A large number of small tables discourages conversation among strangers because there is a great reluctance to join a stranger at his or her table. Even though people might go to a place in hopes of meeting others, such an arrangement will lead them to sit at separate tables, strongly discouraging contacts [273, Chapter 23; 384]. Of course, some people prefer such an arrangement because they do not wish to interact with strangers.

If the purpose is to encourage strangers to converse with each other, the side-by-side arrangement of chairs along a long table or a bar counter is not effective, either. In such a setting, people are more likely to sit immediately next to each other; but the side-by-side seating arrangement hinders them from comfortably having eye contact, which is a necessary part of conversation. Further, even when swivel stools are used, a gregarious stranger has the choice of talking only to the people at his right and left. If he is not interested in either one of them or if his friendly gambits are rebuffed, he is handicapped unless he can move to another location at the counter.

One alternative to these two arrangements is a zig-zag counter with people sitting on both sides. This eliminates the problem of self-consciousness associated with joining a stranger at his or her table, since counters are made to be used by people who may be total strangers to each other. Further, the zig-zag arrangement of the counter allows a friendly loner to sit within comfortable speaking distance of two or three others. This is possible since the angular arrangement of the counter allows one to sit close, but at an angle to others. Sitting at an angle counteracts the possibly excessive intimacy of close seating that would be uncomfortable if we were to face a stranger directly across the counter [18]. The use of swivel stools with a zig-zag arrangement increases flexibility in that each person can turn in several directions to address any one of the several people who may be sitting closest. Figure 2-2 illustrates one such basic module that can be combined with many others to achieve not only high-density seating, but also a very casual and friendly atmosphere.

Notice how person D can take a seat very close to C and initially face the counter, thereby assuming an indirect orientation of approximately 90 degrees to C (that is, they each need to turn through an angle of about 45 degrees to face each other). In this way, through slight turns, D has a choice of conversing with A, C, F, or E. He might even be able to address B, if they together turn a total of about 270 degrees—however, this is a less likely possibility.

The zig-zag counter also has the advantage over a straight one at which people sit on both sides because nobody has to sit directly across from anybody. Sitting directly across from a stranger is too forward; and when a straight counter is used, places directly across from occupied seats remain empty until no others are available. This results in ineffective use of space. Figure 2-3 illustrates one application in which such modules are combined to provide seating in a small restaurant.

With the idea of promoting conversation among strangers, use various combinations of modules like that in Figure 2-2 to design the furniture arrangement for a committee meeting, a university cafeteria, or an outdoor cafe in a park.

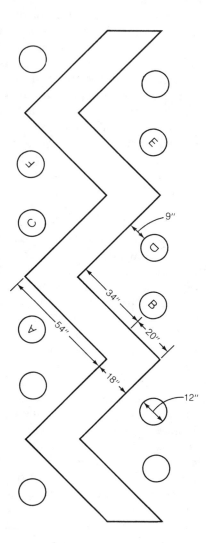

Figure 2-2: A Basic Module for Zig-zag Furniture Arrangements in Public Eating, Drinking, and Entertainment Spots*

*Estimated overall space taken up by this table is 104 ½ square feet (5 ½ feet by 19 feet). To accommodate the twelve people at square tables (assuming 6 ½ feet by 6 ½ feet per table, including seating space) would require 126 ¾ square feet, provided every seat of these square tables was occupied—a very unlikely possibility in actual fact. The zig-zag arrangement is therefore superior in terms of its economical use of space.

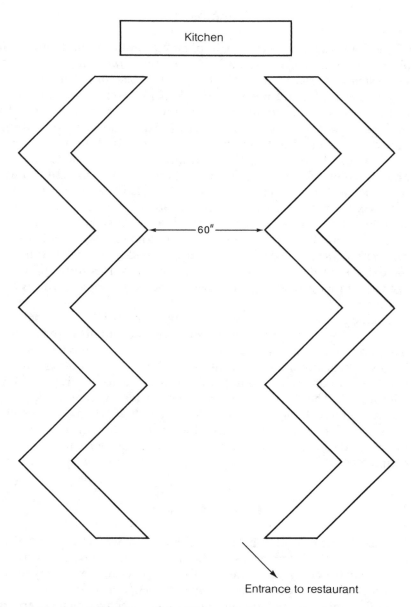

Kitchen

60"

Entrance to restaurant

Figure 2-3: One Application of the Zig-zag Modules in a Small Restaurant

Summary

Of the four major referents of implicit communication, liking of an object, person, or event is probably the most important and is the most straightforward one to infer. Like-dislike subsumes positive-negative attitudes and preference-lack of preference, and can be inferred simply from actual or abbreviated approach-avoidance behaviors. People approach the things they like and avoid others that they dislike. This simple, yet general, hypothesis of a direct correlation between liking and approach (Figure 2-1) allows us to infer degree of like-dislike not only from actual movements toward or away from people, things, and even ideas, but also from observation of abbreviated movements and gestures. Greater liking is conveyed by standing close instead of far, leaning forward instead of back while seated, facing directly instead of turning to one side, touching, having mutual gaze or eye contact, extending bodily contact as during a handshake, prolonging goodbyes, or using gestures during a greeting that imply a reaching out toward the other person who is at a distance.

Such abbreviated movements, postures, and positions not only are useful in inferring somebody else's like-dislike, but also are informative about a person's social style when they are recurrent. Besides her own behaviors, the physical props that surround a person can, without her conscious intent, persistently influence her relationships with others. The furniture arrangement inside the house, the visual accessibility of the interior to outsiders (such as when doors or curtains are left open), or the height of a fence can all affect one's social image and thereby encourage or discourage close interpersonal contacts.

Suggested Readings

Discussions of typical approach-avoidance (or what Edward T. Hall calls "proxemic") behaviors in different cultures and the ways in which such behaviors relate to other aspects of each culture are found in the following works: [21; 154; 155; 156; 157; 395]. Experimental studies related to abbreviated approach-avoidance are reviewed in [14, Chapter 3]. Specific experimental methods and results are also given in [269; 270]. For experimental data on Figure 2-1, see [299, pp. 135–144].

Chapter 3

Inferring Emotions

Each of the emotional dimensions of pleasure-displeasure, arousal-nonarousal, and dominance-submissiveness can be inferred in one of two ways: (1) by knowing the behavioral manifestations of varying degrees of each emotional dimension, or (2) by inferring the emotional state from direct observations of approach-avoidance.

Behavioral Manifestations of Pleasure-Displeasure

We can infer pleasure-displeasure from pleasant versus unpleasant facial expressions (probably the most important set of implicit cues), the pleasant versus unpleasant quality of vocal expressions, and the pleasant versus unpleasant quality of the contents of speech. Thus, smiles, laughter, or generally happy facial expressions imply pleasure, as do jovial and happy voice quality [93; 99; 162; 175; 404; 411]. Although smiling, in particular, indicates pleasant feelings, it is far more consistently a part of interpersonal approach (affiliative) behaviors, thus implying pleasure plus arousal [209]. Frowning, glaring, angry, disgusted, crying, fearful, sneering, smirking, or mocking facial expressions and unhappy, sad, disgusted, or angry vocal expressions in turn readily lead to the inference of displeasure [145, Table 3.4].

In particular, sneers that are distinguished by teeth showing with the center or corners of the upper lip drawn up are reminiscent of preparation to bite (as noted in studies of animals [203; 223]) and are associated with unpleasant (such as hostile) expressions in humans [42; 405].

It is important to note that some facial expressions are extremely brief in duration, lasting ⅕ to ⅛ of a second. These *micromomentary* expressions are evident in slow-motion playback of film or videorecordings [152] and do have a communicative function in actual social interaction—they are noticed and responded to despite their brief duration. Analysis of micromomentary expressions ought to be of considerable interest in studies of communicators who wish to disguise (for example, bluff) or completely withhold (for example, lie about) their feelings in a situation.

Verbal content can explicitly refer to feelings such as "I'm happy," or "I don't feel good." Implicit aspects of verbal content lack such direct references to feelings but instead convey the general emotional tone of the speaker. For instance, a speaker may appear to pursue a general and intellectual discussion of politics, world population problems, or the economic problem of inflation with a friend in a manner that is persistently negative in content. Or, he may discuss these same issues with that friend using positive and constructive contents. The speaker may not actually say anything about how happy or unhappy he feels at the time, but it can be inferred that his emotional state involves displeasure when the contents of his conversation are persistently negative. Conversely, a pleasant emotional state can be inferred when contents are generally positive.

An example of the scoring of verbal content for its implicit reference to pleasant-unpleasant feelings is given in the "problem description," "complaint," "criticize," and "disagree" categories used to score verbal contents in family interaction [419]. Scoring a given speaker frequently in one or more of these four categories indicates implicit communications of displeasure. An "agreement/disagreement" ratio also has been studied extensively in the interactions of couples. Findings show the ratio to be greater for "nondistressed" (namely, happier, less problem-ridden) relationships than for distressed ones [344].

The categories of "verbal reinforcer" (such as "yeah," "uh-huh," "me too," or "same here") and "positive verbal content" (as judged by trained observers on a five-point positiveness scale) have been scored in yet other studies of the spontaneous social interaction of dyads. These two categories have been found to be part of a general approach (affiliative behavior) factor in social interaction [268].

In instances of extreme displeasure, two additional implicit speech cues are useful: speech error rate and halting quality of speech. Speech error rate was originally identified as an indicator of anxiety or as a response to stress in interview or therapeutic situations [228]. Subsequent studies have tended to support a relationship between speech errors and uncertainty, stress, or anxiety [160, Table 2-3; 377]. In our framework, these results mean that speech error rate increases when the speaker feels displeasure, arousal, and submissiveness (that is, anxiety in response to internal cues or environmental stress). Halting quality of speech was used in other studies since it served as a more convenient (more readily scored) measure of the displeasure, arousal, and submissiveness of a speaker [260; 269, Chapter 5 and Appendix A]. Thus, experimental findings have shown that speech error rate or halting speech occur more frequently when a speaker feels displeasure (plus high arousal and submissiveness) because she is communicating about some anxiety-provoking topic, when the interviewer is inducing stress, and when the subject is experiencing discomfort while lying to achieve monetary gain [267; 377].

Additional studies of implicit speech, particularly of high- versus low-pitched voice and of slow- versus fast-rate of speech, have shown higher pitch to have more unpleasant connotations (judged less truthful, less emphatic, more nervous [11; 390]) and slower speech to have more unpleasant connotations (judged less truthful, less fluent [11]).

Behavioral Manifestations of Arousal-Nonarousal

These are not as obvious or as easy to understand in terms of commonsense experiences, but they follow from a definition of arousal. Arousal combines mental alertness and physical activity. Thus, behavioral cues indicative of alertness or activity allow us to infer the arousal level of an individual.

Physical activity can range from strenuous exercise involving high blood pressure, muscle tension, high skin temperature (that is, the various physiological cues associated with arousal), to moderate exercise, to stationary but not relaxed posture (such as being somewhat tense, leaning forward, and being attentive), to a stationary and relaxed (for example, reclining) posture, to a supine and very relaxed position as during rest or sleep. Various degrees of *verbal* activity are superimposed on *physical* activity. These range from rapid and animated speech in loud volume, to slower and less animated speech in softer volume, to occasional, monosyllabic utterances, and on to no speech. In our studies of social interaction, these verbal activity cues were found to be the most prominent indicators of arousal. That is, with some exception, the physical activity of a seated speaker in spontaneous social interaction is not variable enough to be useful for assessing arousal levels. (Exceptions occur with strongly felt emotions, such as when highly arousing topics are discussed; in these cases the expected greater physical activity is evidenced as yet another sign of arousal [362].) However, verbal activity does vary considerably and can be scored readily to assess arousal. Total vocal activity (that is, the animated voice quality during speech or vocal expressiveness), speech rate, and speech volume constitute a factor in social interaction. These cues are standardized and summed to obtain a single measure of speaker arousal [294, p. 82, 93, 137]. Evidence of the significance of verbal activity—speech rate, speech volume, and variation in intonation—has been provided in other studies. These studies have shown that expressions of highly aroused emotions such as anger, fear, surprise were associated with higher speech rates, greater speech volume, and more variability in intonation than expressions of less aroused emotions such as sadness and boredom [75; 369].

In extreme cases, bodily tension serves as a clear indicator of arousal. Also, speech errors, halting speech, and particularly voice tremor, that is, vocal tension, imply high arousal of the speaker.

Pupillary dilation (although it has some relevance for inferring liking since there is greater dilation with more liking [169]) is also a well-established index of arousal. A careful review of the somewhat inconsistent findings on this relationship has led to the conclusion that the pupils dilate more when a person is in a more aroused state [184, p. 41].

As an exercise, make a list of the implicit speech cues associated with displeasure and high arousal. Next, select from these the ones that have been found specifically to be associated with deceitful statements. Now, if you have occasion to question the truthfulness of another's statements in a conversation over the phone, phrase your questions in an open-ended manner so they cannot be answered simply with a yes or no. You will thus be able to apply the available research findings to ascertain the truthfulness of the answers you get to your questions.

Behavioral Manifestations of Dominance-Submissiveness

The implicit messages conveying dominance-submissiveness are diverse and can be elaborate and subtle. Generally, dominance is conveyed with behaviors implying strength, comfort, relaxation, and fearlessness, whereas submissiveness is communicated with behaviors implying weakness, smallness, discomfort, tension, and fearfulness. Studies of dyads in social interaction have consistently revealed postural relaxation to be a subtle indicator of social dominance [259; 269]. In social situations, dominant people assume a relaxed posture whereas submissive people assume a less relaxed or tenser posture. Consistent with this, communicators shown in a more relaxed position have been found to be more influential in eliciting greater opinion change [244].

Postural relaxation is defined and measured in terms of increasing degrees of asymmetry of body and limb position while standing or seated (for example, leaning to one side, placing arms or legs in asymmetrical positions as compared to standing or sitting up straight and placing limbs in a symmetrical position). While seated, a backward lean (a reclining position) is more relaxed than an up-right or forward lean (note the specific scoring criteria for relaxa-tion provided in [260; 269, Appendix A]). Rocking movements of a seated person are also indicative of relaxation and dominance [306]. Other aspects of posture that convey relaxation-tension include head leaning sideways or down versus erect, curved versus erect torso, and drooping versus erect shoulder position. The first instance in each pair is associated with greater relaxation.

If you lean forward in your chair, you will be tenser than if you lean back and cross your legs. This is less relaxed than if you recline considerably and place your legs on another chair or on top of your desk. Picture a "well-bred" schoolgirl in an English boarding school—she sits in an erect posture with her hands clasped in her lap and legs hanging so that her feet are placed flat on the floor. This is in sharp contrast to a teen-age tough's posture as he sits slouched in a classroom. The former embodies the respectful attitude toward authority and established tradition, whereas the latter exudes dis-respect and defiance.

The extreme rigidity of a soldier at attention while being in-spected by a high ranking officer is an unparalleled example of the principle that relates tension to low status. In this case, a casual and relaxed military officer walks past a straight line of soldiers all standing in a rigid symmetrical stance.

To understand the relation of relaxation to dominance, note the emotional components of relaxation (pleasure, low arousal, domi-nance). Bodily relaxation indicates not only dominance, but also pleasure and low arousal. It follows that differences in the relaxation of two people (or of the same individual on two different occasions) can be used to infer dominance, provided pleasure and arousal lev-els are comparable.

Aside from its significance in conveying pleasant feelings, smiling has been found also to be indicative of submissiveness or of a sub-missive role in social situations [10; 98; 106; 306]. Higher rates of head nodding during conversations have also been found to be asso-ciated with greater submissiveness [306].

Among implicit speech cues, quantity of talking (or percentage of the duration of a person's speech in a fixed period of communica-tion) is found to be a good indicator of that person's dominance in the situation. Those who talk more (who, in effect, dominate a con-versation) are more dominant and are perceived as being more dom-inant [385; 386; 388]. Also, louder speech is judged to be more persuasive and more influential [306; 329]. A more recent study showed higher pitch of voice to be judged as more submissive (more nervous) and also slower rate of speech to be an indication of submissiveness (less persuasive, more passive, weaker) [11].

Finally, it has been found that more dominant (confident versus anxious) people have a greater tendency to interrupt their conversational partners [320].

Take a sample of five couples and make a list of the generally dominant individual in each of these five. Next, think back to your casual social interactions with each of these couples and decide which individual in each pair tends to do most of the talking when you get together. Do your own informal observations correspond to the findings noted above?

The more general definition of dominance identifies the following implicit behaviors associated with dominant-submissive feelings: behaviors that convey greater strength (such as assertive voice [46], a greater energy of voice and fewer pauses or hesitations in speech [370]—high speech volume and less halting speech have both been shown to be correlates of a personality measure of dominance [313, p. 37]), control over larger and more desirable territories [394], implied control over large numbers of individuals (such as when a person has many others at her disposal), size (as conveyed through deliberate use of bouffant hair style, massive clothing, and elevated shoes), qualities of voice, speech, or mannerisms that convey relaxation, comfort, confidence, or absence of fear (such as relatively few speech errors and absence of voice tremor), and a free and comfortable life style (for example, a work schedule that is free of constraints and routines, an expansive and convenient home architecture, freedom from intrusion and interruption, and comfort provided by employees) or availability of luxury objects (such as cars, stereos, swimming pools, and other mechanical and electronic gadgets designed to minimize effort and tension and maximize aesthetic appearance, comfort, efficiency, and relaxation) [273, Chapter 6].

Inferring Pleasure, Arousal, and Dominance from Approach

Since the relationship of approach-avoidance to the three basic dimensions of emotion is known, various combinations of the feeling states can be inferred from observation of approach-avoidance.

It is easy to infer pleasure-displeasure from approach-avoidance since the two are positively and strongly correlated. Thus, strong approach generally implies pleasure whereas strong avoidance implies displeasure. There is one important set of exceptions to be considered below.

Arousal level cannot be inferred unambiguously except in the case of extreme approach or avoidance. Figure 1-1 (page 12), which relates pleasure and arousal to liking (and its correlate, approach-avoidance), shows that extreme like-dislike (approach-avoidance) is associated with high arousal: Strong liking is associated with pleasure and high arousal, whereas strong dislike is associated with displeasure and high arousal. When approach is intermediate, high pleasure and moderate arousal, or moderate pleasure and high arousal, are inferred. When avoidance is intermediate, high displeasure and moderate arousal, or moderate displeasure and high arousal, are inferred. Thus, only when approach-avoidance takes on an extreme value can arousal be inferred unambiguously.

Since a particular level of approach-avoidance is a complicated function of pleasure, arousal, and dominance levels, it is difficult to make precise inferences about the three feeling dimensions from approach cues alone. In particular, dominant-submissive feelings cannot be assessed by observing approach, except under the following conditions. A person who feels submissive exhibits limited variability in approach-avoidance as a function of the pleasant-unpleasant and/or arousing-unarousing qualities of stimulation. In contrast, a person who feels dominant exhibits high variability in approach-avoidance [302]. Thus, when someone implicitly or explicitly conveys strong like-dislike, evaluation, or approach-avoidance of others, events, or situations, the implied message is one of dominance. In contrast, less evaluative expressions connote social submissiveness, which may be a general characteristic or a specific feeling induced by a particular situation.

Generally, the inference of emotional states from approach-avoidance is not reliable since it is not always possible to infer values on three variables from observations of a single variable. This is not a problem, however, since the three emotional states can be inferred directly from the behavioral cues we have already noted. In instances when approach-avoidance behaviors are observed readily and emotional states are unclear, the following summary guidelines are useful. Pleasure-displeasure is inferred from approach-avoidance, except when tension accompanies approach (in which case displeasure and high arousal are inferred). Strong approach implies pleasure and high arousal; strong avoidance implies displeasure and high arousal. Submissiveness is inferred when there is small variability in approach-avoidance; dominance is inferred when approach-avoidance varies greatly, as when a person unambiguously expresses liking, attitudes, or preferences.

Exceptions to the Liking-Approach Relationship

The relationships in Figure 1-1 help explain some of the confusion in the literature regarding the significance of various approach cues. Approach cues include eye contact with or looking in the direction of another, turning toward, physically approaching, leaning toward, and touching another. In most everyday interactions such cues are associated with liking. However, there are some important exceptions, such as when one approaches another in anger, yelling, gesturing forcefully, and staring him or her down. Such examples of negative approach necessitate a detailed interpretation of the emotional significance of approach.

Consider eye contact and looking, which have been studied extensively. Several investigators have noted that eye contact or looking can take on different kinds of significance, for instance, as a function of length of the look, the social context of the look, or the presence of other cues associated with the look [17; 100; 101; 102; 103; 109; 195; 196; 205; 352]. Specifically, animal studies have shown eye contact to be associated with aggression [158; 364]. The corresponding phenomenon among humans is the stare, often defined as a long-lasting look, which has been found to signify threat, antagonism, competition, or negative attitude [108; 109; 111; 195; 392; 399].

These contradictions are resolved by noting that (1) approach increases arousal levels of the communicator and addressee whereas avoidance reduces arousal levels, and (2) although approach is generally associated with more pleasure than is avoidance, in a minority of instances, approach may involve displeasure. In the latter, less frequent, instances, the combination of high arousal and approach with the displeasure communicated in various implicit cues, understandably sets off strong dislike and avoidance (Figure 1-1).

Some evidence is now available on the arousing quality of various approach cues. The closeness of others and crowding, both of which are associated with smaller distances and more eye contact, have been found to increase physiological indexes of arousal, such as the GSR [3; 133; 205; 240; 310; 322].

Aggressive, negative, or hostile approach (the downward-slanting line in Figure 1-1), then, is distinguished from the more common, positive, variety (the upward-slanting line in Figure 1-1) by noting the pleasant-unpleasant implicit cues that accompany the approach that tends to be arousing in itself.

Even when the pleasantness-unpleasantness of implicit cues accompanying the approach is difficult to detect, the level of tension-relaxation in the individual who is approaching can serve as a useful and important indicator. For example, in one of our studies, a high level of postural tension was observed in male communicators in the presence of intensely disliked males [256]. Tension may be evident in postural rigidity, muscular tension (muscle tonus), staccato or abrupt rather than flowing gestures and movements, facial tension manifested in frozen or distorted expressions, tics or other erratic and uncontrolled movements, inappropriately high levels of eye contact (that is, intense staring accompanying a bland or negative facial expression [109]), and excessive speech errors, halting speech, or voice tremor.

Tension itself can be analyzed in terms of its emotional components: displeasure, high arousal, submissiveness. When tension is observed, we can directly infer displeasure and arousal (therefore, dislike) without relying on the more tenuous relationships with approach-avoidance and like-dislike.

The shift in the significance of highly arousing cues (proximity, eye contact) depending on the accompanying positive-negative expressions was demonastrated in a study of eye contact [100]. It was found that a high rate of eye contact by the speaker, accompanying pleasant and rewarding verbal contents, led to a very high preference for the speaker; the same rate of eye contact accompanying unpleasant verbal contents led to a very low preference for the speaker. In other words, the arousing impact of the eye contact tended to maximize the differences in the preference for the speaker depending on the positive-negative verbal cues accompanying the eye contact.

In another study employing closeness rather than eye contact as the cue for increasing arousal [371], it was found that, again, consistent with the hypotheses in Figure 1-1, greater closeness increased lack of preference for the other when unpleasant emotional cues were present and that greater closeness increased preference for the other when pleasant emotional cues were present.

The latter findings were corroborated in another study showing that a person who sat close was liked more when she acted friendly or held similar attitudes (note that those who hold more similar attitudes are liked more [51; 52; 271; 290]). In contrast, she was liked less when she sat close and acted in an unfriendly manner or held dissimilar attitudes [389].

Exceptions to the approach-liking relationship can also be understood in terms of the high arousal levels associated with approach. Experimental findings abound showing that humans are physically and psychologically incapable of sustaining high levels of arousal indefinitely and that when such sustained high arousal is unavoidable, illnesses, accidents, and psychological dysfunctions result. For instance, numerous or frequent life changes that require novel adjustments by individuals are arousing (for example, the many adjustments one must make to marriage, undertaking a large mortgage on a house, change of residence, loss of a job) and have been shown to result in increased incidences of physical and psychological dysfunctions [297; 298; 375; 437]. Also, crowding, which tends to increase arousal [273, Chapter 30] because it intensifies affective experience [125], has been found to result in massive die-offs in animal colonies [62] and to lead to dramatic increases in aggression and social disorganization [56].

Humans, particularly those residing in crowded, urban centers and those living under pressured or stressful (highly arousing and unpleasant) social and economic circumstances, understandably do their best to avoid arousal due to crowding or social involvement [241; 273, Chapters 29, 30]. Thus, contact and communication with strangers, even casual greetings, are avoided; there is a relative absence of helpfulness toward those in trouble; and there is a determined effort to minimize various approach cues (eye contact, touching, conversation, access to body odors, breath) when forced into close proximity to others. Even when people voluntarily approach each other, they tend to orient away from one another and to have less eye contact in the closer positions [16; 18; 24; 118; 141; 330; 331; 333]. Alternatively, eye contact increases when good friends interact at larger distances [361].

In one study, when a stranger, the experimenter, took a seat very

close to the subject, that subject left his seat sooner than others who had not been approached in this way [118]. Elevators tend to be uncomfortable for most people; forced into a small space with strangers, they avoid each other's gaze by staring at the floor or watching the lighted, floor-indicator panel above the doors. Some observations suggest that the introduction of some distraction, such as a painting, into an elevator can ease the situation [374, p. 25].

Summary

Implicit behaviors provide information directly about a person's specific emotional state along the dimensions of pleasure, arousal, and dominance. When facial cues are available and are relatively uncensored, pleasant versus unpleasant facial expressions are the most important source of information about feelings of pleasure-displeasure. In addition, the pleasant versus unpleasant quality of vocal expressions and the implicit pleasantness-unpleasantness of verbal contents provide information about a person's level of pleasure. When a speaker seems to be censoring his or her emotions, pleasure-displeasure can still be inferred from approach-avoidance behaviors, since pleasure and approach are positively correlated. The exception to this general relationship is when bodily tension, tense movements, or vocal tension in speech accompany the approach, in which case strong displeasure and high arousal are inferred.

Arousal levels are inferred from level of physical activity and in particular from speech rate, speech volume, vocal expressiveness, and voice tremor. Also, strong approach or avoidance behaviors usually imply high levels of arousal.

More relaxed postures have been found to be associated with dominant rather than with submissive feelings. In other cultures, submissiveness also may be communicated implicitly through behaviors that imply weakness or smallness (speaking very softly, bowing), discomfort and tension (standing or maintaining a rigid seated or standing position while the other is comfortably seated or reclining), and fearfulness (backing out of a room in the presence of one of higher status). Also, submissiveness is inferred when a person manifests little variability in approach-avoidance, whereas dominance is inferred when an individual exhibits a high degree of variability in approach-avoidance, as when expressions of like-dislike are strong and unambiguous.

Suggested Readings

See [273; 280] for experimental evidence and additional discussion of the relations among pleasure, arousal, and approach. For the emotional significance of implicit speech cues, see [160]. See [23; 44] for categories of speech content and [145] for classifications of implicit behaviors, together with a discussion of their significance.

Chapter 4

Dominance

Subtle Expressions of Power

Office doors and differences in visitors' approaches to them can demonstrate the operation of the power metaphor that underlies the inference of dominant-submissive feelings. A visitor may enter without knocking; she may knock briefly and immediately enter; she may knock and wait to be invited in. Stripped of exceptions due to social training (or lack of it) this series of approaches correlates with decreasing degrees of familiarity or with increasing status of the people visited. If the door to an office is open, a comparable series would include simply walking in and taking a seat, hesitating at the threshold for word or gesture of invitation before entering and immediately taking a seat without waiting for specific invitation to do so, or stopping at the threshold until asked to come in and waiting, again, until invited to take a seat. The first example in this series illustrates the behavior of a close friend or a visitor who is of higher status and knows the person she is visiting. The other examples illustrate the behavior of a visitor who is on less intimate terms with or who ranks lower in a status hierarchy than the person visited.

These examples show that people behave in a more formal, considerate, and ritualized fashion in situations involving status differences than they do when interacting with their peers. The underlying principle here, which is based on the power metaphor, is that higher status (that is, socially dominant) people determine the degree of approach permitted in their interactions with others. A person of lower status has less right to approach and touch someone of higher status [163; 165; 166; 167; 383, p. 146].

The clue to status and dominance differences is the degree of hesitation and discomfort shown by the visitor at each stage as he is about to approach the person he visits. If the status differential is significant, he must wait for permission before he makes any major move in coming closer, or risk offending the higher status other. He will be hesitant to presume familiarity by casually dropping into a seat, as this implies relaxation and an intention to stay on. Indeed, even when invited to sit, the visitor will still behave in a way that is consistent with his status in the situation as he sees it. If there is more than one visitor's chair, he will tend to sit at a distance from his host. If the two are intimate or are peers, however, the visitor will feel free to take a seat without being invited to do so, one close to the person he visits [224].

In the American culture, we joke about status symbols, but we are as a general rule uneasily reluctant to discuss our own status relative to others. There are status differences even though our mythology informs us that all people are equal. As these examples show, even the simplest and most common aspects of social life are permeated by actions rather than words that take cognizance of status differences among the participants. More generally, when it is not socially permissible to verbalize a feeling or attitude (in this case, awareness of status differences), actions may reveal the proscribed messages; and if we focus on what we see rather than on the words we hear, we may learn how others really feel. Thus psychoanalysts have sought to understand the unverbalized (or "repressed") feelings of their patients [40; 79; 80; 81; 132; 342].

The ways in which status differences affect people's interactions tend to be particularly pronounced in the more authoritarian and traditional Middle Eastern or Oriental cultures. In these cultures, there is an important and pervasive influence on implicit behaviors due to the greater and more open respect for tradition, the wisdom of old age, and social position. People not only talk about but also act in accordance with certain well-defined social roles corresponding to their status. This reminds me of an instructor at the University of Teheran who once visited me. His behavior strongly emphasized the extreme importance that is placed on status in the Middle East. Throughout our meeting, he spoke softly, almost in a whisper. He did not sit down until I asked him to; and, at the end, instead of turning around to walk out, he backed out of the room. The low volume of his voice metaphorically emphasized the lower status that he felt; his backing out showed the reluctance to "show me his back," a behavior that epitomizes a humble and respectful attitude. As we have seen, the metaphor that underlies communications of status is power, which includes strength and fearlessness. Thus the low volume and passive behaviors of my visitor are analogous to weakness, and the reluctance to turn his back toward me parallels fear in the metaphor.

In the Middle East, the uneasiness about turning one's back even on friends is illustrated by the formalities of making an entrance. There are many arguments at thresholds of entrances, as each of two peers insists that the other should enjoy the privilege of going first. The admiration in a friendship is constantly reiterated through such acts, which convey one's humble and respectful attitude toward one's friends and elders. Even when one of a pair does finally agree to go first, he tends to orient himself sideways as he goes through the entrance to avoid turning his back to the other.

On occasion, vestigial examples of such behaviors crop up in Western cultures. For example, the courtesy of allowing the other person to walk through a narrow entrance first is comparable to the Middle Easterner's conscious aversion to showing his back to a person in a higher position. A man falls back to let a woman precede him; a junior shows deference to his senior in age or position. A striking example in the West is the behavior of guests of the British sovereign at formal court occasions, such as during awards ceremonies. One curtseys or bows low when presented to the queen at formal court occasions and also backs away from her when leaving her presence. The less blatant courtesies, which tend to occur only in formal relationships in the West (that is, those involving status differences), are basically comparable to the "backing out" behaviors in Middle Eastern and Oriental cultures. On the other hand, the "backing out" analogy does not apply in the American armed forces, which are permeated by awareness of status differences to an excruciating degree. In formal situations, when an enlisted person or junior officer is dismissed from the presence of a superior officer, he or she salutes smartly, does an about-face (turning his or her back fully), and marches away. In this context there are many other more obvious ways in which status differences are conveyed. Thus, when there is a clear understanding of who is in charge and who has to listen to orders, the subtle cues that convey status differences become less important.

You may have an opportunity to observe personal interactions in a situation that involves differences in status among a number of people who work in individual offices. If you do, note how people behave as they visit various offices. Who barges into which offices without waiting for an invitation? Who waits at the thresholds of which offices for specific invitations? Notice also how loud or soft a person knocks when she visits someone whose door is closed. Is the knocking softer and less frequent, as though with some reluctance, when the person being visited is of higher status?

Experiments reviewed in Chapter 3 showed that more submissive persons speak in a softer voice in interacting with a stranger [306; 313; 329; 370]. Also, louder speaking persons are judged to be more influential [306; 329]. The implication of smallness by a low voice volume is only one example of a more general metaphorical relationship between large size and power or status. I remember a concert in which all the Oriental musicians were seated on the floor, facing the audience. At the time of applause, when the musicians bowed, the principal performer, who had been introduced as a person of exceptional musical ability, did not bow quite so low as the others in the ensemble. The latter, who were of lesser skill and status, showed their acceptance of their relatively lower status by bowing to a lower position. On some occasions, this phenomenon may be evident also among American actors, dancers, or opera singers during curtain calls.

Body Relaxation

In Western cultures, particularly in the United States, the connotations of democracy run counter to an emphasis on status considerations; there are few overt manifestations of acceptance of status differences. However, in subtle ways, we reveal our arrogance in higher status and our humility in a lower position. Experimental observations in this culture show that body relaxation, which is a much more subtle cue than the ones noted previously, is one very important indicator of status. When two strangers meet, the more relaxed one is probably accepted by both as being of higher status [35; 74; 91; 138; 244; 254; 259; 287; 353]. In our contemporary culture, relaxation is a reminder of the fearlessness of the powerful in times when power (and consequent status) involved life and death. One who is powerful, that is, of higher status, can afford to relax, whereas the weak must remain watchful and tense.

Relaxation and other dominance-related cues are important for understanding communications of respect and disrespect. The definition of respect in our framework as consisting of pleasure, arousal, and submissiveness implies that a small (but not excessive) amount of tension can be a sign of respect and interest whereas excessive or inappropriate relaxation is a sign of disrespect or disinterest [254; 256].

These experimental observations in Western cultures also correlate with certain rules of etiquette in formal situations [337]. Since standing is less relaxed than sitting, it is not surprising that a host seats his most honored guests first. When there are more extreme status differences, guests of lower status remain standing throughout whereas the more distinguished guests are seated. Examples of these are seen in formal political situations in which some attendants of a high-level official remain standing. Similarly, participants in a state dinner rise from their seats when the official party arrives and remain standing until the official party is seated. According to

Emily Post [337], in more casual everyday situations, people of lower status (for example, teen-agers) are supposed to stand up to greet their superiors (for example, anyone over thirty) or to stand whenever they wish to show respect. However, such arbiters of social custom are not often consulted by today's young people.

I recently visited a young dentist, who, as he worked on my teeth, talked a great deal about his "partner," an older man and an internationally distinguished dentist. One day, while the younger dentist was working on my teeth, a man came to the door to talk to him about some routine matter. Although I could not see the man who entered, I could see my dentist clearly. As I heard the visitor's voice, I noticed changes in the posture of my dentist. He moved forward in his seat, leaned forward, moved his knees together, and clasped his hands. These movements were significantly different from his behavior when others stopped at the doorway to talk to him. I had no idea who his visitors were; however, clued by his unusually tense posture during this last exchange, I felt confident enough to say, "That must have been your partner." This was indeed the case.

The noticeable change in his posture more than normally illustrated the idea that increased postural tension (which relates to fear and watchfulness in the power metaphor) occurs when a person addresses someone of higher status. In this situation, the young dentist was quite sensitive to the professional prominence of his partner. The two men had almost certainly never discussed and contrasted their respective professional positions. However, the younger man's postural behavior gave clear indication of his recognition of where he stood in the relationship.

Body tension is not the only abbreviated behavior that is part of a fear reaction signaling lower status. Frequent blinking can also be part of a fear reaction and, when it occurs in normal conversation, can imply weakness and submissiveness. The person who blinks frequently seems to be saying "Please be gentle. Don't disagree with me or hurt my feelings" (in the power metaphor: "Please don't hit me!").

The Prerogative to Approach

It is easy enough to picture an older person in this culture encouraging a younger business partner by patting him or her on the back; but it is very difficult to visualize this situation reversed, that is, with the younger person patting the older and more senior partner. This illustrates a second important way in which status considerations regulate our implicit messages. For two people of different status, the prerogative to approach the other belongs to the one with higher status [165; 166; 167; 179; 378; 402; 412; 431].

In almost any social grouping, there is a status hierarchy the newcomer implicitly discovers and respects. In the context of a working situation, minor status differences may not be immediately evident, but one differential is obvious. The head person, the one with hire-fire power, has highest status in the group. The newcomer in the situation may or may not ever have social contact off the job with a superior; but, if he or she does, the higher-status person initiates the closer relationship. The supervisor of the steno pool may suggest to a typist that they have lunch together. A foreman may invite a machinist to have a beer at the local tavern after the shift ends. A corporation president may invite a junior executive to a cocktail party in her home. There are acceptable exceptions in particular situations, but as a general rule the lower-ranked person does not presume to initiate the approach.

For the junior employee, it would seem (and would probably be) inappropriate to take this step to approach the boss. So, if the superior bypasses this initiative to a more friendly relationship, then the chances are that the two persons will never socialize together off the job.

A related implicit rule is that when the person of higher status provides such an opportunity to approach, the employee is under heavy obligation to accept the invitation. Classically, to reject such an invitation is disrespectful; pragmatically, rejection is probably impolitic for one who wants to do well in a job. So, when a person of lower status is offered an opportunity to approach, he or she generally accepts.

A junior employee may be brash enough to take the initiative to approach even though she does not have that prerogative. In this instance, a rejection of the invitation is also embarrassing but has different connotations. When several such invitations are turned down, the obvious implication is that the superior has a distinct desire to maintain and enforce status differences as well as formality in the relationship.

Interestingly enough, these observations about how humans project status differences in their relationships seem to be true also for primates. In watching a colony of chimpanzees at a zoo, I noticed that the male head of this colony, who was obviously larger and older than the rest, was hardly ever approached by the adolescent males who were constantly playing and wrestling with each other. They especially avoided looking in his direction and tensed slightly as they passed by him, while he remained relaxed and glanced casually in their direction. These informal observations are corroborated in studies of baboons in their natural habitat. Among the baboons, high-status males were the focus of much activity and drew other members of the species, particularly females with young infants, into close interaction with them. The very young animals frequently approached the dominant male, or males, and interacted with them. As these infants became older, however, and entered into the status hierarchy, avoidance and discomfort in the presence of the high-status males were more likely to be observed. Complementary experimental findings have shown that lower status primates indicate submissiveness by allowing greater accessibility to themselves by higher status others [185; 380].

Parallel findings for humans show that although a person of higher status may quite legitimately point out a closer chair to his visiting guest and ask him to take it, thereby inviting approach, people won't spontaneously assume a close position to someone of higher status. Rather, they sit far away and face him directly [224].

Among military personnel in uniform, where rank (and corresponding social status) is unambiguous, the initiator of a conversation assumes a greater distance to addressees of higher rank—the greater the addressee's rank, the greater this distance [77]. Also, passersby are more reluctant to approach closely or intrude upon high-status, compared with low-status, pairs who are in a conversation [207].

Incidentally, temperamentally violent or hostile (that is, unpleasant, arousable, and dominant—see Chapter 6) people have been found to maintain generally greater distances from others [170; 199; 345]. The habitual assumption of greater distances is likely to be determined by displeasure as well as by dominance.

In this context, it is possible to analyze the significance of the position at the head of the table, which in most cultures goes to the most honored or highest status person in the group. Someone sitting at the head of a rectangular table on the average has more ease in achieving eye contact and initiating conversation with others at the table than one sitting along the side. For the latter, establishing eye contact, for instance with someone who sits along the same side of the table, involves bending forward and twisting the neck at an uncomfortable angle. Thus, the end position facilitates eye contacts and the regulation of conversation for its occupant, thereby giving the person more flexibility in regulating this aspect of approach with the others at the table. It is therefore not surprising that the position goes to persons of high status [159; 164; 391].

This kind of status significance led to the elaborate discussions of table shape for the Vietnam peace talks in Paris. Delegates from various nations and political groups at the talks did not wish to be

judged implicitly as being of lower status through an assignment to certain positions at the table. Thus, the extensive preliminary negotiations required to decide on the shape of a table involved necessary compromises on the part of all parties regarding their respective status in the situation.

In addition to the choice of seating, which dictates degree of closeness and directness of orientation, the initiation of a conversation is one common way of approaching another. It is associated with more eye contact and more self-disclosure (expressing one's beliefs, attitudes, or feelings) than is generally possible without conversation. Generally, the option to increase or decrease closeness by initiating or terminating a conversation is left to the person of high status. It is not surprising that when we are addressed by someone of higher status, we tend to be attentive and aroused; failure to do so would be a sign of disrespect. On the other hand, when a lower status person initiates a conversation, the higher status one is not required by custom or her own necessities to be overly aroused and responsive or to have eye contact with the lower status person. She can quite legitimately even turn to one side and seem to be listening without showing much reaction to what she hears.

A friend of mine, Tom, told of an incident that occurred while he was a graduate student. Tom went to the office of a very prominent psychologist in his department to present his ideas for a research project. The status implications in this situation were obvious, and Tom, who was very junior, did not expect to be favored by constant eye contact and verbal response from the senior psychologist, who sat facing away with his head down, quietly listening. There wasn't much reaction as Tom talked on, but this, as we have seen, is not unexpected, so he kept talking. Long before Tom finished his presentation, however, he was startled to hear a gentle snore. Fearing mutual embarrassment, Tom got up and quietly tiptoed away from the slumbering professor.

Inference of status differences from eye contact or looking behavior also follows from the notion that higher status people have the prerogative to increase approach with lower status others. Thus, staring or long-lasting looks are usually directed by higher status persons toward more submissive individuals [18; 20; 69; 131]. Also, when eye contact has been established, the lower status person is the first generally to look away and break eye contact [392]. Parallel findings with primates show that dominant animals are more likely to stare at submissive ones than vice versa [174; 214; 364].

The extreme opposite to staring or prolonged observation of another is avoidance of looking and eye contact. This form of visual behavior is associated with the extreme submissiveness accompanying fear, guilt, shame, or social inferiority (as when someone does not dare look at a terrifying object, hangs his head in shame, or bows and looks down in the presence of a powerful other). More typically, findings that are not altogether consistent show that social submissiveness is evidenced when an individual looks intermittently and briefly toward another of higher status [88; 111].

Status differences are also reflected in subtle aspects of speech [425]. In addressing a doctor of medicine, Robert French, we could say, "Dr. French" (but never "Mr. French"), "Robert," "Bob," or "Frenchie," with increasing degrees of familiarity or equality of status—the last possibly being used only by those who had known him in childhood. Another more subtle example is the occurrence of the word *just* in a request. Use of "I just wanted to borrow this book" instead of "I want to borrow this book," implies a reluctance and hesitation in making the demand. The word *just* suggests an insignificant quality of the demand and is more likely to be used when the other person is of higher status. Even such a small request as this involves approach and is therefore made with some hesitation. The first statement can also imply "I just want the book and plan to leave quickly." This implication is consistent with our general concept in that it indicates a concern about the increased closeness that would result if the requester were to stay on.

Consider some rules of etiquette from the standpoint of these principles that relate implicit behavior to status. Details of the explicit rules have been modified frequently since Emily Post first published her book on etiquette [337] in 1922. However, particularly for formal occasions, the rules still reflect their beginnings in social groupings concerned with power and status. For example, a couple of generations ago people would not introduce themselves to others of high status, but rather would first seek a letter of introduction from those people's equals. This legitimized the approach that was associated with the visit. Today, in seeking a visit with someone of high status, a less direct means of contact, such as a letter or telephone call, is selected to make the request.

Such codes are derived from the etiquette that governed social behavior of court circles and aristocracy of seventeenth-century France and England. The prescribed rules governing introductions (who is presented to whom) are based on relative status and provide some guidelines in a culture that is not characterized by profound concern about status—at least not a formalized overt concern. Few of us today live our social lives under conditions governed by formal rules of etiquette. Most of us are aware of power and status differences, and we act and react accordingly without too much help from handbooks on the subject.

Territoriality

As population density increases, territorial rights become an important prerogative of the higher status people [273]. Experiments with animals have shown that higher status animals visit more locations in their everyday activities than animals of lower status [56]. Thus, the higher status members of a group are afforded a freedom of movement that is less available to those of lower status; furthermore, they have a designated area primarily for their own and their subordinates' use that is larger than areas available to lower status members [13; 223; 239]. The following comments of Edward T. Hall are instructive:

> Dominant animals tend to have larger personal distances than those which occupy lower positions in the social hierarchy, while subordinate animals have been observed to yield room to dominant ones. Glen McBride [239], an Australian professor of animal husbandry, has made detailed observations of the spacing of domestic fowl as a function of dominance. His theory of "social organization and behavior" has as a main element the handling of space. This correlation of personal distance and status in one form or another seems to occur throughout the vertebrate kingdom. It has been reported for birds and many mammals, including the colony of ground-living Old World monkeys at the Japanese Monkey Center near Nagoya [156, p. 14].

These findings can be summarized in terms of the following principle: Higher status people in a social group have access to more, larger, and more desirable locations [154; 224; 384; 391; 394; 433] and, compared with lower status members, have more power to increase or restrict the approach behaviors of others [165; 166; 167; 179; 378; 402; 412; 431]. Also, higher status people tend to assume positions from which they can easily observe (or monitor) the speech and actions of others. People who assume such central or "head of table" positions are in turn viewed by others as being more dominant or as leaders [164; 391].

There are many relevant examples from our everyday observations. For instance, among persons of different status within the same institution, such as a school, a business, or a hospital, higher status individuals are assigned larger and more private quarters.

Think of how much effort it would take to get a personal interview with your boss, one of your state legislators, your governor, a senator, and the president of the United States, in that order. Also, think of how much easier it would be for successive people in this list to regulate (that is, encourage or discourage) approach to themselves.

Besides their contribution in showing a relation between higher status and increased access to a variety of locations or power to regulate others' use of space, experiments with animals have produced some interesting observations of the psychological advantage of having a territory. In one of his experiments, John Calhoun [56] used four interconnected pens and concentrated a large number of rats within them. In a very short time, one of the male rats took over one of these pens and drove out the other males who competed with him for status and for access to females. He was willing to tolerate the presence of other males in his compartment so long as they kept to themselves and did not bother the females. This rat even slept at the entrance to his pen so that he would be awakened by any intruders and could drive them off. Female rats in his pen lived out normal existences; there was a very high mortality rate among the female rats in the other crowded pens. There was also a considerable amount of abnormal behavior among the crowded rats: aggressive tail biting, unstable social hierarchies, transsexuality, and inadequate rearing of the young.

The dominant male that had taken over a pen was readily able to drive away the other males that attempted to enter his premises. He had established his own territory and harem where he was truly king. The fact that he had preserved for himself a more than adequate area seems to have given him not only the upper hand in maintaining his physical well-being but also a psychological advantage in warding off the intruders.

Indeed, evidence shows that there is a psychological advantage in being in one's own territory; an animal who fights in his own territory almost invariably wins. Even a physically stronger and larger animal becomes a less able fighter in another's territory [41; 223]. Thus, status is enhanced within one's own territory and others are reluctant to enter that area and be repulsed. Note that only those who threaten the status or power of the animal within the territory are repulsed. In the example of the rat who took over one pen, weaker males who did not interfere with his power in the situation were allowed to stay on. Among the baboons, the very young approached and played with the high-status males, but the adolescents who were beginning to enter the status hierarchy avoided approaching the latter. Finally, among birds, territorial defense is usually engaged in against birds with similar food needs and not against species with dissimilar food needs. Thus, when power and prerogatives are not threatened by the intruding animal, the intruder is allowed to stay; otherwise, the intruder is repulsed from a position of psychological advantage.

The psychological advantage that we have within our own territories (homes, offices) is lost when we visit elsewhere. Since higher status people can claim greater areas and facilities as their own territories, they have a better chance of retaining this psychological advantage in dealing with others. So, we have a two-sided relationship. People of high status claim and regulate access to larger territories and facilities and those who already have access to large territories are able thereby to assume the advantages of high status.

The following experimental findings are relevant in this context. Men were grouped into pairs and were socially isolated by living in a restricted space for a few days [8]. Personality test scores for members of these pairs were available, including a measure of each subject's level of dominance (an analogue of status). All three combinations of high-high, high-low, and low-low dominance pairs were observed in this setting. It was found that relative to the other pairs, high-high pairs tended to increase their territorial behavior over time. In these high-dominant pairs, each individual was more likely to develop exclusive use of locations and furniture in the area where the two were isolated. These findings are not surprising, since only in the high-high pairs was there a good chance that one member's dominant position would be threatened. Thus, the territorial behavior was a means that both used to cling to the limited psychological advantages provided by the setting.

Violated Territories

The concept of territoriality goes beyond "staking out" a piece of land for yourself. People possess areas, such as desks, favorite chairs, rooms that are not to be intruded upon, or even particular seats at the eating table.

Sometime, if you care to risk an episode of unpleasantness, appropriate the favorite lounge chair of a friend whom you visit at home. Note her reactions, if she reveals them, and any change in her behavior toward you. I suggest this as an informal experiment that could be fun to discuss afterward with a good (and forgiving) friend, but I would be very reluctant to suggest such recurrent experiments with your family at home.

Some of the most persistent irritants for people who live together are their occasional violations of each other's territorial rights. The magnitude of hurt feelings and irritations from such violations can be appreciated when we consider that even John Calhoun's rats under normal population density conditions showed a great deal of respect for each other's limited territorial rights within the same pen [56]. Only under conditions of excessive crowding within a pen did they begin to intrude on each other's territories so that these had to be maintained through fighting.

The analogy to the home environment can be striking. Crowding within the same dwelling unit can result in violation of inhabitants' territorial rights, and the violations may arouse hostility and aggression. When the crowding is excessive, the hostility becomes a frequent problem and grows into psychological and general social maladjustments. Chombart de Lauwe [61] found that in France when the number of people within a given dwelling unit approaches a point where less than 8 to 10 square meters of floor space are available per person, physical and social dysfunction suddenly doubles. At least part of the social disturbances resulting from crowding that have been obtained in various studies [134; 424] can be attributed to the violations of cohabitants' territorial rights and associated recurrent problems.

On the other hand, insistence on territorial rights can be viewed as a way of minimizing stress, and therefore could be expected to be more forceful when people are under stress, that is, while experiencing displeasure, high arousal, and submissiveness. In line with this, extreme territorial behavior was observed in Green Beret camps in Vietnam [39]. Each man had an area of his own within the camp and at certain times would prohibit entry into this area by anyone. There was an implicit understanding that at such times entry into the area would result in violent repulsion and such periods of seclusion of each soldier were carefully respected.

Even when the setting (for instance, the apartment or house) provides a considerable amount of space for the inhabitants, violation of territorial rights is not necessarily precluded. Some people seem completely oblivious to another's implicit rights to a given part of a living space. Worse yet, their violations may be part of a more or less conscious attempt to take over more space and to assume a more dominant position in the situation. They move from one area of the house to another, successively claiming each from their victims. Such people seem to note a favorite "territory" (a working, music-listening, or reading area; a chair or desk); and, when it is vacated, they take it over. One of the maneuvers to claim space involves leaving some of their possessions in the appropriated area. We can tell a systematic takeover from simple carelessness by trying to reclaim some area—the resistance we get is a measure of the interloper's expansive intentions. Dominant victims may fight back; submissive victims may relinquish their claims to those particular areas and move on to other territories where they can attain some privacy and where their belongings will remain undisturbed.

Summary

The ideas introduced in this chapter to explain the kinds of actions that reflect status differences in this culture form a coherent framework. The metaphor of power and fearlessness underlies the representation of status. Thus, lower status people assume postures that indicate weakness; they speak softly and are more watchful and tenser in the presence of higher status others.

Also, in terms of the metaphor, a fearful person does not spontaneously select a position close to one whom he or she fears and who is more powerful. However, when asked to do so, the person obeys and remains watchful. It is therefore not surprising that the prerogative to approach and increase contact remains with the higher status member in a situation and that when he or she offers this option to another, it is generally accepted.

In a related way, the phenomenon of territoriality is a by-product of the prerogative of high-status members of a group to regulate the approach of others. Under conditions of crowding, the more powerful members insist on this prerogative and stake out relatively large areas that are out of bounds for the weaker members. Such territories are generally respected under normal conditions of crowding, but need to be forcefully maintained under conditions of overcrowding. Animal studies also show that female or weaker male members of the species who do not threaten the integrity of the territory are welcome to visit and to stay.

Suggested Readings

For reviews of the experimental findings on how people convey dominance or status, see [259; 383; 394]. Informal discussion of the prerogative to approach lower status others is given by Goffman [139; 140] and by Henley [167]. Examples of territorial behavior from observations of animals are given in [13; 239]. Hall [156] presents a readable account of the differences in the territorial behavior of various cultures. See Chapter 30 of my *Public Places and Private Spaces* [273] for a detailed analysis of the emotional consequences of crowding.

Chapter 5

The Double-edged Message

Most of us have had accidents in social situations—a drink or a cup of coffee spilled, a vase or a lamp overturned. There are many possible reactions to such mishaps from companions and hostesses. But sometimes we've heard from good friends such reactions as "Clumsy!" "Slob!" and "Oh, you schlemiel!" said with a smile and in a tone of exasperated affection. The verbal message, the epithet, expresses the distress and dismay of the speaker; the smile and the voice tone assure us that we have not fallen from favor. It would be difficult, if not impossible for most of us, to put across the complexities of that message in words alone: "I really don't like what you did; it hurts my feelings, but I still like you." Such a verbalization would sound phony at best, and few of us would be inclined to try it. However, some psychotherapists actually suggest that such messages are a healthy way to communicate.

We are not at our most lovable best when we do it, but most of us on occasion use the two-edged message when we wish to convey heavy sarcasm that can be blandly denied when we are called on it. The formula is unfortunately as overused in real life as it is in domestic situation comedies on television. Person A (man or woman) makes a sarcastic statement. Person B protests, takes exception to the remark. Person A replies, usually starting with "But all I said was . . ." and repeats the words in a matter-of-fact tone of voice and a more neutral facial expression instead of the original negative one.

Part of the problem is that in our culture, we are excessively sensitized to words and have very few terms for characterizing implicit behavior. It is therefore very difficult, unless we have an audio-video record, to identify and cope with implicit expressions of hostility that are cloaked by simultaneous verbal expressions to which we cannot legitimately take exception.

About two decades ago psychologists and psychiatrists working in family therapy became aware of the significance of inconsistent communication [153; 415], and many of them routinely tape-recorded their therapy sessions. On occasion, they played back recorded segments of previous sessions to their patients to point out the ways in which the family members implicitly hurt each other, while making seemingly positive or innocuous statements. Such informal inquiries by psychotherapists pointed out that inconsistent communications do indeed serve special functions, and they motivated researchers to try to understand why people use these messages.

In order to describe these special functions of inconsistent communication, we need first to establish a more general definition of it. Inconsistent communications are those in which contradictory messages are being conveyed simultaneously by words and other behaviors. That is, we may express something verbally while our facial expressions [33; 98], postures and positions [259; 270], tone of voice [178; 351; 387; 440], or gestures [90; 126] indicate the opposite. Since the kinds of messages that we can communicate implicitly are pleasure-displeasure, arousal-nonarousal, dominance-submissiveness, and like-dislike (with the latter also inferred from various combinations of the first three), inconsistency can be measured in terms of each of these separately.

Watch for two-edged messages—as others talk, as others speak to you, as you speak to others. How often is the verbal message contradicted by voice tone, facial expression, posture, gestures? Are people more prone to use inconsistent messages in some situations than others? Can you spot an expression of liking contradicted? How? Can you find an expression of dominance contradicted by behavior of submissiveness? If you do not observe a situation of contradictory messages about arousal, can you remember or imagine such?

Resolution of Inconsistent Messages

As noted, people can convey varying degrees of liking by simultaneously using words, facial and vocal expressions, postures, and gestures. They may also convey different degrees of dominance with these behaviors. Many a politician has stood before the voters, chest proudly thrust forward, posture erect, and in a booming voice declared, "If elected, I will be the humble servant of the people." The demeanor of such a candidate, his manner of dress, and the props surrounding him more often than not have indicated a high status and a dominant position. The objective observer could hardly believe that the candidate is capable of being a truly humble servant of the people, or that he has any intention of trying to be. He might, however, think of him as a person in a position of power who will take great care to seem considerate of the needs and feelings of others, particularly his constituents.

Behaviors can be used simultaneously with speech to convey different degrees of arousal. The fast-talking auctioneer is a champion of inconsistency here. His voluble and almost incessant speech shows a great deal of arousal, but his bland expressions and monotonous voice are at the other extreme—low arousal.

An interesting question now arises: Is there a systematic and coherent approach to resolving the general meaning or impact of an inconsistent message? Indeed there is. Our experimental results [269, Chapter 6; 286; 305] show:

Total liking = 7% verbal liking + 38% vocal liking + 55% facial liking

Thus, the impact of facial expression is greatest, then the impact of the tone of voice (or vocal expression), and finally that of words. If the facial expression is inconsistent with the words, the degree of liking conveyed by the facial expression will prevail and determine the impact of the total message. On the other hand, in an audiorecorded message or a conversation on the phone, if the vocal expression happens to contradict the words, then the former determines the total impact. This can work either way: The words may be positive and the vocal expression negative, in which case the total sarcastic message is a negative one; or the vocal expression may be positive and the words negative, in which case the total message is a positive one.

Experiments conducted in England [15] confirmed our findings reported in the above equation that implicit cues have about twelve times the power of verbal cues. Support was obtained for a similar relationship when the messages referred to dominance [19]; a person's implicit behavior far outweighs the importance of his words (about four to five times as much) when he uses contradictory messages showing dominance-submissiveness. For instance, if a person's facial expression and posture are domineering, no matter how submissive her words imply her to be, the message will be interpreted in a manner consistent with the dominance revealed by her facial expression and posture.

There are as yet no experimental results for analysis of inconsistent messages of arousal; but those results, once obtained, probably will conform to what has been found for liking and dominance.

In an employment interview, the applicant may say all the right things, but his contradictory behavior may cost him the job. He may say positively that he is interested in the job, that he will work hard and believes very much in what the company is doing; that is, verbally express liking. But the interviewer may find that his bland and expressionless face and voice do little to confirm this verbalized enthusiasm, and may intuitively decide that he does not really mean what he says; there was insufficient arousal in these implicit cues. Remember that the most liking is conveyed implicitly when both

pleasure and arousal levels are high (Figure 1-1). In trying to estimate how enthusiastic an applicant really is about getting a particular job, an interviewer tends to give more weight to the applicant's
implicitly expressed, rather than verbally expressed, arousal.

Generalizing, we can say that people's implicit behavior has more
bearing than their words on communicating feelings or attitudes to
others. So we have rewritten our equation for any *feeling*.

Total feeling = 7% verbal feeling + 38% vocal feeling + 55% facial feeling

Numerical values in this equation are only approximate. However,
the order of importance of words, vocal expressions, and facial expressions is likely to be upheld in future experiments. To use this
equation, we have to restrict ourselves to the analysis of only one
dimension at a time. This dimension could be like-dislike, pleasure-
displeasure, dominance-submissiveness, or arousal-nonarousal; or it
could be even very specific feelings such as joy, anxiety, hurt, anger,
depression, or curiosity.

Additional experimental support for the relationships given in the
equation has been provided by findings showing that facial expressions of feelings are more important than vocal expressions in
terms of their contribution to the total message [47]. And, vocal expressions contribute more than words [439], particularly when the
tone of voice in itself is judged spontaneous and believable [45]. Further, in the case of overall judgments of communicated empathy, implicit cues contribute more than verbal ones [151]. This last result
clearly illustrates the applicability of our equation to specific emotions that combine various degrees of pleasure, arousal, and dominance.

In a comprehensive study of inconsistent messages of pleasure-
displeasure and dominance-submissiveness in vocal and visual (face
and/or body) cues, it was established that visual cues were more
powerful than vocal cues in determining the overall effect inferred
from moderately inconsistent messages. This effect was greater
when the visual cues involved the face. However, in the case of extreme inconsistency, visual cues were weighted less than vocal cues
[78]. The latter reversal was interpreted by noting that subjects are
less likely to believe and rely upon visual cues (which are easier to
control [266; 440]) when visual and vocal cues are extremely discrepant, thus implying deception.

It is important to note also that even though more complex models have been proposed to explain the decoding of inconsistent messages, the simple linear model given in our equation (and variants
thereof) consistently works best [438]. In using the equation to estimate the total emotion or level of liking communicated, it is first

necessary to measure the impact of each behavior by itself and on the same scale. The equation is then used to compute the total impact.

In the laboratory situation, we obtain videotapes of subjects delivering verbal messages, then have several people separately evaluate the various aspects of communication in terms of the impression made on the receiver of the message, using a scale from −3 to +3. The procedure is, of course, artificial and could not readily be used outside the laboratory, but it gives us more objective data than those based on unstructured intuition. For example, in estimating the feeling of happiness communicated by a subject, we play back the videotaped message without the sound; a group of judges observes the soundless picture and rates his facial expression on a scale from −3 (extremely unhappy) to +3 (extremely happy). Next, a typed transcription of the message (just the words on paper—no sound, no picture) is rated on the same scale. Finally, the audiorecording is played back through an electronic device (for example, a Krohn-Hite Model 3500 Band Pass Filter) to make the words of the speech incomprehensible while retaining the quality of vocal expression; and this filtered audio message is rated on the same happiness scale.

Let us say that for this example we had a score of −2 for the facial expression, a score of +2 for the words, and a score of −2 for the vocal expression. Inserting these values into the equation gives an overall value for the feeling of happiness communicated by the subject of −1.72 on the scale. In this case, since the vocal expression and facial expression were both judged as unhappy (−2), the impact of the total message is very close to the impact made by these two, and the relative happiness (+2) of the words has very little effect.

We have written the second and more general equation only for combinations of words, vocal expressions, and facial expressions. If we extrapolate from these results, we can obtain the following, reasonably safe, generalization: When any implicit behavior contradicts speech, it is more likely to determine the total impact of the message. In other words, touching, positions (distance, forward lean, or eye contact), postures, gestures, as well as facial and vocal expressions, can all outweigh words and determine the feelings conveyed by a message.

Suppose an engaged couple encounters a woman whom the man had formerly dated frequently. She has news of a mutual friend, who is unknown to the fiancée. As they pause for the exchange of pleasantries, he reaches out and grasps the hand of his fiancée. Even though he has turned his face and his direct attention from her, the clasping of her hand is reassurance that she is more important to him than the other woman and is preferred to her. One implication here is that touching is a very important clue to liking; and, even when it contradicts postures, positions, and words, it still determines the total impact of a message.

We have all been interrupted in social and business conversations by phone calls. On some occasions and for any of a number of reasons, the interruption may be protracted. As we continue the phone conversation, however, we turn in the direction of our visitor, make eye contact, smile, or use other facial expressions that indicate our regret about the interruption. The implicit messages assure the visitor that we have not forgotten and are not neglecting him even though we are talking to someone else. Here again, the importance of facial expressions becomes evident, since generally they are quite sufficient to keep the visitor from feeling restless and uneasy as he occupies his enforced social vacuum.

Incidentally, we should be careful to note that these assertions about the disproportionate contribution of implicit, relative to verbal, cues is limited to feelings (pleasure, arousal, dominance) and like-dislike. Obviously, implicit expressions are not always more important than words. In fact, implicit cues are ineffective for communicating most referents denoted by words (for example, "I'll see you tomorrow afternoon at 2:00 P.M.," "I was wearing my new velour suit yesterday," or "$x + y = z$").

The basic metaphors that underlie implicit messages, together with some other aspects of our culture, help us to understand why people assign greater weight to the implicit part of inconsistently communicated feelings. Two pervasive traditions of Western society bear on this issue. The first and probably more important of these traditions is restraint in the expression of feelings, particularly negative ones (such as anger, jealously, resentment, or weakness) outside the sphere of intimate relationships [343]. The second is the absence of explicit instruction on the subject of implicit communication within the framework of formal education. The continued emphasis on language skills both at home and in school contrasts sharply with the neglect of training in implicit communication.

How do these two traditions relate to one another in affecting communication? We assume that the human organism cannot totally "conceal" emotion—that emotions denied expression in one channel find another outlet [95; 267; 390]. Both negative feelings (frustration, irritation, hostility) and positive feelings (pleasure, desire, love) are part of social life, so if expression is discouraged, feelings are conveyed less overtly (and often without conscious volition) by implicit behaviors. These are more subtle; nonetheless, they assume a greater significance for many who rely more on these less-censored expressions. The lack of emphasis on implicit communication in education helps to perpetuate a situation in which socially unacceptable feelings must be expressed in behaviors other than speech and cannot be recognized "officially" as part of a person's communication. We learn to express a variety of feelings in these more subtle ways to avoid detectable transgression of the social norms.

General Function of Inconsistent Messages

We sometimes say, "That's great!" with a sarcastic tone of voice when we could simply say, "That's lousy!" Sometimes a wife exclaims to her husband, "I hate you!" with a positive expression when she could use a consistent message to express liking. Even though both the inconsistent and consistent messages convey liking to the husband, in some situations the wife finds the inconsistent one more expressive of her intended meaning. Some special function must be served by such inconsistent messages that cannot operate with consistent ones. This function becomes apparent when we think of the wife who says, "I hate you!" with a loving expression. In this instance, there may be a certain degree of resignation in her message. She might use this particular form when he has done something that will cause her extra work or inconvenience and yet in no way affects her love for him. For example, he might have come home with an adorable puppy, for which the children have been clamoring for months and which she also has wanted—covertly. Although her words convey her dismay over the prospect of housebreaking, muddy paw prints, and desecrated flowerbeds, her soft laugh and the warmth of her voice tell him that he has in no way forfeited her

love and approval [266]. As we have already seen, despite the negativeness of the words, the total impact is positive.

On the other hand, an inconsistent message can have a negative impact. Darlene, a secretary, in talking about the office manager may say to a coworker, "Oh yes! I really like her!" with a sarcastic tone of voice. The message received by Harry is that Darlene dislikes their supervisor; this inference is consistent with the vocal expression that Darlene used in expressing the words. The words may be simply a playful continuation of an earlier segment of the conversation—something like, "What's the matter, don't you like her?" from Harry. Chances are that the office manager is someone who cannot be openly and directly criticized by underlings. In this informal conversation between Darlene and Harry, the words playfully maintain a façade that has to be put up in her presence, but they are clearly contradicted by actions and tone of voice.

These examples bring out another aspect of inconsistent messages—they are more likely to be used in an informal and casual setting than in a formal one [266]. A situation is informal when we are with friends rather than acquaintances or people we barely know, or when we are with people of whom we can be openly critical as we cannot be with others who tend to be readily hurt and are intolerant of criticism. Private, face-to-face conversations are generally more informal than those conducted where strangers are nearby and where arguments could be embarrassing. In other words, when the situation or the person you converse with is "uptight," inconsistent messages of any kind are discouraged. In such circumstances, the humor of an unpleasant comment spoken jokingly will not be appreciated, and consistent negative messages of any kind can only "put people off."

In welcoming a new employee to his job, the department head says, "We are all equal here and can openly express our feelings. I want you to let your feelings be known and especially to let me know if you have reservations about anything or feel that something is wrong." As he speaks, his posture, facial expression, and vocal expression convey his awareness of his dominant relationship relative to the new member of his department, who comes away from this pep talk with the feeling that the boss is a bit of a phony, that he is trying to be a nice guy, but that he doesn't really mean what he says. In other words, the new man feels that he will be wise not to be critical of anything the boss says or does.

We have already discussed how self-conscious Americans feel about the issue of status. Some aspects of the youth culture notwithstanding, it is still legitimate in many parts of this culture to actively seek status—but not to talk about it or to flaunt it. In our socially prescribed dealings with others, good manners include much behavior that is deferential, considerate of the needs, wishes, and egos of others. Very few who use these social mannerisms, which might appear to the uninitiated as evidence of humility and submissiveness, are at all humble or submissive. The American who flaunts his or her power or higher status in one context or another does not get along well with other Americans. As with expressions of dislike, verbal or blatant implicit communication of a dominant attitude is discouraged. The social bully is offensive and wins no popularity contests.

When a police officer says, "Pull over!" most of us have an inclination to retort, "Say, 'Please.'" An imperious demand, a direct order, or a command generally sparks in most of us a disinclination to comply. A folk saying notes: "Honey attracts more flies than vinegar." The reaction is not peculiar to twentieth-century Americans; Aesop's fable about the relative persuasiveness of the North Wind and the Sun has been known for at least 2500 years. We are not taught to grovel, to kowtow, or to be servile. However, we are taught to say "Excuse me," "Please," and "Thank you." As status goes in our culture, many (though not all) children of highest status strata are most carefully trained in these and other social amenities. Our peers of childhood teach us more surely than our families about the relative effectiveness of requests and demands; children who try to boss others around are not acceptable to their peer groups.

We do not use words and behaviors of dominance, if for no other reason than that they are not generally effective in getting us what we want and need from others. If the verbal message and the behaviors that accompany it convey an impression of dominance, most of us almost instinctively balk and cooperate no more than we absolutely must. We have to make demands on others; others constantly make demands on us. We ask favors of others; others ask favors of us. Often, however, orders and demands are phrased as requests or as quasi-requests. If they are starkly phrased ("Do this . . . ," "Give me that . . ."), they are often communicated as requests because of the quality of facial expression and tone of voice.

Sometimes the social roles make it clear that these covert expressions of request are clearly a sign of polite consideration: An executive says pleasantly to her secretary, "Miss Carlson, would you please bring me the file on the construction contract?" The verbal message and the implicit behaviors convey nothing of dominance. But that is an order—both know it. There is no question in either mind about the dominant and submissive roles in the situation.

Generally, we are well aware of status and of the relative power of others to affect our lives for good or ill; and we tend to modify our behaviors accordingly. The submissive aspects of our implicit behavior associated with requests tend to be intensified, however slightly, when we deal with a person who has the power to injure us (as through loss of employment or of social favor). The submissive overtones are often less evident when the other person is in a dependent or subordinate position, such as a child. Nevertheless, some people, even in dealing with a dependent other, use excessively pleading expressions as they make a request. It is tempting to say that such people are just trying to be considerate. A more accurate description, however, is that they are submissive people who have an unrealistic concern about possible rebuff and rejection, even when their social position legitimately allows them to make a request.

Our discussion and examples show that inconsistent messages come into play in this culture when we have mixed feelings about something [266]. Implicit and explicit social rules sometimes dictate ways of acting that are strongly at odds with our true feelings in given situations. At these times, we often send inconsistent messages in which we quite literally pay lip service (verbal message) to social convention, while implicit messages betray our real feelings. Experimental findings confirm folk wisdom: "Actions speak louder than words." Generally speaking, others weigh our actions more than our words as they try to understand what we feel.

Inconsistent Messages and Social Influence

Inconsistent messages assume a specific function in situations in which people influence one another [264]. Even though we don't like to talk about it, our dealings with others frequently involve influencing them or being influenced by them. Our behavior is influenced more than most of us care to admit even to ourselves by our friends and our foes, by our coworkers as well as our superiors in our employment situation, by our neighbors (even if we don't know them), by "people" (as in ". . . but what will people think!").

We accept persuasion as a legitimate, if sometimes annoying, part of living—sometimes we enjoy being coaxed. Efforts to persuade others are essential in human interaction; some of us are more skillful than others. However, we tend to be outraged by efforts to influence that go beyond persuasion, which is acceptable, and become manipulation, which is repugnant. There is a subtle difference between "He persuaded me" and "He conned me into it." We speak of "credibility gaps" and "manipulation of news," and our disapproval probably reflects our resentment of manipulation—not of news but of us.

We don't like to think about or discuss what might be considered "undue and improper" influence. Manipulation of others is a socially disapproved activity, and we prefer to believe that we would not do it (or at least not be caught doing it). Most of us are sufficient egoists to be foolishly certain that we cannot be manipulated by others. As with other aspects of social interaction, unwillingness or inability to verbalize about something, to discuss it, makes implicit behavior related to it a more important vehicle of communication. In other words, when the words fail to convey some important fact in a social situation, actions take over this function.

A psychotherapist's relationship with adult clients is an example to consider. If therapists are to be worth what they charge, they must influence their clients' behaviors, but must do so without being too obvious about it. At least this is the feeling of most of the more traditional and psychoanalytically oriented therapists [129; 346].

Such therapists make sure their clients know that they will not provide any suggestions or guidelines. They say very little, and that little is mostly restricted to carefully worded neutral questions like "How?" and "Why you?" and "Then what did you do?" If a client chooses not to talk, they can sit in patient silence for the whole of a fifty-minute hour. If the therapists carry this rationale to its logical extreme, they would be just as guarded in what they revealed implicitly by voice tone, facial expression, posture, and gesture. However, their implicit behavior generally does reveal some differential preference for certain things that their clients do or report. Even when, in traditional Freudian style [129], therapists sit at the head of the couch and behind reclining clients so the clients cannot see them, they can still show varying degrees of interest and preference through vocal expressions. In most therapy sessions, however, therapists are actually fully visible to their clients and can subtly reveal information about their preferences for or like-dislike of different things reported by clients. Since, as we have already seen, the impact of implicit behavior outweighs the impact of words, it follows that therapists are in a position to guide their clients' progress implicitly without actually requesting the clients to do anything specific [408].

The function of psychoanalytically oriented therapists is to help clients help themselves. They do not tell their clients what is wrong and what should be done about it because, according to their theoretical orientation, it is futile to do so—clients must work things out for themselves, and premature disclosure and interpretation by therapists may harm the clients rather than help them. Also, the nonintervention, nondirective approach protects these therapists from loss of face and against rebellion or antagonism from clients. Since the therapists do not make suggestions or demands, clients cannot shift the responsibility for their social problems to their therapists, nor can they set about to prove their therapists wrong, thus delaying their own progress.

As with therapists who deny being directive in relation to their clients, talk about the "self-determination" of a group is suspect in some situations, especially when the speaker has a stake in the outcome of self-determination. The person who stresses self-determination may be a den mother of a Cub Scout pack, a union leader, a grade-school teacher, or a boss of a political machine. Such people know full well that any open and aggressive efforts on their part, or on the part of their organizations, to dictate the actions of the group in question, may well fail or even backfire. Thus, they talk about self-determination while unobtrusively, perhaps ruthlessly, manipulating the group in the desired direction.

Inconsistent Messages and Psychological Disturbance

Attention was first drawn to the significance of inconsistent messages in the context of work with schizophrenics [153; 415]. Psychotherapists who interviewed schizophrenic patients along with their families began to notice a certain peculiarity in the way in which parents addressed their maladjusted children. There seemed to be a predominance of inconsistent messages; many of the parents, for example, repeatedly said reasonably pleasant things about their children while implicitly conveying negative feelings. This kind of message was interpreted by therapists as being confusing and probably the major source of psychological disturbance. For instance, when a mother tells her son, "Come and give your mommy a kiss" and then turns away from him as he approaches because his hands are dirty, the child is confused. He thinks that he's wanted, and yet he is also rejected. He does not know what to do. He loses either way. If he reacts to the implicit behavior—the turning away—by crying and shrinking back, his mother will be offended because she has told him to come over and kiss her. On the other hand, if he reacts to what she said and tries to come to her and kiss her, she will be offended by his dirty hands and reject him.

This "double-bind" situation, repeated over and over again, gives the child no clear choice for action and leads him to a point where he himself begins to use very peculiar inconsistent messages. For example, a son sends a birthday card to his mother and signs it "Napoleon." This action lets his mother know, on the one hand, that he has remembered her birthday and is being affectionate, but signing a name not his own implies that it was not really he who sent the card. This bizarre behavior is consistent with his other strange and maladaptive ways of dealing with people.

Double-bind theorists' basic assumption about the relation between psychological disturbance and inconsistent messages was that the latter were ambiguous and difficult to interpret [153; 373; 415]. However, we now know that this is not true. People do quite readily understand the true meaning when the verbal and implicit parts of a message are inconsistent—they rely on the implicit part and make their judgment accordingly [15; 19; 48; 49; 221; 286; 305].

We now also know that parents of maladjusted children do not necessarily use more frequent inconsistent messages than parents of normal children, but they do use more negative messages [4; 29; 393]. Analysis of the anecdotal evidence cited by the double-bind therapists to support their thesis shows that they were struck by the inconsistent sarcastic messages and not by the inconsistent positive ones. In other words, the messages that drew their attention had an overall negative impact. Present experimental findings show that parents of more maladjusted or delinquent children do communicate more negative feelings to these children and that they sometimes use sarcastic messages to do so [4; 29; 393].

There are two ways to understand the latter result. First, the parents' initial negative attitude toward their own children may be the cause of maladjustment in the children; second, they may be more negative toward their disturbed children since these are a greater source of frustration to them. It is also possible that both of these processes are involved and together function to perpetuate an unhealthy parent-child relationship. A vicious cycle is maintained whereby the child is constantly criticized and feels his parents do not like him, so he does not cooperate or meet their demands. As the child is disobedient and rebellious in relation to his parents, the parents become even more frustrated and have more reasons for being negative to him; he in turn becomes even less cooperative, and so forth; the difficulty is easily perpetuated [264].

We must be cautious in identifying inconsistent messages with psychological disturbance. With our implicit social rules and prohibitions about the expressions of feelings (particularly negative ones), people frequently must use inconsistent messages. They may also use these to achieve efficient communication or even to be funny. Our discussion suggests that we should focus, not on the inconsistency as such, but rather on the total impact of a message. Is the overall quality positive or negative? Unusually frequent negative messages are indicative of frustrated and frustrating relationships, whether these be of married couples or of parents and their children.

The vicious cycle of a negative relationship can be easily modified. With outside help, parents can gain some feeling of adequacy and control over the relationship with the child. This minimizes their sense of frustration and allows them to be more positive. At this more positive stage of the relationship, the child, in turn, may become more amenable to influence and more willing to make some effort; social influence is enhanced by liking and positive feelings in a relationship and is discouraged by negative feelings [263; 289; 294]. The response of the child provides the parents with an even greater sense of accomplishment and control and reduces their frustration further. So, they are even more positive, and so forth. The vicious cycle is broken and a positive cycle thereby initiated [264].

Summary

One of the more common examples of contradictory verbal and implicit behavior is sarcasm. "How wonderful!" said with a negative tone of voice is interpreted as "How bad!" because the vocal expression is more important than the words. The same phrase, "How wonderful!" said with a negative vocal expression *and* a disgruntled frown implies even a stronger negative feeling and is more likely to imply "How utterly miserable!" The negative message in the vocal expression, as well as the facial expression, accounts for this stronger result.

The opposite of sarcasm, for which we don't have a word in English, is involved when we, for instance, tell a friend, "You idiot!" with a smile and positive tone of voice. The overall result is more of a joke than an insult. "You little monster!" said to a child with a smile implies "You lovable little creature!"

The general rule for understanding the effects of such inconsistent messages is that, when actions contradict words, people rely more heavily on actions to infer another's feelings. In other words, less-controllable behaviors are generally assigned greater weight.

Of course, if both our words and facial expressions show pleasure, a different effect is produced than if only the words show pleasure. It has been demonstrated that redundancy of messages in different behaviors intensifies the impact [286]. In a number of African languages, this rule is exemplified as a formal grammatical device [420]. An adjective is repeated successively to emphasize a certain quality of an object or person. Applying this to English, we would say, "She was a happy, happy woman," to stress great happiness. The effect of redundancy explains why a person is more convincing when he uses an expressive face and voice to say, "No, that doesn't bother me at all," than when he says it with bland vocal and facial expressions.

Our implicit messages may contradict or reinforce what we say in words; in either event, they are more potent in communication than the words we speak.

Suggested Readings

For specific experimental reports of how inconsistent messages are resolved, see [15; 19; 45; 47; 48; 49; 78; 151; 221; 286; 305; 438; 439]. Experimental results of preferences for consistent and inconsistent messages are given in [266]. The following works contain data and reviews of studies that relate inconsistent messages to psychopathology: [4; 29; 373; 393].

Chapter 6

Social Style

We form distinct first impressions of many people whom we meet; we feel that they are extroverted, introverted, domineering, pleasant, obnoxious, self-assured, active, argumentative, hostile, or even bland. There is something about each person, a pervasive style that applies to almost everything he or she does that enables us to form an impression before any exchange of words [7].

Observe your own reactions as you meet people for the first time. You may find yourself forming certain ideas of what you can expect from each or how much you feel you might like each one. You may think to yourself, "Here's a timid and passive type" or "There's an intolerable snob!"

The way an extrovert enters a gathering is very different from the entrance made by an introvert. Compared with submissive or passive people, dominant individuals take their seats in a more visible position—one from which they can more readily survey the whole scene [383]. The gestures and movements of these different people suggest the character or style of their personalities without the aid of words. In addition to implicit behavior, the physical props that people use—in their home or work environment—and their manner of dress provide the necessary background for a more complete impression [156; 273].

What specifically is it about the implicit behavior or favorite props of different people that creates such distinct impressions? How, for instance, does a domineering person convey this image even before speaking? As you take a seat next to a stranger on a plane, what is it about the person that leads you to think, "This looks like it's going to be an interesting trip" instead of "I wish they had given me another seat"?

Of course, manner of dress and general physical appearance (such as cleanliness, physical attractiveness) have a definite effect on the impression made. However, here we are more interested in the behaviors that supplement, or even override, this appearance in presenting an overall picture. For instance, aside from clothing, what is it in a man's mannerisms that label him a flirt? Is it the greater intimacy he conveys to women? Does he indulge in more eye contact with unfamiliar females? Does he stand unduly close to women who are only casual acquaintances? Or is it because his behavior fluctuates in positiveness—warm and intimate at times and aloof at others?

So far, the importance of people's actions has been highlighted by considering the impression they make before they speak. We can also form an impression of someone whom we have not seen, but whose speech or writings are familiar. Actually meeting someone with whom we have corresponded but have never met before can have a jarring effect. A favorite author, eloquent and fluent on paper, may turn out to be a shy woman who stutters and stammers; she may be young, although we had imagined her as old and serious. The impression that has been drawn from the communications involving words (that is, her writings only) simply does not fit with our face-to-face observations.

Newscasters and announcers who can employ vocal expressions as well as words on radio provide us with only a very sketchy impression of what they are like. An announcer's voice might give us the impression of a tall and domineering person, but he may actually be small and quite friendly and unimposing. A person with a "flat" voice may turn out to be very interesting.

More interesting still is how a person's home or office may contribute largely to overall impression. In fact, some of us feel that we do not really know someone until we have visited the person's home ground. We may find that a woman who is apparently interested in nothing but tennis has a good library and a classical record collection at home. A television star who plays tough killer-type roles may be revealed by a feature story in a fan magazine as a father who spends most of his free time with his young children and their pets.

Several interrelated questions need to be answered in order to formulate what factors go into making an overall picture of a person. Probably, it is not just one isolated behavior here or there that gives us an impression but rather a composite of behaviors that are indicative of a certain style. One question therefore is "What are these clusters?" or "What are the categories of social behavior?" A second question is "What are the personality attributes, qualities such as extroversion or introversion, that underlie distinct social styles?" Finally, "How are the various personality attributes related to the categories of social behavior?"

Elements of Social Behavior

To answer such questions, we devised situations similar to the following one in several experiments [71; 268; 282; 283; 293; 294]. Pairs of students who were subjects in our experiments and perfect strangers to each other were led into a room by an experimenter. She told them that they were going to listen to some music and that she had to prepare the tape. For five minutes, while they waited for the experimenter to return with the tape, each pair was observed from an adjacent room through a one-way mirror. The subjects were unaware of being observed, and what transpired was a natural exchange between pairs of strangers. Everything they said and did during the five-minute period was recorded on videotape.

At the end of this waiting, they did actually listen to some music and were asked to judge its pleasantness. They then answered some questions covering personality measures, which included such statements as "I like to know people who have a lot of friends" and "When someone does something to hurt my feelings, it takes me a long time to get over it."

These measures were available to us from other experiments and had been devised to describe various aspects of personality. One of these, a measure of affiliative tendency [265; 274], can be used to assign a score to each person that shows how friendly or unfriendly he is. A second one measures the sensitivity of a person to rejection [265; 274]; that is, how much he fears being slighted in a social setting and how hard he tries to avoid this possibility. Other personality questionnaires can be used to measure a person's achieving tendency [255; 258; 281], dominance [288], and dependency, impulsivity, aggressiveness, or desire for social recognition [181].

Once they had completed the questionnaires, the subjects were given a thorough briefing on the experiment. Their questionnaire answers provided us with a description of their personalities, while their behavior in the waiting situation provided us with data that could be scored [260] and used to formulate the categories of social behavior. With these data, we could try to define clusters of social behavior and, more importantly, relate these clusters to personality attributes.

In observing the pairs of subjects through the one-way mirror, it was readily apparent that there were striking differences between them. One of the most fascinating aspects of psychological research is the opportunity to observe the differences in the behavior of people in the same experimental situation. This can be interesting and instructive even for the casual onlooker.

As you have opportunity, take a few minutes to observe different behaviors of people in standardized situations; for example, as they approach a cashier's booth to buy tickets to a performance that is sold out, or as they respond to the stewardess on boarding or leaving a plane.

Tellers, cashiers, and waitresses have the opportunity to see differences in how people act in similar situations. For instance, one man at a snack-bar counter asks courteously, "May I please have a hot dog?" Another says, "Give me a hot dog," in a matter-of-fact tone. A third and friendly man says, "Let's have a hot dog." A fourth belligerently demands, "Give me a hot dog, will you?" The short-order cook who serves them gets a real education in psychology, provided these brief exchanges are typical of each stranger's personality. His experience with many people in this situation allows him to assess each instance as being unusual or normal. Although he may be unable to conclude much about the person who acts like most others, he can certainly make educated assumptions about the personality of one who belligerently demands a hot dog from a perfect stranger [252].

In the case of the experiment just described, one objective was to see whether it is possible to make such generalizations. Is it possible to observe someone for five minutes and predict accurately the kind of person she is, that is, predict her scores on a personality questionnaire?

To test this, we first analyzed the videorecordings and scored each person's behavior on some three dozen measures, including how frequently he smiled and gestured, how pleasant his speech was, how relaxed he appeared, and how close he stood to his partner. In scoring, we tried to include as many different aspects of behavior as we thought were a meaningful part of social interaction. Given these scores, it was possible to determine which sets of behaviors clustered together to define a category of social behavior.

The most important cluster that we identified was *affiliative behavior* [268; 283; 292; 293]. This included the frequency of declarative statements (which served as a measure of how much a person

spoke), percentage of the waiting time that was spent looking in the direction of the partner, the frequency of head nods and hand gestures, and the pleasant versus unpleasant quality of what was said. As is characteristic of a cluster, these behaviors were found to change together. That is, when someone had more of one of these behaviors, he also exhibited more of the rest. Alternatively, a person who talked very little also had very few of the other qualities in his behavior.

All the behaviors on this list show like-dislike or approach and pleasure. If we dislike someone or wish to make a negative impression, we intuitively tend to avoid all the behaviors in this cluster. These findings, together with others, lead us to conclude that affiliation consists of pleasure and approach cues. People affiliate more with liked than with disliked persons; and if we affiliate a lot with someone, he or she can reasonably infer that we like them [173]. In sum, this first category of social interaction, gregarious behavior, is generally perpetuated through the exchange of pleasant feelings and approach cues and cannot be maintained, or is lacking, in the absence of such an exchange [28; 127; 215; 294; 349; 414].

Since one major category of social behavior is closely intertwined with a primary feeling dimension, pleasure, we wondered if other categories of social behavior corresponded to the remaining feeling dimensions, dominance-submissiveness and arousal-nonarousal [275]. Indeed, we identified two additional clusters that paralleled these two qualities.

The cluster of behaviors that defined *arousal level* consisted of the total expressive quality of the tone of voice, including positive and negative vocal expressions, speech volume, and speech rate measured in number of words per minute [268; 292]. Facial activity, which includes positive as well as negative facial expressions, has also been identified as part of this cluster in some of our experiments [306]. Thus, one aspect of our social behavior is how aroused we seem to others, and these are the specific cues that reflect it.

We found, for instance, that when people try to persuade someone else of something, there is a sharp increase in their arousal levels compared to when they simply try to be informative [306]. Such findings show that even though high arousal can be part of an individual's general style, arousal can also increase or decrease depending on the circumstances in which that person interacts with others. Nevertheless, if we say that someone is "arousable," we mean that he or she is more readily aroused than others.

The third cluster of behaviors related to the *dominant-submissive dimension* and included all the relaxation cues [268]: reclining or leaning sideways while seated and an asymmetrical placement of the arms and legs. Greater relaxation, as we have already seen, is associated with a higher status and a more dominant feeling. In contrast, tension, which is indexed by a symmetrical placement of the arms and legs and an upright posture, is more characteristic of the social behavior of those who are lower in status and more subordinate.

There were several other clusters, one of which represented *distress*. In one experiment in which the subjects were standing, greater distress was indexed by the percentage of the waiting period during which the subject walked about or preoccupied himself with various objects in the room; wrote on a blackboard, examined the thermostat, or looked behind things [293].

One of the remaining clusters, *ingratiating behavior*, deserves more discussion. This cluster included frequent questioning, smiling, and other pleasant vocal and facial expressions, frequent verbal agreements such "Uh-huh," "Yes," or "Same here," and the complete exclusion of negative and unpleasant remarks [293].

Due to its positive quality, ingratiation can be, and has been found to be, a positive correlate of affiliation. However, there is a distinctive quality about ingratiating behavior and the feeling which it projects that keeps it apart from affiliation.

I once spent an evening with a friend and her date whom I met for the first time that night. Throughout the evening, he asked me an unusually large number of questions, which quickly became a considerable burden, and which I was unable to discourage. He was not unpleasant but seemed rather interested, smiled a lot, and had a very positive tone of voice; however, he gave me the impression of being dependent and clinging. His frequent questions and related mannerisms exemplified an almost pure case of ingratiating style. More common instances of ingratiation are likely to be considerably toned down. People sometimes behave in an ingratiating way at the beginning of a somewhat formal or awkward social situation but change to a more relaxed and casual manner with increasing familiarity.

In sum, ingratiating behaviors, despite their pleasant quality, are conducive to a strained and uncomfortable interaction. The pleasantness is excessive and demands reciprocation. The ingratiator is judged as somewhat false and insincere, and his or her victim feels forced to smile and be pleasant. The frequent questioning and the implicit behaviors, which are part of the ingratiator's attempt to ensure a positive reaction, hint at dependency. Ingratiating behavior thus combines pleasure and approach cues with submissiveness.

The three dimensions of pleasure-displeasure, level of arousal, and dominance-submissiveness, thus, provide a framework for describing social behaviors, in addition to characterizing emotional states. In the top half of Figure 6-1, for instance, a combination of unpleasant and dominant qualities yields aggressive behavior, which in turn implies the anger that underlies such behavior. In a vigilant state, a person is slightly tense (feeling unpleasant and submissive) [256], which may be due to apprehension about rejection or to lack of self-confidence. A very different quality, benevolence, is obtained

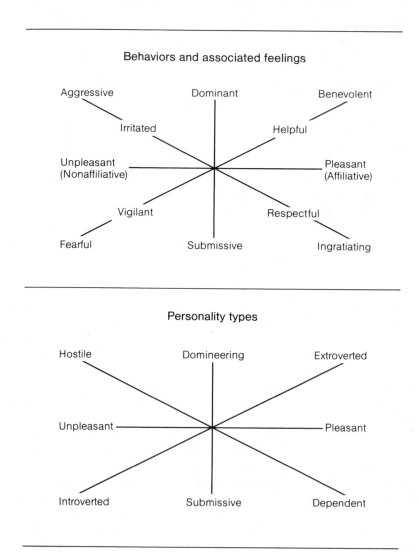

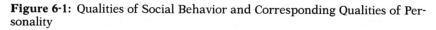

Figure 6-1: Qualities of Social Behavior and Corresponding Qualities of Personality

by combining high degrees of pleasantness and dominance. This again is a way of describing a behavior and its concomitant feeling.

To portray three-dimensional relationships in Figure 6-1, we used the following device: adjectives further out along each spoke represent higher levels of arousal. Thus, the intensity or arousal level accompanying pleasant and submissive feelings varies and can result in different emotional states or social behaviors—respectful being less intense than ingratiating. Or, being vigilant is a less aroused state than being fearful, although both states include displeasure and submissiveness.

Elements of Social Style

One of the main questions we asked ourselves in doing this study was how to describe the social styles of different personality types. Relations between personality scores and the behaviors of various subjects provided some of this information. For example, those who had received high scores on the measure of affiliative tendency behaved in a friendly and affiliative way in the waiting situation [268; 293]. Other experiments have also shown more affiliative persons to exhibit more pleasant implicit cues, such as more eye contact [112]. The second half of Figure 6-1 provides a description based on our recent studies [279; 295].

For every kind of behavior in the top section of the figure, there is a corresponding personality type listed in the bottom section. For instance, Carl Jung [191] introduced the concepts of introversion and extroversion to distinguish important aspects of social style. Extroverts are more outgoing, friendly, and approachable; they are also more likely to take charge of social situations. Introverts are passive, shy, and withdrawn [114]. Accordingly, Figure 6-1 shows that an extrovert's characteristic behaviors are both dominant and pleasant, whereas an introvert's typical behaviors are unpleasant and submissive. The extrovert, then, unlike the introvert, is likely to make a good leader. Such a person not only shows self-assurance in this position but can also generate and maintain good feelings in the group.

The style of a pleasant person characteristically conveys liking and positive expectations to others and also elicits these [283; 294; 382]. It is therefore conducive to the perpetuation of good feelings and comfortable social relationships. At the other extreme, an unpleasant person generally relates to others in a negative way. Such an individual either expects to be hurt or is in the process of retaliating against imaginary aggression. Further, negative behaviors provide some of the stimulus to confirm and uphold negative expectations; those who come into contact with someone who is unpleasant do not enjoy that person's company and might occasionally express irritation and anger toward him or her.

The pure dominant or submissive types of Figure 6-1 are not as interesting as some of the kinds of people we have already considered. A dominant person has a controlling and relaxed style that is neither pleasant nor unpleasant in the effect it has on others. The submissive person, who also fails to leave a clear pleasant or unpleasant impression, is simply passive and a follower.

Some of the most consistent results in our research on social styles bear on sex differences. In line with other data from personality test scores [227], women are generally more pleasant and less dominant than men. Their implicit style of interaction conveys more pleasant feelings and includes more eye contact and more approach cues [108; 113; 188; 268] and less relaxation and more submissiveness [259; 268]. Consistent with these results are the findings that they get higher scores than men on measures of affiliative tendency [9; 227] and emotional empathy [284].

Just for fun, make a list of your ten best-liked friends and relatives. Categorize their styles and personalities using the concepts of Figure 6-1. Is there any consistent pattern in the kinds of people you like? If there seems to be a certain type of person you are drawn to, how does this type compare with your own style and personality?

Temperament*

Following the studies described in the last section, a considerable amount of research was conducted in our laboratory that was aimed at achieving a comprehensive system for personality description. Essentially, our recent findings show that we can describe basic personality dimensions (together with their correlated social styles) by building on the system for describing emotions. First, one makes a distinction between emotional *states* (that is, transitory, such as situationally determined, feelings) and emotional *traits* (that is, characteristic emotional states of a person). Emotional traits help describe the emotional makeup of an individual; they allow us to describe

---

*This section includes rewritten portions taken from the paper by A. Mehrabian and E. O'Reilly, "Analysis of personality measures in terms of basic dimensions of temperament," *Journal of Personality and Social Psychology,* 1980, *38,* 492–503. Copyright 1980 by the American Psychological Association. Reprinted by permission.

which moods or emotions tend to be characteristic, habitual, or prevalent in a person. In short, emotional traits provide a description of *temperament*. Some people are habitually slow and careful, others are active and energetic; some are happy and pleasant, others are unhappy, distressed, and problem-laden; some are dominant and controlling, others are submissive or dependent.

Just as emotional states are comprehensively described in terms of the three independent dimensions of pleasure-displeasure, arousal-nonarousal, and dominance-submissiveness, emotional traits are described in terms of the following three independent dimensions: trait pleasure, arousability, and trait dominance. "Trait pleasure" refers to a person's habitual or characteristic level of pleasure-displeasure across a large variety of life situations [279]. "Arousability" refers to the ease with which a person becomes aroused and how long it takes him or her to return to a normal or baseline level of arousal—the longer it takes, the more arousable the person is [272; 276; 277; 285]. "Trait dominance" refers to the habitual or characteristic degree of dominant-submissive (controlling) feeling a person exhibits across a variety of life situations [279; 288].

Employing measures produced in our laboratory for each of these three dimensions of temperament, we obtained specific descriptions of a large number of commonly employed personality measures. The following list illustrates some of the findings [295]. In the list, high versus low trait pleasure is referred to as "pleasant" versus "unpleasant"; high versus low arousability is referred to as "arousable" versus "unarousable"; and high versus low trait dominance is referred to as "dominant" versus "submissive."

Anxious	=	unpleasant arousable	submissive
Neurotic	=	unpleasant arousable	submissive
Achiever	=	pleasant	dominant
Affiliative	=	pleasant arousable	
Sensitive to Rejection	=	arousable	submissive
Empathic	=	pleasant arousable	
"Arousal Seeker"	=	pleasant arousable	dominant
Extrovert	=	pleasant arousable	dominant
Aggressive	=	unpleasant arousable	dominant
Autonomous	=		dominant
Impulsive	=	arousable	dominant
Depressive	=	unpleasant unarousable	submissive

Each of the personality terms in the left-hand column is defined in terms of one or more of the temperament dimensions. Thus, habitually anxious or neurotic persons are temperamentally unpleasant, arousable, and submissive. High achievers are pleasant and dominant, but they are neither arousable nor unarousable to a significant degree. A temperament attribute is mentioned in defining each trait only when it is a significant correlate of that trait. Our findings also provided the specific strengths of each of the three components (regression coefficients, in statistical terminology) in defining each personality trait [280; 295].

The three measures of temperament used here as reference dimensions define a three-dimensional space. The octants of this space represent all possible combinations of trait pleasure × arousability × trait dominance. Other personality dimensions can be viewed as diagonal lines in this three-dimensional space and may be grouped according to the octant into which the major pole of a diagonal projects. Thus, for example, various measures of trait anxiety and related traits can be grouped within the octant combining unpleasant, arousable, and submissive attributes.

When personality is viewed in the context of the three independent dimensions of temperament, and each of the latter is dichotomized, eight broad groupings of personality result. These eight temperament types represent the following four diagonals in the temperament space:

Exuberant-Depressed:	pleasant, arousable, dominant vs. unpleasant, unarousable, submissive
Relaxed-Anxious:	pleasant, unarousable, dominant vs. unpleasant, arousable, submissive
Disdainful-Dependent:	unpleasant, unarousable, dominant vs. pleasant, arousable, submissive
Hostile-Docile:	unpleasant, arousable, dominant vs. pleasant, unarousable, submissive

Each of the four diagonals relates to and helps clarify some basic issues in personality description. For example, the natural opposition of exuberance and depression is evident in manic-depressive psychosis, and physiological determination of the latter [309] is suggestive of a physiological base for temperament variations along exuberance-depression.

Clinicians have sometimes attempted to identify "healthy" personality traits and to distinguish these from the "unhealthy" traits of anxiety or neuroticism. One such attempt resulted in the concept of "competence" [423]. In our present terminology, a relaxed temperament is the most direct opposite to an anxious one and is thus most likely to be associated with a sense of well-being and psychological health.

A relaxed temperament also provides the greatest amount of immunity to environmentally induced stress and its consequent effects on both psychological and physical functioning. "Stress" induces displeasure, high arousal, and submissiveness, and has been shown to be an important determinant of physical illness [297; 298; 375; 437]. The temperament constellation that is most likely to negate the effects of stress is one that is conducive to pleasure, low arousal, and dominance—namely, a relaxed temperament. Thus, from two independent sources (the fact of its opposition to anxiety and its counteracting effect on stress) a relaxed temperament is most likely to be associated with physical and psychological well-being.

The concept of a "disdainful" personality or temperament is not encountered as often as that of a "dependent" one in studies of personality. Nevertheless, "disdainful" provides an interesting perspective on the definition of "dependent," while identifying an important distinction to a "hostile" temperament. Disdainful and hostile temperaments both involve displeasure and dominance but are distinguished in terms of arousability: Hostile people are arousable, disdainful ones are unarousable. Thus, for example, the antisocial behavior associated with a disdainful temperament is more likely to be "cold and calculating," involving elaborate planning and careful consideration of risks; antisocial behavior associated with hostility might involve a greater degree of physical violence and subjectively uncontrollable aggressive or destructive behavior.

Docility is partially defined by considering its opposite pole, hostility. Also, some of the following emotion terms that correspond to the combination of pleasant, unaroused, and submissive feelings are helpful for devising items for measures of docility: consoled, sleepy, tranquilized, sheltered, protected. Thus, although the distinction between the terms *docile* and *dependent* is somewhat difficult in terms of linguistic meaning, their theoretical distinction is important: docility and dependency both involve pleasant and submissive attributes, but dependent people are arousable, docile ones are unarousable. From a pragmatic standpoint, personality measures of docility might be useful for identifying very poor negotiators or individuals most susceptible to extreme forms of social influence, as in brainwashing.

To discover the relevance to your personal life of these findings on temperament, make a list of a dozen persons best known to you. Then, carefully rate each of these individuals on trait pleasure-displeasure (high, neutral, low), arousability (high, neutral, low), and trait domi-

nance-submissiveness (high, neutral, low). Use the labels correspond-
ing to the eight temperament types given on page 100 to characterize
the twelve individuals. Does any one of the eight general types (such as
exuberant or dependent) predominate in your list and if so what does
this tell you about yourself? How would you rate your own tempera-
ment in this scheme?

In devising measures, each of the eight temperament types would
ideally receive equal absolute weightings from trait pleasure,
arousability, and trait dominance. However, personality measures
actually in use involve varying weights and represent subtle variations in temperament within each of the octants. Measures for each
of the four diagonal dimensions can be derived easily once an individual's scores on trait pleasure, arousability, and trait dominance
are available. The latter scores can be standardized and employed in
the following equations to obtain the desired estimates.*

Exuberant-depressed	=	$+P \ +A \ +D$
Relaxed-anxious	=	$+P \ -A \ +D$
Disdainful-dependent	=	$-P \ -A \ +D$
Hostile-docile	=	$-P \ +A \ +D$

Social styles, as well as personality characteristics, can thus be
viewed in terms of a temperament framework. Social styles relating
to trait pleasure are evident in pleasant and unpleasant implicit cues
(smiles, frowns, tone of voice) and of course in the pleasant-unpleasant quality of the contents of speech. Varying degrees of arousability
are evident in a person's habitual activity and alertness levels: Some
are typically more active, energetic, and alert; others tend to be slow-
moving, lethargic, or slow-paced. Dominance-submissiveness differences are evident in how much a person takes control of the situations or people about him or her as distinct from going along and
allowing situations and others to control and determine his or her
behaviors. [See Chapter 3 for detailed lists of implicit cues relating
to pleasure-displeasure, arousal-nonarousal, and dominance-submissiveness.]

If we know the three fundamental dimensions of temperament,
we know what to watch for to assess social styles. And, using the
octant labels, we know how to provide consistent and distinct de-

---

*Requests for a complete set of the three basic temperament scales, administration
instructions, scoring procedures, and norms should be addressed in writing to Albert Mehrabian.

scriptions of social styles that combine two or more of the temperament qualities.

Future studies can use the available measures for each of the
three temperament dimensions to identify the implicit social style
correlates of various temperament types. In such studies, subjects
would first be administered the three temperament measures. Then
their verbal and implicit behaviors would be recorded and scored in
various social situations. Data analyses would then help identify
those implicit behavioral cues that exhibited the highest correlations
with each of the three dimensions of temperament. Alternatively, if
investigators were interested specifically in one or more of the diagonal dimensions (such as relaxed-anxious), derived scores based on
the three temperament measures could be correlated with the social
style measures. For example, anxious people would be expected to
display tension in their implicit speech cues and in their postures
and movements. Depressed types would be expected to be interper-
sonally unpleasant and avoiding (or less approaching), and generally
to lack expressive and lively qualities of face and voice.

Problem Styles

An educator once told me that teachers who habitually gesture get
better results with their students. This puzzling observation can be
explained in terms of what we already know. A pleasant and aroused
(affiliative) style, which elicits liking and cooperation from others,
includes frequent gesturing and other behaviors that also convey
positive feelings [268]. The gesturing of these more effective teachers is probably only one aspect of a generally pleasant style that
leads students to like them and thus to become more cooperative and
involved in their class work [193; 263]. Of course, the opposite is
more likely to be the case for teachers who do not possess an affiliative style.

In a classroom, a teacher can inadvertently exclude some of her
students from participation, by simply looking more in the direction
of those who sit up front or those who are the better students and
whom she likes. While the brighter and more interested students
continue to receive the bulk of the teacher's attention and remain
interested and aroused, the less able ones receive little attention, feel
left out, and continue to perform poorly. Thus, the teacher's implicit
behavior subtly functions to enforce a dichotomy between "good"
and "poor" students, even though the initial intuitive assignment of
a student to one of these two groups may have been quite accidental.
If this teacher were to improve her style by distributing her atten-

tion more evenly, some of the "poor" students could surprise her. These may be capable students whose performances are especially affected by the emotional ties in a work situation and who perform poorly because they feel rejected and unimportant.

Implicit style can, in very indirect ways, affect work effectiveness or other dealings outside social situations. In addition to job history or level of competence, a person's implicit style can influence his success in getting a desired position. People who conduct job interviews know that applicants are not likely to volunteer information about their own weaknesses. So, interviewers look for weaknesses, as well as strengths, in the style in which the applicants relate to them. An ingratiating applicant may be judged unsuited because he gives the impression of being much too dependent. Another applicant might try to appear casual and assume such a relaxed posture as to suggest disrespect and a rebellious quality unsuited for the job.

One of my graduate students, Mark, who was accustomed to an informal relationship with me, had an important request to make of another professor who was visiting our department from England. While making his request in the professor's office, Mark slouched in his chair and braced his foot against the professor's desk. The man was so enraged that he practically threw Mark out of his office.

To this Englishman, Mark's behavior seemed obviously unreasonable and deliberately insulting. In his culture, people are more careful about adhering to the prescribed standards of behavior associated with levels of status, and he felt little restraint in expressing his annoyance. Had the professor been American, Mark's foot on his desk might not have been sufficiently offensive to seem insulting, but it would probably have aroused a negative reaction—seeming "out of place." Nothing would have been said about it, and Mark would have had little opportunity to understand a possibly uncooperative attitude toward his request.

The behaviors of lonely people provide another example of problem styles. Some people are alone by choice; but those who are unhappily aware of loneliness may be the source of their own misery. The factors that seem to hold others at a distance consist of lonely people's failure to be sufficiently pleasant and their tendency to make others feel uncomfortable [263; 291; 294].

In our experiments [282; 283], we have repeatedly seen the following rapid succession of events when two strangers are asked to wait in a room together. As they enter that room, there is usually a brief mutual glance, and frequently one or both smile. As they sit down, some resolve the initial discomfort by looking about and seeming to become interested in the objects around them. This kind of "escape" makes it even more difficult to start a conversation later on, and consequently a long and painful silence ensues. Others look at the other person and smile as they enter and, soon after being seated, say something. A brief comment at this time is usually sufficient to break the ice; the conversation then starts with topics that are relevant to the immediate situation and proceeds to more personal issues.

Lonely people who would like to make new friends fail because they do the wrong things during these initial and critical moments. They avoid the other person's gaze, they do not smile, and they seem tense or preoccupied with other things. All of this discourages any comment from the other person, who does not realize that this apparent unfriendliness is due to a considerable discomfort and an inability to cope with it.

National Styles

We all, as we travel, enjoy observing people, and the following are some informal observations of my own, described in terms of the concepts proposed in this volume.

The sidewalk cafes that are so much a part of life in France are indicative of a general and distinctive aspect of the French social style. The prevalence of these sidewalk cafes indicates a lesser tendency to set up social barriers and the lack of reservation of the French about exposing themselves to strangers. What the French eat, how they eat it, and whom they eat with are part of a public spectacle accessible to any passerby. The pinnacle of the phenomenon is the small French town, where loudspeakers are strategically placed in the central square so that the local radio station can be heard clearly throughout this busy area. This central square functions almost as a living room, where people spend a lot of their leisure time, seated at cafe tables or on public benches, socializing, and listening to the music.

The characteristic willingness to expose intimate affairs to strangers is evident in an incident that I witnessed. While I sat in a cafe, the lady owner yelled almost continuously in irritation at a young girl who was working for her. This public expression of negative feelings, which would have drawn others' attention and concern in the United States, did not seem to have any effect on the French people in that cafe. The whole thing seemed to be taken for granted.

These examples illustrate the French people's greater preference for arousing social interactions and less emphasis on privacy as compared to Americans. Of course, such observations are expected more in small towns, among the French, and when familiar faces are around than otherwise.

The English also spend a considerable amount of time socializing in public places. They differ from the French, however, in that the pubs and restaurants where they meet are indoors. The one facet of their social style that distinguishes them from North Americans is their extreme emphasis on pleasant exchanges (affiliation), particularly among social equals. The general atmosphere that prevails in the English pub, a public beer parlor, is the liveliness of a friendly cocktail party. People stand at the bar, sit at the tables, or stand in available open spaces, wherever they wish, and converse in groups, moving about with their drinks.

The informality of these pubs is considerably enhanced by the absence of waiters and waitresses, and the complete freedom to move the furniture about to suit one's needs. Pubs, which are frequent gathering places, epitomize the great desire of the English for informal affiliation and characterize their friendliness—remember our cluster of affiliative behavior and what it includes. The contrasting stereotype of the "aloof" British may have arisen in situations where there were clear-cut status differences, as in the British colonies.

Edward T. Hall [154; 156] has described the social styles of various other cultural groups. One striking difference between Arabs and Americans is that the former are more likely to stand closer, touch, orient more directly, and speak louder; in other words, Arabs engage in highly arousing exchanges [413]. In fact, they sometimes stand close enough to use the quality of each other's breath as an important and personal source of information. Latin Americans prefer a closer talking position than do North Americans. Thus, if a Latin American and a North American converse standing up, the Latin tends to move closer and the North American tends to back away, each seeking to maintain his own habitual distance [154]. They both come away from an interaction thinking there is something wrong with the other.

A distinctive pattern of emphases in implicit social style is revealed in studies of the Japanese. Since proper, respectful, and pleasant social attitudes are considered most desirable in this culture, the Japanese tend to evidence pleasant facial expressions (smiling) even in uncomfortable or stressful situations [37; 316]. Also, their postures during interaction with Americans are less relaxed than those of the Americans [397]. Compared with Americans, too, the Japanese interact at greater distances from one another and are less likely to touch one another [26; 104]. All in all, the social manner of the Japanese compared to that of Westerners can be said to be more formal and respectful (that is, primarily more submissive) in quality.

Since the acceptable standards for implicit social behavior vary from culture to culture, certain behaviors that are normal for other cultures but alien in our own can assume great importance for us. Alternatively, a behavior that seems common and insignificant in our culture may have great implications for foreigners [90; 154; 213, Chapter 13].

The most dramatic cultural differences in implicit communication codes relate to "emblems," that is, very specific expressions or gestures that have wordlike functions in communication. For example, the Japanese use the little finger pointed straight up to mean girlfriend, wife, or mistress; rapid crossing of the index fingers to mean a fight; and licking the index finger briefly and moving it across an eyebrow to mean someone is a liar [316]. Such wordlike implicit symbols are culturally determined and arbitrary, as in the case of verbal codes. Understandably, then, wide variations are expected in these codes across cultures.

Nevertheless, it is easy to overstress differences in the implicit communication codes of various cultures. Remember that the largest differences occur in the use of emblems and when broad social attitudes dictate certain trends in social style. For the most part, the basic metaphors that we have described for understanding implicit behaviors in this culture can be applied equally to other cultures. The differences in the interpretation of a certain behavior arise from the different standards that have been set, in terms of what is acceptable and what is not. For example, for Latins the acceptable distance range is generally closer to others than it is for North Americans.

Summary

Our social style can be described in terms of its pleasant-unpleasant, aroused-unaroused, and dominant-submissive qualities. Each of these qualities is a composite of several interrelated behaviors, which together describe a unified theme. People differ from one another in terms of how much of each of these qualities they consistently exhibit across a variety of situations. Some are affiliative most of the time; they are comfortable to associate with and are good company. Others are ingratiating no matter what the circumstances; and their excessive positiveness, frequent questioning, and eagerness to please make them appear clinging and dependent. Yet others are sensitive to rejection; these people are so tense that they are unapproachable. Then there are the domineering and relaxed people, who contrast sharply with the tense and timid ones.

These qualities may also blend together. For example, not only is the extrovert affiliative, but he is also likely to assume a more dominant role, such as taking the lead in guiding a relationship or situation into a pleasant course. In contrast, the introvert is not only passive and submissive but also seems unable or unwilling to affiliate. Further, compared with men, women not only are generally pleasanter, but also are more submissive and arousable in their social style.

These social styles, which are uncontrolled and often unintended parts of our behavior, can have persistent beneficial or disturbing effects not only in social but also work-related situations. An undesirable style can be corrected through simple feedback about how one seems to others (such as watching a videorecording of oneself in the presence of others). Other methods, which rely on a more active role-playing of styles that are different from one's own, can be even more effective in bringing about a greater awareness and a change for the better.

Suggested Readings

For experimental reports of the scoring and grouping of implicit behaviors that define various social styles, see [23; 145; 347; 348] and related work done in our laboratory [260; 268; 294]. Experiments dealing with sex differences in social style that showed females to be personally more approaching and approachable (that is, more pleasant and more arousable) than males are represented by [112; 148; 222; 268; 293; 431] and were reviewed in [105].

Studies dealing with the social styles of various personality types include those showing extroverts to prefer greater approach than introverts [331] (a finding not replicated in [308]) and studies relating social styles to affiliative tendency and sensitivity to rejection [294]. See [38; 123; 172; 176; 226; 403] for studies showing that disturbed individuals (whom we would assume to be neurotic or highly anxious) approach others less and avoid others more. Discussions of ethnic and cultural differences in social styles are given in the work of a variety of investigators [26; 27; 90; 104; 154; 156; 213; 220; 316; 413].

Chapter 7

Environments and Social
Interaction

Does the effectiveness of our social style change as we move from one situation to another? Are there cities, towns, or specific locations in which we find it easier to initiate and maintain intimate conversations that are not only meaningful but also fun?

In recent years, psychologists have focused increasing attention on the effects of environments [70; 273; 338; 434]. In this chapter, we consider the specific issue of the beneficial or adverse effects of environments on social interaction. In some very subtle though persistent ways, people's surroundings affect their implicit behavior and social interaction.

In small towns, where most people are only too well acquainted with each other, adequate social interactions present no problem. However, with the massive movement of populations into large metropolitan centers, problems of loneliness and social alienation have become increasingly prominent. Much has been written about the destructive and inhuman quality of cities [135; 136]: People are somehow kept apart, intimacy is discouraged, and meaningful relationships with neighbors, coworkers, or strangers one might meet on a bus or train, in a park or a museum are nonexistent. However, little has been learned about the causes of this alienation and how to counteract them.

The problem of alienation is not restricted to our relationships with strangers. Even with our acquaintances, and whether we are in someone else's home or our own, in a restaurant, or simply taking a walk, there is a constant struggle to somehow maintain meaningful relationships.

To see how the physical environment can help or hinder in this struggle, let us examine some situations in which, for no apparent reason, there is a quality of discomfort.

We all know places in which conversation and spontaneous good times occur with great regularity and others in which the conversation never seems to get off the ground, where every verbal exchange is an uphill labor, and a vague discomfort pervades. What makes the difference? Is it the different people in each place? Not entirely—we have all been part of gatherings that subtly changed character with only a change of setting: from the dining room to the living room, from the automobile to the restaurant, from the parlor to the patio.

Evidently, tasteful and even comfortable furnishings are not the answer either. We are reminded of countless "living" rooms, as beautifully furnished as a showroom but left just as unoccupied while the guests clustered happily in the kitchen and enjoyed themselves there. At the University of California, Berkeley, the public rooms in the college dormitories—spacious, airy, well lighted and handsomely furnished—were intended to be a place for the dormies to "rap," to become acquainted, to "live" in. Regrettably, these lounges are somehow afflicted with the same living room malady—the dormies stay away in droves [410].

Put simply, some rooms are avoided and others are sought. Why? What are the factors that make some rooms succeed as social spaces and others fail?

Humphry Osmond was one of the first to consider these questions [327; 328]. In his studies of hospitals, he described as *sociofugal* areas that seemed to drive people apart and as *sociopetal* those that seemed to bring people closer together. However, he did not describe the physical attributes of the two areas—how a sociofugal space differs from a sociopetal one. So the question now becomes "What physical factors in a given space inhibit or facilitate social interaction?"

To study this question, it is first necessary to identify the major components of social interaction. The evidence already reviewed in Chapter 6 shows that, although there are other important parts, affiliative behavior is the most important aspect of social interaction. Our own studies of affiliation led to its definition as a composite of the following behaviors: amount of conversation, eye contact (or mutual gaze) between the people involved, positiveness of their statements to one another, pleasantness of their facial expressions, and the frequency of their head nodding and hand and arm gesturing [294].

The correlated cues that define affiliation include almost all the subtle verbal and nonverbal behaviors that people use to communicate liking to one another. Thus, affiliation can be considered a process of exchanging positive reinforcers, or liking. The perpetuation of affiliation, in turn, depends on the variety of means available for conveying pleasure cues and approaching others.

Of course, a person's reaction in a specific instance varies, depending on her general predisposition to be pleasant to others, and depending on the person with whom she is interacting. This is understandable intuitively and has also been experimentally verified [274]. However, of more interest here is how the behavior of a person is further influenced by her physical environment. Any setting, be it an office, a park, or a whole city, can influence the affiliation that people exhibit in many ways. For instance, the design of certain neighborhoods or apartment buildings seems to make it easier for neighbors to get to know each other; offices, both in terms of architecture and interior design, can be planned to minimize or maximize social interaction.

Environmentally Facilitated Pleasant Approach

The concept of "environmentally facilitated approach" refers to one important effect of spaces in which people meet and/or interact. It refers to the extent to which a setting facilitates mutual sensory stimulation among persons within it and is measured in terms of the spatio-temporal proximity or by the number of "communication channels" available to the individuals in that setting. Communication channels are the means by which we convey our thoughts and feelings to another—words, facial expressions, tone of voice, postures, movements, and so on. Greater approach tends to be associated with communication in more channels and the resulting increase in information has been found to be arousing [3; 133; 205; 240; 310; 322]. For example, telegrams and letters involve the least approach as far as communication media are concerned, since they permit the verbal channel alone. These are followed in order by telephone conversations (verbal and vocal channels), conversations on a picturephone (verbal, vocal, and facial), and face-to-face meetings.

Since interpersonal approach, contact, and mutual stimulation are arousing, it follows that the pleasantness-unpleasantness of the setting in which such approach occurs can be a key determinant of whether the approach results in mutual liking and rewarding relationships versus mutual dislike, discomfort, and antagonism. This follows from Figure 1-1, which shows that the effects on pleasure-displeasure or like-dislike are maximized under highly arousing conditions.

Humans are generally more of a source of rewarding and reinforcing (pleasant) experiences for each other than they are sources of punishing and negatively reinforcing (unpleasant) experiences [294, Chapter 3]. This implies that across all possible pleasant plus unpleasant situations, increased social contact and approach is more likely to result in liking than in dislike. Thus, for instance, in neutrally pleasant (or even slightly unpleasant) settings, the inherent pleasantness of social contact yields a resultant level of pleasantness that, together with the greater arousal from contact, leads to liking. However, when situations are clearly unpleasant and/or resources (such as food, shelter) are scarce, we expect the arousing quality of social contact to be disliked and avoided (note the downward-slanting line in Figure 1-1).

In this section, we review studies showing that when clearly unpleasant environmental cues are absent, situations that facilitate contact and approach result in liking and greater affiliation. In the following section we consider studies of the less frequently encountered unpleasant situations in which contact and approach that are environmentally enforced (as with crowding) result in dislike and the avoidance of affiliation.

Let us consider the effects of communication media. A review of studies that compared the effects of face-to-face, audiovisual, and audio-only channels of communication showed that (1) "audio-only conversations were ... more depersonalized, argumentative, and narrow in focus, compared with face-to-face conversations" [428, p. 972], (2) "media which are richer in nonverbal cues lead to more favorable impressions" [428, p. 969], and (3) there is a tendency toward more self-disclosure in face-to-face compared with audio-only communications [428]. Thus, media that permit more approach tend to result in greater affiliation, pleasantness, and rewarding relationships.

In fact, when pleasantness predominates (that is, the resultant pleasantness from environmental and social cues is positive rather than negative), there is a two-way relationship between approach and liking: Approach produces more liking and liking leads people to approach one another more.

Research evidence reviewed in Chapter 2 has shown that when people like each other or when they are basically more friendly or affiliative, they choose to approach one another. When together, they sit closer, orient more directly, lean toward each other, touch, have more eye contact, and converse more. Everyday observations suggest that people who like each other and live in different cities choose the closest means of communicating (subject, of course, to cost considerations); visits are preferred over telephone conversations, and telephone conversations over letters. And whatever means they use, they use it more often the more they like someone.

Conversely, opportunities for increased approach can foster greater liking [32; 180; 314; 441]. For instance, studies of college students have shown that people who had more opportunities to be closer together, whether in their dormitories, apartments, or classes, more often tended to form friendships and like one another [50; 54; 120; 232; 427]. Similarly, people in various occupations who were assigned working positions closer to one another were more likely to develop closer relationships and to like each other more [149; 200; 442]. The following comments of Leon Festinger, which were quoted by Ellen Berscheid and Elaine Walster [32], are based on a study of developing friendships in a new housing project, where few residents had previously known each other. It is evident that the architecturally determined and accidental arrangement of people can have dramatic effects on their relationships [119; 121].

> It is a fair summary to say that the two major factors affecting the friendships which developed were (1) sheer distance between houses and (2) the direction in which a house faced. Friendships developed more frequently between next-door neighbors, less frequently between people whose houses were separated by another house, and so on. As the distance between houses increased, the number of friendships fell off so rapidly that it was rare to find a friendship between persons who lived in houses that were separated by more than four or five other houses. . . .
>
> There were instances in which the site plan of the project had more profound effects than merely to determine with whom one associated. Indeed, on occasion the arrangements of the houses severely limited the social life of their occupants. . . . In order to have the street appear "lived on," ten of the houses near the street had been turned so that they faced the street rather than the court area as did the other houses. This apparently small change in the direction in which a house faced had a considerable effect on the lives of the people who, by accident, happened to occupy these end houses. They had less than half as many friends in the project as did those whose houses faced the court area. The consistency of this finding left no doubt that the turning of these houses toward the street had made involuntary social isolates out of the persons who lived in them [119, pp. 156–157].

The results from some of these studies can be attributed to the fact that some of the people were friends to begin with and elected to become close neighbors because of this friendship. However, in a number of the studies, strangers were accidentally assigned close or far positions to one another and it was found that closeness led to greater liking [121; 321]. Thus, it follows that the greater approach and contact among persons facilitated by architecture and housing arrangements were indeed instrumental in enhancing the possibility of liking and friendships.

Some of the classical prejudice studies have shown also that housing projects that permit people of different races to live in close proximity lessen the prejudices of these people toward one another [432; 436]. In these studies, approach and contact afforded by the design of the movement paths and the availability of common work and recreation areas served to increase liking. If increased contact can reduce initially unpleasant (prejudicial) feelings, then its effect should be even more profound in cases where the initial attitudes are positive.

One important exception, however, should be noted: When *hostile* groups of persons are brought together, the increased contact does nothing to improve their relations [376].

Check out the relation between approach and liking for yourself by first listing the names of ten acquaintances. Next rate each of these on a scale of liking that ranges from − 3 (extreme dislike) to + 3 (extreme liking). Now divide these people into two groups: the five whom you meet most frequently and the others whom you encounter least frequently. What is the average liking score you have assigned to each of these two groups?

Relations Between Dwelling Units   Given these general ideas, it is possible to illustrate the ways in which man-made environments can be optimally designed to encourage social interaction, particularly among people who are strangers to each other. A consideration of environmentally facilitated approach can influence the design of living spaces at all levels—from urban renewal projects, to the architecture of a building or apartment complex, to interior design and furniture arrangement. When the design of living and working spaces minimizes the frequency and duration of meetings, it minimizes approach. On the other hand, if the environment permits opportunities for frequent and prolonged contacts among its inhabitants, perhaps by common paths, common shopping, work, hobby, and recreation areas or attractive gathering places, it can be conducive to better feelings. In short, areas that attract people and hold them in close proximity lay the groundwork for affiliation. Consider some good and bad instances.

Typical apartment buildings, with several stacked floors of apartments opening off long hallways, decrease chances for approach. In such buildings people meet only briefly when riding the elevator or passing in a hallway. These encounters are few, compared to meetings in other apartment complexes in which units open on courtyards through which each resident must go in order to enter his apartment. In this second case, lawn chairs placed in the yard can enhance contacts, provided, of course, that residents use them.

A large academic department recently acquired a "beautiful" new building—and experienced a surprising and drastic reduction in the number of contacts among the faculty. Before the expansion, most of the faculty were concentrated on three floors, had offices close together, and were continually passing one another in the hallways. Now they are scattered throughout a ten-story building and only occasionally meet in passing. Had anyone considered the advantages

of environmentally facilitated contacts and approach, the design of the new building could have included arrangements to maintain the frequent interactions. Perhaps offices could have been concentrated on only a few floors, or open central spaces could have been included and furnished comfortably to allow informal contacts.

The primary reason for visiting such comfortably furnished areas (or the courtyard with the lawn chairs in the case of the apartments) may not be to socialize, but social interaction would be likely. Some people use the swimming pool of an apartment complex for a daily workout, but often residents visit the pool area without any intention of actually swimming. For them, the pool's apparent function is actually quite secondary to that of bringing strangers together and providing an excuse to maintain proximity.

One aspect of personality that has an effect in such situations is what we have called "sensitivity to rejection." Whenever people meet, a factor that influences the nature and extent of their interaction is the fear of being slighted [294]. This fear acts as a deterrent, so that even though two or more people may be interested in getting acquainted, they still feel hesitant about initiating contact without some reassurance from the others. Most of the findings in affiliation research can be understood in terms of this approach-avoidance model: Each person is drawn to others, but at the same time fear of rejection discourages him or her from making contact [289; 294].

There are vast individual differences in the desire to affiliate and the tendency to fear rejection, and the proper environment can exert a great influence on how people act. For instance, an environment that enhances approach could provide those who are excessively sensitive with an excuse to be close to others, while simultaneously inducing more frequent contacts among those who simply lack the desire to affiliate. Those who are sensitive have a chance to probe new relations cautiously, and the less affiliative persons might find the contacts rewarding.

Many puzzling phenomena in today's lonely societies can be better understood in terms of the idea that some settings or occasions, ostensibly planned for another purpose, perform the important function of bringing people together and fostering interaction. For instance, political or ideological convictions are only part of the reason why so many people actively participate in demonstrations or other gatherings. An important function of these gatherings—and one that has not been stressed—is that they bring together great numbers of people who hold similar beliefs and attitudes, who share a life style. Findings from different sources have shown that contacts with similar, rather than dissimilar, others are sought more because these are more likely to be successful or mutually rewarding [51; 52; 263; 271; 290].

Relations Within Dwelling Units   So far, we have developed the conceptual tools to analyze the quality of environments that is conducive to socializing and have briefly sketched how these tools may be applied to the design of buildings or the relations among dwelling units. How about the application of these ideas to the interior space of a single room? What can be done to the furnishings of a room to foster interaction? Let us consider in some detail the findings from a few experiments [282; 283]. In these experiments, we concerned ourselves primarily with two questions: (1) How does a close arrangement of furniture (that is, the distance between the various seats and the relative angles at which seats are placed) affect social interaction? (2) What do decorative objects in a room do to the interaction that occurs there?

In terms of what has already been said about environmentally facilitated approach, it was expected that closer positions and more direct orientations would enhance conversation, provided that the combined contribution of closeness and directness was not excessive. Four distances (3, 4.5, 6, and 9 feet) and three orientations (zero degrees or face to face, 90 degrees or at right angles, and 180 degrees or side by side) were selected so that the twelve resulting combinations would provide a considerable range of approach in seating arrangement. For instance, the 3-foot, face-to-face position would represent extreme closeness, and the 9-foot, 180-degree position would be too distant. For the entire range, then, it was expected that conversation would increase with increasing approach, except for the excessively close positions.

Concerning our second question, it seemed that room furnishings and decorative objects could be described in two groups: those, such as artwork, that are unusual, interesting, and the subject of conversation, in contrast to those such as books, magazines, or puzzles that are the objects of individual preoccupation. We therefore introduced an example of each type into one of the experiments [283].

To avoid the confounding of results by already existing friendly relationships or by physical attraction, 400 pairs of same-sexed strangers were employed as subjects in the experiments. The subjects' affiliative tendency and sensitivity to rejection were assessed with questionnaire measures [265; 274] so that we could explore the ways in which the environmental variables affected different kinds of persons.

For our first two experiments, we used the same basic design but used different rooms and different instructions. In the first, a pair of strangers entered a room in which there were two comfortable, upholstered armchairs placed in one of the twelve possible arrangements (four distances × three orientations). The pair were asked to sit down and wait for a few minutes until we returned to begin the experiment. Five minutes were allowed to elapse before the experimenter returned with the personality questionnaires and asked the subjects to complete them. Presumably, taking these tests constituted the experiment. However, during the five-minute period, the subjects' interaction was observed through a one-way mirror and recorded. Later, a composite affiliative behavior score was computed for each member of the pair, based on each person's amount of conversation and pleasantness, using cues that were noted in Chapter 6.

In the second experiment, we used the same chairs in the same twelve positions; but the room was smaller and carpeted, and the one-way mirrors were camouflaged. This time, subjects thought they were participating in a music-listening experiment, and during their five minutes alone together they were supposedly waiting for the experimenter to prepare the tape recorder for the music. They actually listened to some music, rated it, and also filled out the personality questionnaires.

The results of the two experiments were similar. Subjects who had obtained high scores on the affiliative-tendency measure were more affiliative in the waiting situation. In the more stressful and ambiguous first experiment, subjects with high scores on sensitivity to rejection were less affiliative during the waiting period. These results support the commonsense idea that people do indeed consistently differ from one another in terms of their affiliative patterns.

In both experiments, orientation had the greatest effect on conversation. The 180-degree or side-by-side position consistently produced less affiliation, whereas the 90-degree angle was only slightly less conducive to conversation than the face-to-face position. Neither experiment showed an overall effect for distance. The second experiment did, however, show that when both subjects in a pair were sensitive to rejection, they affiliated less when they were seated at greater distances. This same effect was obtained in another experiment involving four strangers waiting in a group [282]. Thus, if we ignore the personality differences of participants, distance alone does not have a strong enough effect to show up in the averages; but it can be detrimental to conversation for those who are sensitive to rejection—people who could be expected to gain most from environmental improvements.

Both experiments suggested strongly that our traditional practice of furnishing the living room with a long sofa leaves much to be desired, since sitting on a sofa involves the conversation-crippling 180-degree orientation. When two persons sit on the same sofa, they tend to occupy the end seats. If they wish to interact, they shift sideways so as to assume a more direct orientation. This action essentially inactivates the seating spaces still remaining between them, because a third person is reluctant to place himself in the center of their communication lane. Thus, the conversationally effective seating capacity of a straight sofa, whatever its length, is only two people. It inhibits interaction still more when those seated on it are strangers. The postural adjustments that friends would casually make to gain more eye contact indicate a greater commitment and more informality than one can readily assume with a stranger, at least until the other has demonstrated some interest.

In plain words, to minimize interaction in a room, furnish it with straight sofas, preferably around the perimeter. Photographs of the dorm lounges at Berkeley reveal that this is precisely how they were arranged [410]. The same plan is also typical of day rooms in mental hospitals. While such an arrangement may be convenient for the cleaning staff or the nurses and attendants of a hospital, it is less easily justified in our living rooms—places where pleasant social interaction is intended to be the primary function.

The first useful principle for designing seating areas, then, is that a maximum number of pairs of seats should be placed for intermediate levels of closeness (that is, about 4 feet apart and oriented from face-to-face position to 90-degree angle). In fact, any arrangement can be characterized in terms of the average distance and orientation between all possible pairs of seats. The average approach afforded by all pairs could serve as a measure of the conversation-facilitating effect of the arrangement.

Our third experiment explored the contribution of decorative objects to conversation. We used a waiting situation such as that in the

second experiment, with subjects always seated 4½ feet apart at right angles. An abstract sculpture, serving as a conversation piece, and a difficult puzzle poster were readily visible to both subjects. The experiment focused more on those who are sensitive to rejection. We had already seen how smaller distances helped the conversation of pairs who were sensitive to rejection. Could a "conversation piece" have been of any special value to such persons? Would it be easier to initiate a conversation, since venturing a remark about the object, rather than about some personal matter, would not leave one so vulnerable to rebuff? The puzzle was also introduced to maximize individual differences. It was expected that a less affiliative person would tend to busy herself with the puzzle and ignore the stranger waiting with her.

Affiliative behavior was measured from audiorecordings, as in the previous experiments. In addition, separate notations were made of the lengths of time each subject spent looking at the sculpture and the puzzle. Preoccupation with the puzzle was indeed found to be inversely related to affiliation; those who affiliated more spent less time with the puzzle. The sculpture was not equally important and did not have the same effect for all different pairings of subjects. Only pairs whose members were both sensitive to rejection seemed to benefit measurably from its presence. It was somehow instrumental in allowing them to agree more often (that is, reinforce each other), to be generally more pleasant, and to converse more.

A second useful principle in the design of seating areas, then, is that an environment can facilitate interaction if it provides an excuse for people to engage in a similar activity in close proximity to one another. This activity can be, and perhaps must be, ostensibly unrelated to socializing; it is especially helpful to people who need the most help in these matters—those who are sensitive to rejection.

Consider the arrangement of furniture in your own living room, in various living rooms of homes you have visited, in various family or recreation rooms. Do the arrangements tend to foster or to inhibit interaction? Recall waiting rooms you may have known (doctor's office, airport terminal, the local laundromat, hotel lobbies)—do they encourage or discourage approach and contact between strangers? If you have the opportunity, note the conversations of those who sit in front of an aquarium at a bar. How do these differ from conversations initiated between strangers in spots where there is no ready conversation piece available? Or just think of the homes of your different friends who have done their own interior designing. How do the "warm and inviting" living rooms differ physically from those that seem cold and reserved?

Environmentally Enforced Unpleasant Approach

The preceding section on the positive correlation between environmentally facilitated approach and liking (affiliation) applies also to settings that are, at worst, slightly unpleasant. A second, and seemingly unrelated, set of findings bears on the detrimental effects of crowding. Within our framework, the first set of findings discussed relates to the majority of situations and is explained in terms of the upward-slanting line in Figure 1-1; this second set is understood in terms of the downward-slanting line of that figure.

As already noted, environmentally facilitated contacts do not always reduce prejudice and dislike. When feelings of antagonism are initially strong (that is, displeasure levels are high), increased contact simply reinforces those feelings [376].

Generally, unpleasant cues predominate when (1) interactants already know and dislike each other, (2) the setting in which interaction occurs is unpleasant (dirty, noisy, polluted, ugly, hot, uncomfortable, lacking in resources, and so on), and (3) one or more of the interactants has an unpleasant temperament [see Chapter 6].

John Calhoun [56] carried out the pioneering work on the detrimental effects of crowding for rats. Numerous experimental and survey studies have since been conducted with humans in an effort to show parallel effects [134; 424]. However, a general review of findings led to the conclusion that crowding in itself is neither desirable nor undesirable; rather, it tends to *intensify* emotional reactions and corresponding behaviors [125]. Thus, crowding is best conceptualized as being an important source of arousal [273, Chapter 30]. Considerable direct evidence is available on this point: Experiments show that having others in close proximity tends to be more arousing than having them at a distance. The arousing effect of closeness to others has been demonstrated with animals [235; 236] as well as with humans [3; 133; 205; 240; 310; 322]. It follows from Figure 1-1 that, relative to uncrowded conditions, crowded ones tend to amplify the effects of pleasant-unpleasant cues on like-dislike and affiliation. Understandably, then, crowding enhances positive social exchanges and affiliation in generally pleasant physical and social surroundings. Alternatively, crowding leads to indifferent or antagonistic exchanges (such as impolite or inconsiderate behavior, crime, hostility, maladaptive functioning, social disorganization) in generally unpleasant circumstances.

Environmentally Induced Emotions and Affiliation*

The importance of environmentally induced pleasant-unpleasant feelings on social attitudes and social interaction has been demonstrated. Studies have shown that others are evaluated more positively (liked more) and approached more in pleasant compared with unpleasant settings [146; 147; 183; 234; 340; 341]. Thus, the good feelings induced by a setting generalize [198] to the people within it; alternatively, situationally induced unpleasant feelings also generalize to the people in such places.

A seemingly contradictory line of evidence was provided by Stanley Schachter [363], some of whose subjects showed a greater desire to affiliate while anticipating an unpleasant shock than while anticipating no shock. This effect was not general in that it was only observed among firstborn females and not among the laterborns. Our review of related findings led to the conclusion that birth order differences, obtained twenty to twenty-five years ago when Schachter conducted his experiments, primarily reflected individual differences in dependency [294, pp. 7–9]. That is, his firstborn, more dependent, subjects preferred to be with others and to engage others in conversation while anticipating a painful experience.

Specific findings supporting the latter conclusion were provided in another study [294, pp. 48–50]. These findings showed that in general, across all subjects, there was more affiliation with others while anticipating a pleasant than a neutral (neither pleasant nor unpleas-

*Parts of this section have been taken from A. Mehrabian and J. A. Russell, "Environmental effects on affiliation among strangers." *Humanitas*, 1975, *11*, 219–230. Reproduced by permission.

ant) experience; and there was more affiliation while anticipating a neutral than an unpleasant experience. As predicted, among subjects who were anticipating an unpleasant experience, the dependent ones showed more affiliation than independent ones. Nevertheless, even in the case of these dependent people, there was greater affiliation while anticipating a pleasant than an unpleasant experience. The following figure taken from [294, Figure 3.1] summarizes those findings.

The results in Figure 7-1 show that the effects of stress (anticipated shock) on affiliation that were noted by Schachter [363] are small compared with the effects of pleasant-unpleasant feelings. Further, the effects of stress are found primarily for one segment of the population—more dependent people.

Findings such as these demonstrated the need for a more comprehensive test of the effects of precisely defined (and environmentally induced) emotional states on affiliation. The following experiments systematically varied pleasure-displeasure and arousal-nonarousal of subjects and explored the effects of these on affiliation. The mea-

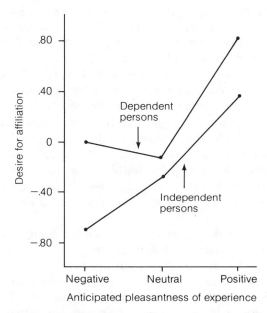

Figure 7-1: Affiliation as a Function of Pleasantness-Unpleasantness of an Anticipated Experience and a Person's Dependency*

*From A. Mehrabian and J. A. Russell, "Environmental effects on affiliation among strangers." *Humanitas*, 1975, *11*, 219–230. Reproduced by permission.

sure of affiliation used tapped a general feeling of friendliness and approach toward strangers, plus a specific desire to talk to them.

In the initial set of experiments, environments were presented to subjects using vivid written descriptions. One such description was as follows:

> You are sitting on a deserted beach in the late afternoon. The water is dark blue, and the waves are crashing loudly. The beach is hidden completely from the outside by the sand dunes behind it.

There were sixty-five such verbally described settings [299, Appendix A]. In the second set of experiments, settings were presented to subjects using photographic slides [357; 359].

The results from each one of the six experiments (three using verbal descriptions of places and three using slides) consistently showed the expected effect of pleasure on affiliation: Subjects reported a greater desire to interact with others in pleasant compared with unpleasant places. Additional and representative findings from one of the experiments that used slides [359] are given in Figure 7-2. Since the dominant-submissive feelings induced by a setting strongly affected the other results that were due to the pleasantness and arousing quality of settings, Figure 7-2 shows separate graphs for dominance-eliciting settings in the right half, and for submissiveness-eliciting settings in the left half.

The three curves in the right half of Figure 7-2 show a strong increase in desire to affiliate with increasing pleasantness of situations. This is the pleasure effect on affiliation. Further, the curve relating affiliation to arousal is positively sloped for pleasant settings; affiliation is unaffected by arousing quality in neutrally pleasant settings; and the curve is generally negatively sloped for unpleasant settings, but shows an increase for highly arousing settings. The latter increase is the stress effect originally noted by Schachter—the combination of displeasure and high arousal yields an increment in affiliation.

The right half of the figure also shows that among highly pleasant settings, more affiliation occurs in exciting places (those that are not only pleasant but also arousing) than in calming settings (those that are pleasant but unarousing). For instance, more excitement at a party—provided it is pleasant—should enhance the friendliness of the guests. Changes in arousal have no significant effect on affiliation in neutrally pleasant situations. For unpleasant settings, the relationship between arousing quality and affiliation has the following implications. Depressing or boring (that is, unpleasant and unarousing) settings elicit more affiliation than unpleasant and moderately arous-

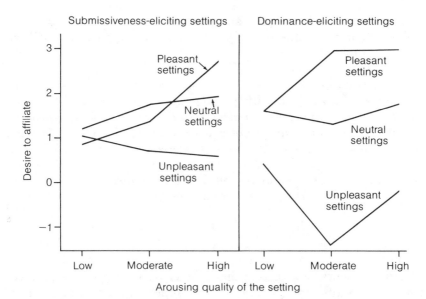

Figure 7-2: Arousing Quality by Dominance-Eliciting Quality by Pleasant-ness Interaction on Desire to Affiliate*

ing settings. This suggests that affiliation is used to relieve depression or boredom. Highly arousing and unpleasant settings also elicit more affiliation than moderately arousing and unpleasant places; however, here the reasons for the increased affiliation are different. While feeling displeasure and arousal (stress), people seek others to reduce uncertainty, and the reduction of uncertainty lowers arousal. Furthermore, the pleasant exchanges associated with affiliation far exceed the unpleasant emotional exchanges [294, pp. 53–54]. Thus, on both these counts—uncertainty reduction and contribution to pleasant feelings—affiliation counteracts the high arousal and displeasure associated with stress.

The left half of Figure 7-2 summarizes the findings for submissiveness-eliciting settings. The closeness of the three curves for the three levels of setting pleasantness shows that differences in setting pleasantness have a weaker effect on people's affiliation when they feel submissive than when they feel dominant. Also, the stress effect is absent in submissiveness-eliciting situations.

Altogether, these results show that the more dominant people are made to feel, the more preferences they express regarding where they want to affiliate (for example, seeking affiliation in pleasant, but

*From A. Mehrabian and J. A. Russell, "Environmental effects on affiliation among strangers." *Humanitas*, 1975, *11*, 219–230. Reproduced by permission.

avoiding affiliation in unpleasant, places). In contrast, the more submissive people feel, the fewer preferences they express as to where they want to affiliate.

List three examples of each of the following four types of situations: pleasant and arousing (exciting, invigorating); pleasant and unarousing (relaxing, comfortable); unpleasant and arousing (anxiety-producing, uncomfortable); unpleasant and unarousing (depressing, boring). Now write out a sentence or two to describe specifically how you would feel toward and react to strangers in each of these twelve situations. Do your descriptions of your affiliative patterns in these situations correspond to the findings we just reported?

Summary

The experiments described in this chapter have only touched the perimeter of a vast and unexplored area; they indicate that environmentally facilitated approach does indeed affect social interaction. Strangers who happen to occupy rooms, apartments, or working areas that increase the frequency of their contacts because of closeness are found to get to like each other more. These findings have many implications for the design of cities and buildings, as well as the interiors of buildings. For instance, in the case of furniture arrangement, more direct orientations and closer positions facilitate conversation. Even though excessively close, that is, face-to-face and very close, positions do not hinder conversation, they are not conducive to comfort; people tend to be less relaxed in these positions.

The findings involving distance and sensitivity to rejection help clarify why strangers have so much trouble interacting at large distances, such as across vast expanses of living room. Large distances discourage the conversation of those who are sensitive to rejection, particularly when others are present. Our interpretation is that in these situations, fear of seeming silly or unintelligent makes it difficult just to say something outright. For those who are sensitive to rejection this problem is even more accentuated.

The objects in a setting can also affect social interaction. Such objects can be grouped broadly into those that encourage isolated activity and those that can mediate the relationship between two people. Thus, the swimming pool in the apartment complex or the sculpture in a living room provide means of implicitly communicating a shared interest, by highlighting the common theme in the participants' actions—they are all out to relax beside the pool, or they are both interested in a piece of art. In the context of the greater proximity and shared activity, it is easier to initiate conversation with an offhand comment. Further, agreements with such comments (remember the mutual reinforcements of those who were sensitive to rejection in one of the experiments) provide the necessary reassurance to proceed with a more meaningful exchange.

General effects of the environment on affiliation are described best in terms of the hypotheses of Figure 1-1: Under pleasant (or even neutral) circumstances, liking and approach are positively correlated; under unpleasant circumstances, liking and approach are negatively correlated. Thus, in most normal social situations where pleasant or neutral cues are present, greater contact and approach lead to more liking among the participants. However, under unpleasant social or physical conditions, enforced approach due to crowding leads to hostile, aggressive, and generally negative and maladaptive social exchanges.

Studies were described that directly explored these effects of pleasure-displeasure and arousal-nonarousal on social interaction. The findings showed that affiliation is greater in pleasant than in unpleasant settings. Also, affiliation increases with increases in the arousing quality of pleasant settings, and decreases with increases in the arousing quality of unpleasant settings. Thus, the most marked environmental effects on affiliation are noted in highly arousing and pleasant settings compared to highly arousing and unpleasant ones. These effects of the pleasure- and arousal-eliciting qualities of environments are maximized in those situations where the participants feel dominant and are minimized in situations where they feel submissive.

Suggested Readings

General treatments of the effects of environments on a variety of behaviors including interpersonal ones are given in [115; 116; 280; 338]. Details of some interesting studies of the effects of closeness and contacts on liking among strangers are given in [25; 32; 121; 321]. Experimental studies of the contribution of seating arrangement to social interaction are given in [282; 283; 384].

Reviews of the experimental findings on crowding are provided in [125; 160, pp. 285–295]. My volume [273] on the general topic of environmental psychology contains discussions of the effects of environments on social interaction in apartments and public housing (Chapters 10 and 11), offices (Chapter 13), at sporting events (Chapter 25), and as a function of the qualities of cities (Chapter 30). See [117] for measures of the emotional environments created by parental attitudes, and see [115] for a review of the consequences of various emotional conditions on child-parent interactions.

Chapter 8

A Language within Language

In describing what her boy friend did, Joan could say, "Sally was dancing with him," "He was dancing with Sally," or "They were dancing together." These three statements show increasing degrees of Joan's acceptance of what her boy friend did. Bob could describe his activity to his wife as follows: "Alice and I danced," "She and I danced," "I danced with her," "She danced with me," or "I had to dance with her," depending, perhaps, on his feelings about liking Alice or about his wife's reaction—the last statement being, of course, the most cautious.

Talking about a party you attended, you say, "The food was pretty good," "They had a good time," "They were having a good time," "We had a good time," or "I had a good time." All these are different ways of making a positive statement about the party; however, when analyzed in some detail, they show interesting differences in liking.

Previous chapters have emphasized the role of implicit messages in social interaction. In cultures like ours, these constant companions of what we say are an important way of conveying feelings and like-dislike, the expression of which would otherwise sometimes be unacceptable. Increased focus on implicit modes may help overcome the handicapping reliance on words in communication, at least as communication skills are formally taught, and may contribute to a better understanding of the significance of various gestures, postures, and expressions. Let us now note the numerous and frequently overlooked subtleties of speech itself that are part of the expression of feelings and like-dislike [76; 231; 251].

Distance in Time and Place

The stylistic differences of the sentences selected to express a certain idea can be used to infer (1) liking of the thing being described, (2) liking of the listener, or (3) liking of, or preference for, the act of saying certain things to a certain listener [425]. Here again, we shall use the important concept of approach-avoidance to make inferences about the like-dislike revealed in any of these three cases. Notice the difference in each of the following pairs: "Here they are," "There they are"; "These people need help," "Those people need help"; "I can't understand this man," "I can't understand that man"; "I am showing Liz my collection of etchings," "I have been showing

Liz my collection of etchings." In each example, the first sentence of the pair involves greater approach. This is due to the particular use of demonstrative pronouns ("this" or "these" versus "that" or "those"), adjectives ("here," "there"), or verb tense (present versus past).

There are many situations in which forms varying in approach-avoidance can effectively be used to communicate the verbal message, and thus the particular usage becomes significant [304]. For instance, in talking about a minority group, the speaker who says, "Those people need help" is putting the group further away from himself in this very subtle verbal form than when he says, "These people need help." Consider another example: As a woman enters a crowded room, two men exclaim simultaneously. One says, "Here's Kathy"; the other says, "There's Kathy." It turns out that the first is her current favored escort; the second used to be.

When the form of demonstrative pronoun or tense used is incongruous with the time or place of the actual event, it suggests some special feelings of the speaker [257]. For example, a person says, "I don't understand those people," about some people in the room with her. Her demonstrative "those" is incongruous for the situation, which is here and now. In another example, John is showing Mary his cherished collection of plants when his wife, Tina, joins them. When he says, "I am showing Mary the plants," he places the entire activity in the present tense and doubtless is easy in his own mind about the activity. This is closer in time to the actual activity than if he were to say, "I have been showing Mary the plants" or "I showed Mary the plants." If John uses one of the "avoidant," meaning avoidance-involving, forms, he may be revealing his awareness of Tina's jealousy of Mary's attentiveness to him or, even though Tina does not mind what she considers to be an innocent relationship, he may feel some edge of uneasiness about his own interest in Mary.

This kind of avoidance involves putting something at a physical distance through the use of demonstrative pronouns or at a temporal distance through the use of past tenses. But avoidance can be indicated in other ways, one of which is mention of the more unpleasant, or less pleasant, things later in a sequence [257]. Such ordering can occur when we describe different parts of an event or situation. We might refer to a couple we know as "John and Marge," to another couple as "Jane and Jack," and yet another couple as "the Browns." In the first case, chances are that John is the more important, better known, or better liked member of the pair. In the second case, Jane may be the more important or better liked member. In the last case, perhaps neither one of the pair is well known to the speaker, or there is a certain formality and social distance in the relationship with these people.

In describing a day's activities I could say, "We went to the bank, shopped, and visited some friends"; or I could say, "We visited some friends, shopped, and also went to the bank." Assuming that neither one of these orders corresponds to the actual sequence of events, it is safe to infer that the first item mentioned is probably the more important or the more liked part of the day's activities. In some situations, we may have the necessary information to be able to consider the actual sequence of events and the way in which it is recited in a description. If an event that actually occurred first in the sequence is mentioned last, perhaps the speaker does not like it as well as she does the other items and has delayed mentioning it quite unintentionally. Even stronger dislike is implied when she leaves out an item entirely.

If you've had psychotherapy, remember the order in which you described your problems to the therapist in the initial interview.

In the psychotherapy situation, when we mention something first it is not because we like it more but rather because it is easiest for us to mention that particular problem to a stranger. Thus, another value of the order in which things are mentioned is that it shows how easily certain things can be described to someone else. The general rule for making such interpretations is that avoidance through delay can be due to discomfort about saying a particular thing to a particular listener.

There is a related way in which avoidance comes into play in speech. Hesitant and halting speech with errors, incomplete sentences, and repetition of words indicate anxiety and negative feelings [192; 228; 231; 377]. We tend to make more errors when talking about a distressing subject than a pleasant one. *Note:* "How did it go at the dentist's?" "Well, uh (pause) it went fine"; "Did you cook dinner?" "I, I thought . . . uh, we could go out tonight." This is reminiscent of Freud's [128] discussion of slips of the tongue—a special kind of error that, in his view, reveals conflicts in the speaker and dislike of aspects of the current situation. What, indeed, is the function of halting and faltering speech? Halting speech delays the completion of a statement. Errors associated with such speech make the descriptions less effective, more difficult to understand, and generally inhibit the communication process. In this sense, the errors delay what a person has to say and lead us to infer that he has at least some reservations about saying it.

Form of Reference

We can show less liking of something by putting it at a distance; by avoiding any mention of it; or, as in the following examples, by referring to it in ambiguous ways [247]. This ambiguity makes it more difficult for our listeners to understand what exactly our statement refers to and reflects our unwillingness to express a certain idea in a certain situation.

One important source of ambiguity of reference is the *overinclusive* statement. Suppose a friend has recommended a certain restaurant; and, to your chagrin, you have tried it. You have put off mentioning anything about it to her (already, one kind of avoidance), but she asks you, "How did you like your dinner at One-Eyed Joe's?" You say, "It was a pleasant evening" instead of "It was a pleasant dinner." You use the more inclusive term "evening," which involves a broader set of events, thus making an ambiguous positive remark. With this kind of overinclusive statement the involvement with a particular event is minimized since the stated relation includes many parts in addition to the specific referent in question (for example, "evening" includes other events apart from "dinner").

There are two ways of making such overinclusive statements: (1) placing the referent within a more comprehensive category and (2) including oneself within a larger group of people. If I am asked, "How do you like Wanda?" and answer, "I like the Smiths," I have not specifically referred to Wanda in my answer but rather have referred to her and her husband, the Smiths, thereby minimizing involvement. It could be that I have reservations about Wanda or that I am unwilling to say what I feel about her to the person who asked me the question. On the other hand, I could have answered, "We like Wanda," implying that my friends and I like her. Using an inclusive "we" instead of "I" in the statement dilutes the relation with Wanda, which is again indicative of less liking.

The use of "we" instead of "I" is a familiar rhetorical device. If a speaker uses both "I" and "we," we can infer which of his statements he feels more strongly about and which are token statements to placate or gratify his listeners. When a speaker feels strongly about the accuracy of some statement or wishes to be identified with a certain proposition, he is more likely to start that sentence with "I." But when he feels less confident about something and does not want to be held responsible for it, he may use the pronoun "we." *Note:* "I believe that the national economy will respond favorably to an increase in the money supply" versus "We believe . . ." The "we" may refer to the speaker and his wife, to many Americans, or to some economists; it is not altogether clear to the listeners that this is the speaker's particular stand on the issue.

Euphemisms are a rich source of overinclusive references, and their use is motivated by the desire to diminish the negative or distasteful quality of the expression they replace. "Tickets are available at . . ." instead of "Tickets are sold at . . ." may be popular in advertisements that seek to minimize the implied exchange of money. Familiar examples of such expressions are "passed away" instead of "died"; "exceptional child" instead of "retarded child"; "donation" instead of "price"; "to wash hands" instead of "to go to the bathroom"; "detention center" instead of "prison"; and "sanitation engineer" instead of "garbage collector."

Many people make up their own euphemisms to refer to disliked persons or events. Can you think of any expressions of this kind that you use only with persons who share the particular negative feeling?

Another way, perhaps more extreme, of diluting the relationship between self and the referent is to make a statement that touches only tangentially on the person or issue being considered. A question like "What do you think of their marriage?" may be answered with remarks such as "My husband thinks it's great" or "Don't you think it's great?" rather than "I think it's great." In the first two instances, the speaker is implying that not she but someone else thinks the marriage is exceptionally suitable. We may infer that she has some reservations about the soundness of this marriage—or perhaps is simply not particularly interested. Quite frequently, the negative significance of such answers is overlooked, but experimental findings have consistently shown that this kind of avoidance through tangential reference is a powerful indicator of a speaker's negative feelings about what she is discussing. The difference between "I lost control of the car" and the more avoidant form, "The car went out of control," can be similarly interpreted. It is evident that the person making the latter statement is unwilling to accept responsibility for the accident.

Elaborate and adept applications of such tangential references to oneself are very common in public speeches and debates when the speaker feels that a remark may be controversial or that it is only weakly supported by facts and reasoning. Common examples are "You would expect," "You'd think," "It would seem to be," "It would be expected," all of which serve as substitutes for "I think" or "I expect." Similar hedging also occurs frequently in scientific writings, in which it is especially important to emphasize the tentative quality of one's ideas.

The complement of tangential reference to self occurs when a

The car went out of control.

subject of distaste is described in such a way that it is unclear who or what is being described. A mother, in referring to her son's fiancée, could say, "our daughter-to-be," "our son's fiancée," "his fiancée," "his lady-friend," "his friend," "she," or "that thing"—showing increasing avoidance and dislike of the girl. Similarly, across the generation gap, a shaven and shorn solid citizen may refer to his hirsute son as "that bum," while the youth may reciprocate with "that reactionary" or "that uptight square" (if he uses printable epithets).

An interesting variant of the overinclusive statement is *negation*. Following a brief encounter with someone whom we do not really care to meet again, we say, "Why don't we get together sometime?" instead of "Let's get together." If we are enthusiastic about meeting this person again, we actually suggest a time and place for the next meeting. Less preference for a listener or a feeling that the listener will not like to comply with a request can also become evident in examples such as this: "Why don't you type this one first and then go back to what you were doing." In this instance, the executive uses this particular form to request that the secretary change priorities because she is aware that the secretary will be inconvenienced and won't like her request.

More generally, the "why don't you" statement is likely to occur when the speaker doubts that her request or suggestion will be complied with, either because she feels that the request may sound imposing or demanding, as in the case of the employer, or because she shares little mutual feeling of goodwill with the listener, as in our first example.

Another kind of negation that reveals one's reservations is illustrated by "How did you like the movie?" answered with "It wasn't bad." This answer conveys a feeling different from that indicated by

"It was fine." We can understand the difference in terms of the over-inclusive quality of "not bad" relative to "fine." The former includes "fine" as well as "so-so," and more than likely the feeling was indeed "so-so." Other examples are "We're not exactly buddies" and "The movie is not the best I've seen."

Think back to the times when you have answered a question in just this way or made such a statement. You probably used this kind of negation because you did not really care for the experience you were describing but, as a matter of politeness or caution, preferred not to express your strong feelings to your listener.

The exact opposite of the overinclusive statement is yet another source of information about feelings. "I enjoy being with her, for an evening" shows how, in addition to using overinclusive reference, a speaker can also minimize his relation to a referent by using *over-specific* statements. In this case, the "enjoying" is restricted to an evening, rather than left unqualified. Overspecification arises when we refer to a part of the referent in a context that requires a more complete statement: "How did you like my new production?" is answered with "I liked the acting" instead of simply "I liked it." In saying "I liked (or enjoyed) the acting," the speaker has managed to pick out the one part of the production that he liked best or, which is more likely to be the case, disliked least. An astute and straightforward producer at this point might say, "What was the matter with the rest of it?" More than likely, however, he will simply go on with a discussion of the acting and will fail to consider the possible weaknesses in his play that are implied by the remark.

Someone asks you about the ball game he had suggested you go to: "How was the game?" You say, "It was a nice day, and it was fun to be outdoors." These references to the weather and to the outdoors touch only in part on the game and reveal a low level of liking, or even dislike, of the game by you.

Just as overspecificity shows dislike and lack of preference when it involves the referent, the same kind of implication is made when it involves the speaker [246]. After an accident, I could say, "My car slid out of control and struck her" instead of "I struck her with my car." In the first statement something associated with me, "my car," is the implied agent responsible for this action; in the second, "I," the actor, am the responsible agent. Someone says, "The thoughts that come to my mind are . . ." instead of "I think . . .," thus implying that only a part of her, "her thoughts," should be held responsible for what she is to say. A more straightforward example of over-specificity is "Her hands touched his hair" instead of "She touched his hair."

In all these cases, a part of the person speaking (her thoughts) or something that belongs to or is associated with the speaker (her car) is the ostensible actor and the responsible agent in a situation. Thus, we can infer that the speaker does not feel very comfortable about a statement she is going to make, since she is unwilling to assume full responsibility. Indeed, an entire set of avoidant statements can be analyzed directly in terms of the desire to minimize responsibility.

Responsibility

As he brings his date back home, a young man says, "I would like to see you again," instead of the less conditional "I want to see you again." In this case, he probably uses the conditional (more avoid-ant) form because he does not want to seem too forward with a girl he has taken out for the first time or lay himself on the line to be rejected. In other words, he has trouble expressing his enthusiasm about the girl, not because he does not like her, but because there are social sanctions against it or because of the possibility of being turned down.

Usually, the conditional is used when the speaker does not like what he is going to say [248]. *Note:* "You'd think they would do some-thing to improve the quality of service here" instead of "I think they ought to improve the quality of service here." Of course, this exam-ple involves at least two kinds of avoidance. One is the use of "you" instead of "I," and the other is the use of the conditional. Here the speaker is trying to avoid seeming domineering or authoritarian to his addressee. Alternatively, the addressee in this case may be con-nected with the management of the place being criticized, and the speaker may be uncomfortable about being directly critical. What-ever the reason for making such conditional statements, it is obvious that the speaker is trying to imply a lack of familiarity and a weaker relationship with the object being discussed.

When an author sends his manuscript to a publisher and receives the following kind of initial response, he has some reason to wonder whether his manuscript will be accepted. "The manuscript seems very interesting and apparently does a very good job of portraying youth in our society. Our readers are now giving your manuscript a closer look, and I will be getting in touch with you about it." The words "seems" and "apparently" indicate that the editor has some reserve about the manuscript. In this case, even though the editor is making a number of positive statements, the author probably should not take the letter as an enthusiastic reception of his manuscript.

In a similar minimizing of responsibility, a speaker makes no direct reference to herself: "It is evident that . . .," "It is obvious that . . .," or "Most people realize that she's an intolerable bitch." The implication here is that others are responsible for the view being expressed and that the speaker merely shares that view. This device is likely to be used by a speaker who does not wish to be held answerable for what she is going to say and is especially concerned about possible disagreement from her listener. By protecting herself from rebuff in this way, she hints at the quality of her relationship with the listener: They are not likely to agree on this and perhaps many other matters. Experimental findings have consistently shown that people tend to dislike others who hold different opinions and attitudes, that is, those they would disagree with frequently [51; 52; 271; 290; 294]. So in this instance, the implication of expected disagreement of the listener is indicative of dislike or a low level of liking toward him.

Of course, another way to avoid responsibility for what we say is to qualify our statements. Common forms are "I feel . . .," "I think . . .," "It seems to me . . .," or "It is possible that she's pregnant." With such qualification, the speaker shows his reluctance to make the particular statement as a matter of established fact and again highlights this awareness of possible disagreement from his listeners. This device is also used in gossip. By prefacing a scandalous thought with "I think . . ." or "They say . . .," the speaker technically avoids responsibility for the truth or falsehood of his statement, yet he still gets the benefit of saying it.

In some situations, the avoidance and associated dislike of the speaker is evident in statements that very obviously seek to minimize her responsibility [144]. A woman who is asked for a date by someone whom she does not like says, "I have to go with someone else," instead of the more straightforward "I prefer (or want) to go with someone else." The avoidance of responsibility in "I have to" reflects her difficulty in being frank with him.

In departing from a friend's house, we could say "I am leaving now" or "I want to leave now" instead of "I should leave now," or "I have to leave now," or "I really should leave now." The second set of statements implies that we are leaving, not because we want to, but because of some extraneous circumstances that force us to do so. In other words, something other than our own desires is responsible for the fact that we must leave. This kind of avoidant statement is used if the relationship with the listener is more formal, less straightforward, and generally one in which feelings cannot be clearly and directly expressed without fear of hurting others.

People tend to attribute responsibility to some external agent in their statement for departing, especially because the act of departure is tantamount to avoidance. If we leave a party at 11:00 P.M. instead of 2:00 A.M., or if we are first rather than last to leave, this departure time indicates something about how much we are enjoying the party. So, when we do leave at a time that we think is too early and might lead the host to think we did not like and enjoy the party (which is actually the case), a statement such as "We've got to get back" helps to save face for the host and provides an easy out for the guest.

When a couple is going to get married, and they tell their friends, "We have to get married," it doesn't take much psychological training for friends to wonder about possible reservations and negative feelings of the engaged couple toward the marriage. But when someone says, "I can't come because I have to see a friend off at the airport," the negative affect is less likely to be detected without knowledge of avoidant speech forms. We know that he could have said, "I can't come because I am going to see a friend off at the airport."

Another way in which responsibility for an action or a statement is minimized is through the use of the passive rather than the active form. I could say, "The results of my experiments have led me to this conclusion" instead of "I conclude this from my experiments." I would be more likely to use the passive form if I were not quite sure about the results or how they should be interpreted. The use of the passive form in this case implies that anybody else, just like myself, could have been led to the same conclusion, and that I should not be held responsible for making the particular interpretation. However, if I were to use the active form, I would not provide myself with this "out."

You may be able to think of some of your friends or acquaintances who are generally prone to using the passive form when they talk about certain topics. This should give you a clue about their sense of helplessness and consequent negative feelings when these topics are mentioned. Alternatively, if an individual resorts to the passive form more than most others, this could be a sign of his general unwillingness to assume responsibility for his actions.

Examples so far in this section show how avoiding responsibility generally indicates dislike of, or lack of preference for, the contents of one's communication. There are other times, however, when the sharing of responsibility with the listener, a form of *mutuality*, can be informative about the relation between speaker and listener. *Note:* "Remember what we decided about the office?" instead of "Remember what I suggested about the office?" In the first case, the decision is a mutual one involving the speaker and the listener, whereas in the second the decision is a unilateral one. It involves the speaker alone and implies her separation from the listener, at least in terms of their contribution to this activity [246].

When such expressions occur frequently in a relationship, they can serve as clues about how two people, who are closely involved in either a social or working relationship, feel toward each other. The statements implying mutuality are likely to arise in relationships where there is mutual liking, since they indicate a more intense involvement of the pair in the activity in which they are engaged. Let us say that two people are having lunch and a third person joins them. At his point, one of the two says, "John and I have been discussing your project" instead of "I have been telling John about your project." Either one of these two statements could be quite legitimate in the situation, but the former implies equality of status between John and the speaker and a more intimate feeling.

This concept allows us to interpret "I was dancing with her" or "She was dancing with me" differently from "We were dancing." The first statement implies that she really was not participating much, possibly because she does not like the speaker. The second statement implies that the speaker does not like her or that he does not want to let his listener know that he likes her. The last statement shows no reservation about dancing with this particular person or the act of mentioning it to someone else.

Guarded Expressions of Liking

So far most of our discussion has focused on how avoidant forms of speech reflect less liking or greater dislike. On some occasions, a more avoidant statement is used because the speaker feels uncomfortable about saying what she wants to say to her listener. This idea can be turned to our advantage. In a number of social situations, it may seem too forward to make clear and direct statements of liking or interest to a stranger or a casual acquaintance, but a more avoidant form would be socially acceptable.

A man sees an interesting woman in the hallway of the office building where he works and wishes to get to know her. The first chance he gets, he says, "That's a nice dress you have on." In this instance, the remark involves less approach than the simple "I like you," but serves as an indirect and socially more acceptable way of conveying liking. The avoidant form of the remark reflects his uneasiness, not because he dislikes her, but because he feels uncomfortable about this initial contact with a stranger.

Other examples: "I heard that you have a marvelous wine cellar" or "Someone told me that you grow prize-winning camellias." The speaker desires to somehow compliment his listener but feels that he cannot do so in a very direct and obvious way. So he selects something related to the listener to compliment, because the more indirect statement involving less approach happens to be more socially appropriate. The avoidant form of his statement still shows that the speaker feels uncomfortable in the situation, which is indeed why this kind of statement is more acceptable in formal relationships or contacts with a stranger.

Relations of Verbal and Nonverbal Approach-Avoidance

Our analyses of speech here and of actions in Chapter 2 have been based on the same basic metaphor: People seek out and get involved with things they like and they try to minimize their relationship or, if possible, entirely avoid contact with things they dislike or fear. We have examined the many special devices that are available in speech to reflect a speaker's negative feelings. At this point, let us consider some analogues of these avoidant speech forms in implicit messages.

For example, the times at which various participants at major political negotiations arrive for a specific meeting can be important cues, provided the people whose behaviors are under scrutiny have some prepared remarks for that session. Thus, if one of the participants comes with prepared remarks of a hopeful quality, but makes her entrance late (relative to other sessions), she is providing grounds for questioning the sincerity of her remarks. Her delay shows a reluctance to make those remarks. On the other hand, if she delivers some prepared negative remarks, her delay will constitute a positive sign and show her reluctance to seem antagonistic. In either case, the delay can also be a function of the importance of the remarks (she was busy up to the last minute preparing them) or a variety of other factors. This is of course true, but suppose we make these observations repeatedly over a large number of instances, say weekly meetings. In this case, the extraneous and unsystematic effect of some of these factors (for example, she was delayed in traffic) is washed out in the averaging process, and the underlying level of liking tends to become evident from the implicit or the verbal behavior of the participants. This is exactly what is done in any experiment where such ideas are tested. We do not rely on a single incident to make a judgment, so most of our experiments employ large numbers of subjects to test these ideas.

In a somewhat different context, Freud's [128] discussion of forgetting provides another point of similarity between verbal and nonverbal forms of approach-avoidance. The verbal analogues of forgetting are the speech errors and other obstructions that delay the expression of an idea [192; 377]. As in the case of forgetting, such phenomena make it possible for the speaker or the actor to put off or avoid saying something that is unpleasant. Freud did not interpret forgetting or slips specifically in terms of approach and avoidance. Nevertheless, his analyses always implied that the unconscious conflicts that led to these errors or even more serious symptoms were motivated by dislike and negative feelings. In the case of forgetting, the negative feelings were toward the forgotten object. Thus, forgetting to mail a letter we have written helps delay contact with the intended receiver of the letter and shows the writer's reservations about the contents of his letter or toward the person who would receive it.

I have frequently and painfully been reminded of the validity of this idea when I have belatedly come across a disliked chore I had forgotten to get done on time. It seems much easier to forget an unpleasant or time-consuming chore than a liked one.

Keep a tally of all the things you forget, listing the liked ones separately from the disliked ones. You will probably find that the disliked ones far outnumber the liked ones. Close examination of such a list can provide valuable insights into feelings that you are not so willing to recognize in yourself.

After hearing a lecture on the present topic, a student asked if the approach-avoidance concept could help explain why her boy friend was invariably about half an hour late for their dates. She said that this was very annoying for her but that otherwise the relationship was perfect. I suggested that this was a way for him to express some negative feelings that he was otherwise unable to convey. As we discussed her problem, it became apparent that he had a great deal of trouble refusing her requests. It also became apparent that he was especially late to their dates when these also involved her parents, so that on such occasions his tardiness was especially embarrassing to her. She concluded that most of the time she had gotten her way in the relationship. The possibility of marriage, which was also her idea initially, was highlighted by those evenings spent with her parents and accounted for his greater tardiness when the parents were involved. Considering his inability to refuse her requests, the boy was resisting in the only way that he knew how—on a most important issue.

Approach-Avoidance and Context

More accurate estimates of the speaker's feelings can be made provided knowledge of the situation in which he makes those statements is available. When a psychotherapist listens to his patient list a series of problems in an initial interview, he has no knowledge of the sequence in which these problems occurred. Therefore, he can rely only on the sequence in which they are given to infer the corresponding ease with which his patient can discuss them (that is, the less negative quality of the problems mentioned earlier in the series). However, if the therapist has an independent source of information, such as a relative of the person whom he is interviewing, then he is in an even better position to estimate the patient's feelings from the sequence in which he relates his problems. So, if the problems occurred in the sequence A, B, C and are described in the sequence C, A, B, he knows that the patient feels less dislike toward C than toward A.

In applying approach-avoidance analysis to infer level of liking, the person doing the analysis can himself create the situation within which he can make a more accurate interpretation. This is done with a careful selection of the wording of the question. If I ask you, "How did you like the movie?" and you say, "I like it," there is a striking tense shift in your answer. It shows your desire to bring this experience closer to yourself than the context allows and leads me to infer that you really like the movie. On the other hand, if I ask, "How do you like my tie?" and, as you stand in front of me, you answer, "That one is OK," then despite the closeness or approach in the situation, your statement implies distance and avoidance—a desire to place this object farther away.

Table 8-1 illustrates the different categories of approach-avoidance used in the analysis of speech and provides all possible combinations of approach or avoidance involving situation and speech. In the first example, a man standing on the edge of a pool comments, "Go ahead and jump into this pool," which is congruent with the greater closeness (approach) in the situation. Or he could say, "Go ahead and jump into that pool," which is avoidant and shows dislike.

Table 8-1: Approach-Avoidance: Situations and Speech Forms*

Category	Approach/Avoidance Situation	Approaching/Avoidant Speech Form
Distance: spatial distance between communicator and object of communication.	A man standing on the edge of a pool comments to a friend standing beside him./A man standing on the patio some distance from a pool comments . . .	"Go ahead and jump into this pool."/"Go ahead and jump into that pool."
Time: temporal distance between communicator and object.	Question asked of communicator: "Do you think about X?"/"Have you been thinking about X?"	"I think about X."/"I used to think about X."
Order of occurrence: order of interaction with the object in an interaction sequence.	Question asked of communicator: "Did you visit X and Y?"/"Did you visit Y and X?"	"I visited X and Y."/"I visited Y and X."
Duration: duration of interaction or duration (e.g., length) of communication about interaction.	A is asked to write a long letter about B./A is asked to write a short letter about B.	A writes a long letter about B./A writes a short letter about B.
Activity-passivity: willingness vs. an obligatory quality of communicator-object interaction.	X stopped to help someone fix a flat tire./X had to stop to help someone fix . . .	X says, "I stopped to help someone fix a flat tire."/"I had to stop to help . . ."
Mutuality-unilaterality: degree of reciprocity of communicator-object interaction.	Question asked of communicator: "Have you and X met each other?"/"Have you met X?"	"X and I met yesterday."/"I met X yesterday."
Probability: degree of certainty of communicator-object interaction.	Question asked of communicator: "Are you taking physical education courses?"/"Could you take physical education courses?"	"I am taking physical education courses."/"I could take physical . . ."
Communicator participation₁: the totality vs. only a part, aspect or acquaintance of the communicator interacts with the object.	Question asked of communicator: "Are you going to the store?"/"Is your friend going to the store?"	"I am going to the store."/"My friend is going to the store."
Communicator participation₂: the communicator interacts individually with the object vs. being part of a group of people who interact with the object.	Question asked of communicator: "Did you go to the beach last summer?"/"Did you people go to the beach last summer?"	"I went to the beach last summer."/"We went to the beach last summer."
Object participation₁: the totality vs. only a part, aspect or acquaintance of the object interacts with the communicator.	X is asked to write a letter and describe Y's personality./X . . . describe some of Y's habits.	In his letter, X describes Y's personality./In his letter, X describes some of Y's habits.

Table 8-1: Approach-Avoidance: Situations and Speech Forms (*continued*)

Category	Approach/Avoidance Situation	Approaching/Avoidant Speech Form
Object participation₂: the object interacts individually with the communicator vs. being part of a group of people who interact with the communicator.	A and B are talking about C, and A asks, "Do you see C near the pool?"/"Do you see the people near the pool?"	B says, "I see C near the pool."/"I see the people near the pool."
Communicator-object participation: the presence vs. the absence of participation of the communicator (or object) in the interaction.	Question asked of communicator: "How are you and B doing at school?"/"How are you doing at school?"	"B and I are doing well at school."/"I am doing well at school."

*From A Mehrabian, "The effect of context on judgments of speaker attitude." *Journal of Personality,* 1968, *36,* 21–32. Copyright 1968 Duke University Press. Reproduced by permission.

On the other hand, a man standing on the patio some distance from the pool could say, "Go ahead and jump into this pool," which shows more liking than if he were to say, "Go ahead and jump into that pool," in which case the avoidant speech form is congruent with the situation.

The finer points illustrated in Table 8-1 can be useful when a cautious scrutiny of material is required. Most everyday situations provide obvious and blatantly avoidant forms that can be interpreted readily. So we'll close with the following instance: "One would think that those people could do something to help themselves!" Such a statement made in reference to minority groups reveals an underlying prejudicial attitude that may not be evident from a casual perusal of the meaning of the words but is readily detected from the excessive avoidance in the phrasing.

Applications

Jacobo Varela,* a colleague in Uruguay, has applied some of these approach-avoidance concepts to the analysis of Shakespearean plays. According to him, Shakespeare made considerable use of avoidant forms in the speeches of some of his characters to subtly imply their dislike of persons of high status. Varela has found that Shakespeare became even more proficient in using avoidant forms

*Private communication.

as a literary device in his later plays. Indeed, he suggests that certain aspects of approach-avoidance in the speech of various characters can be used as a test of authorship for some of the Shakespearean plays where this is uncertain. Incidentally, a similar analysis can be applied to important speeches and documents of questionable authorship, especially in the political field.

In the context of analyzing political documents, historians and present-day political analysts can use approaching versus avoidant forms to infer the feelings of a speaker, particularly when the speech is extemporaneous. There are very few people whose behavior and attitudes are not somehow affected by social mores and social scrutiny. This is especially the case with political leaders who may not be able to say what they feel because of various social pressures. Indeed, since the behavior of important political persons is the subject of constant scrutiny, what they say publicly is likely to be dictated by many considerations other than their private feelings.

Sometimes it is interesting to examine, in historical perspective, the feelings of a certain president or an important political figure with regard to a major social issue. When a film or videorecord is not available, it is possible to apply our analysis to his extemporaneous speech. This is done most readily for answers that are given to specific questions, for instance, in a press conference. A suitable question is the open-ended one, which can permit considerable variation in approach-avoidance in the answer. For example, the question could be "Mr. President, what is your opinion on the economic outlook for the near future?" The answer could be any one of the following, which illustrate increasing degrees of avoidance: "I think our economy is sound," "I think our economy is basically sound," "I have reason to believe that our economy is basically sound," "We have reason to believe that . . . ," "The information which is available to us at present shows that . . . ," or "Most of the major economic indicators suggest that. . . ." In developing this progression of answers, we used the overinclusive "we" instead of "I"; the more tangential reference to oneself with the use of "the information shows" rather than "I conclude"; the introduction of "basically," which refers to a part or an aspect of the subject of discussion (the implication here is that superficially it may not seem so, but the economy is basically sound); and we used the word "suggest" instead of "show," which introduces uncertainty about the assertion.

The implication of increasing avoidance in this series of statements is the unwillingness of the speaker to assume full responsibility for the conclusion that he draws from the economic indicators. Avoidance reveals his own doubts—and possible disagreement with the opinions of his economic advisors—about this answer to the question.

Considerably more interesting analyses can be performed on the records of previous political speeches as well as current ones to arrive at some ideas about how important leaders feel about the hotly debated issues of the day.

Approach-avoidance analysis can be applied, for instance, to union contract negotiations in which participants seldom can express all they feel or think. The negotiators in such situations who are better able to understand the unverbalized attitude of the other side are in a better position to deal at the negotiation table. In a way, the process resembles a bridge or poker game, where the more knowledge the player has of her opponent's cards, the better are her chances of winning. In the negotiation situation, the astute observer should be able to infer the issues on which the other side will compromise before there is any verbal indication of willingness to yield.

In addition to scrutinizing answers to specific questions, our analysis can also rely on the possible changes in the manner in which the same question is answered, over the course of negotiations. For example, it would be interesting to observe the amount of avoidance associated with "hard-line" statements by representatives of one side. Over the course of negotiations, such aggressive and uncompromising statements may begin to become associated with avoidance (speech errors, pauses, or some other forms of verbal avoidance and nonverbal variants of avoidance such as less eye contact with the person asking the question or turning to one side while answering it). This would be a hopeful sign, indicating that the representative is having trouble maintaining the hard-line approach, possibly because she knows that this is not the present "true" stand of her group, but is simply a manipulative device at the negotiation table.

Summary

We have seen how the concept of approach-avoidance is helpful in understanding some of the seemingly arbitrary and stylistic aspects of speech, as well as the apparently inconsequential variations in implicit behavior. The association of approach with liking, preference, and generally good feelings on the one hand and the association of avoidance with dislike, discomfort, and other unpleasant feelings lead to numerous applications. In addition to the commonly known interpretation of speech errors, our analysis allows the interpretation of many other kinds of variations. These indicate the speaker's attempt to place something at a spatial or temporal distance or otherwise to minimize his relation to, or involvement with, the thing he describes. Variants of verbal avoidance subtly minimize the speaker's responsibility for what he says by implying that the contents of his message are obvious to everyone including himself; or the contrary, that these statements are conditional and doubtful. Alternatively, responsibility is minimized by implying that the events were beyond the control of the actors, one of whom may be the speaker.

Suggested Readings

General discussion of the phenomena of approach-avoidance forms in speech is given in [269, Chapter 3; 425]. Reports of specific work conducted in our laboratory [144; 245; 246; 247; 248; 249; 257; 304] contain details of experimental results. Subsequent work bearing on these ideas has been reported in [67].

Chapter 9

Applications

Implicit communication comes into play in almost all of our every-day social encounters. This chapter illustrates some of the general principles we have already examined, by applying them to some common and important categories of social interaction.

Selling

Many subtleties in implicit behavior become evident in the face-to-face promotion of a product. A salesperson would certainly seem strange if she were to knock on a door and say, "I like you and there-fore want to tell you something about our new product." It would seem inappropriate and insincere; and she might get the door slammed in her face. How can you meet someone and in the first moment, even before you get a good look at her, say that you like her? No one would believe it. Yet a good salesperson does just this and gets away with it. She uses implicit behavior so she does not need words to get this message across.

Why does a door-to-door salesperson go to all this bother? She knows that to make a sale, she must not only show enthusiasm about her product but also somehow get the potential buyer to feel the same. This means getting someone to think differently about her product—acquire a new attitude toward it or change an existing one. Most salespeople intuitively, and quite correctly, know that if you wish to influence someone, then it helps to have him get to like you. This is because people who like each other have a greater tendency to meet each others' demands [263; 294]. In the case of the salesperson and her customer, the salesperson must somehow elicit liking from the total stranger in a very short time. She does so by implicitly showing pleasant feelings. You have heard the expression "The customer is always right." She may assume a very respectful attitude and smile or be extra attentive when the customer talks. She hopes that this will pay off through reciprocation and compliance from a customer who will buy the product.

This method of being pleasant to a customer is necessary when the product will not sell itself, that is, when it is indeed necessary to bring about a change in the attitudes and behavior of a customer. On the other hand, a different method can be effective if the products are of high quality.

In sales rooms of prestigious stores in more affluent districts, usually nobody even approaches the shopper, who may feel lost to some degree because it is not clear where things are situated or whom to ask about prices and terms. There frequently are salespeople around who are casually talking to one another or to some other customer and seem to be preoccupied. Their aloofness implies "This furniture is good enough to sell itself; I don't have to sell it to you." In this situation when one asks for help, the salesperson behaves in a very businesslike and matter-of-fact manner, with a good chance of making his sale.

Indeed, a shopper in one of these more expensive stores who is not well dressed may sometimes find the salesperson slightly disrespectful, with the implication that their products are not within the shopper's budget. Some such customers may be tempted to prove them wrong, even though they do not particularly like anything on display.

The same kind of situation can occur in an expensive restaurant if the diners are not "properly" dressed. The maître d' will seat them in "Siberia," where the waiter will take little care in serving them. Again the implicit communication is "You obviously do not belong here." The diner is thus challenged to prove that he does belong by buying an expensive meal he may not actually prefer.

Whether any of these sales methods succeeds depends on the quality of the product and the sophistication of the customer. When there is no obvious need for the product or when the product is of poor quality, the traditional selling approach is more effective: the salesperson conveys liking and thereby elicits cooperation and buying behavior. When the product is of high quality, high levels of pleasantness are unnecessary and may even have an adverse effect. For instance, a well-known gourmet who made it a habit to remain anonymous once accidentally revealed his identity while in his favorite Chinese restaurant. The maître d' then tried excessively hard to please the man. He virtually ignored what was ordered and served special dishes he thought would be sure to please. He even went so far as to serve one of the most expensive champagnes available. The gourmet felt this was the worst meal he'd ever had at that restaurant. As far as the champagne was concerned, he just happened to prefer beer with Chinese food.

Persuasion

Although social psychologists have conducted numerous studies of types and organization of verbal contents on the persuasive impact of messages, few studies of the implicit aspects of persuasion are available. Nevertheless, we can predict the effectiveness of persuasive messages by noting the emotional states that accompany high levels of suggestibility. Excited or angry crowds and panic group behavior share the common element of extremely high arousal of group members and illustrate conditions of heightened individual susceptibility to influence.

The function of arousal in attitude change was demonstrated in an important study where tranquilizer (arousal-reducing) and amphetamine (arousal-increasing) drugs were administered to subjects [68]. The findings showed that attitude change was minimized when subjects received tranquilizers whereas it was maximized when they received amphetamines, thus clearly showing that increased arousal tends to enhance attitude change.

It follows that the implicit style of an effective persuasive communication ought to create a highly aroused state in the listener. Consistent with this prediction, strong relationships have been found between arousal cues (facial and vocal activity, speech rate, and speech volume) of the speaker and the intended and judged (or perceived) persuasiveness of the accompanying messages [306].

Consistent with the latter, findings from another study show that faster talking individuals are more persuasive [312]. Also, speakers whose voice pitch varies less and tends to be monotonic (that is, those with less vocal activity) were judged less credible and less persuasive [1] and louder statements were more persuasive [329]. Thus, when an individual attempts to be persuasive, he tends to become highly aroused and his style of communication is, in turn, more arousing and more persuasive to the listener.

Additional, though weaker, relationships have been found between pleasantness and approach cues of the speaker and his or her persuasiveness [306]. Indeed, physically more attractive communicators also have been found to be more persuasive [59].

In sum, the implicit communication style associated with attempts to persuade and the degree of success at persuasion incorporate two primary style factors: arousing quality and pleasantness. Effective styles of persuasion can thus be said to be "exciting."

List two friends or acquaintances whom you have observed to be most effective in influencing others; also list two others whom you know are least able to persuade others in various situations. Describe briefly the implicit social style of each of these four people and specifically note their implicit behaviors during discussions or disagreements with oth-

ers. Do your casual observations of the implicit styles of the more per-suasive and less persuasive pairs correspond to the findings noted above?

Deceit

What are the implicit cues most likely to accompany deceit? To answer this question we need first to identify the likely emotional states of a deceitful communicator. In instances of "high risk" deceit, where the reward for successful deceit, or punishment and loss following unsuccessful deceit, is great, the expected emotional reactions are guardedness, discomfort, tension, vigilance, or anxiety. All of these emotional states involve displeasure, high arousal, and submissiveness. It is therefore readily possible to define the implicit cues expected to accompany high-risk deceit.

Among implicit speech cues, we expect more speech errors, more halting speech, and more tremor in the voice. Indeed, the expected positive correlation between speech error rate and deceitful versus truthful statements has been found [267]. More generally, deceitful, compared with truthful, communicators nod and gesture less, exhibit less frequent leg and foot movements while seated, assume less approaching (that is, less body lean toward, less eye contact) positions relative to their addressees, talk less, talk more slowly, have more speech errors, and smile more [267; 269, Chapter 5].

Studies have also consistently shown a higher pitch of voice to be judged more deceitful and actually to be associated with more deceitful statements [11; 390]. Also, consistent with results already noted, slower speakers are judged as less truthful [11].

Finally, increased self-manipulation (touching of body parts) is yet another index of deceit. There are more of these "adjustments" (as with scratching or holding a part of the body), probably in response to the greater discomfort associated with deceit [206; 242].

For the most part, these distinguishing characteristics of deceitful behavior, together with a vigilant or tense quality of movements and speech, imply guardedness. Being guarded, the speaker says as little as possible, says it carefully and slowly, and moves less so as not to accidentally reveal any information.

The only exception to the hypothesized relationship of a guarded, tense, or uncomfortable feeling and deceit was the finding that subjects smiled more while being deceitful [267]. Additional findings in these experiments, however, showed that anxious subjects (and females who tend to be temperamentally more anxious than males [9]) smiled less while being deceitful whereas nonanxious (and male) subjects smiled more while being deceitful. Thus, implicit cues that the subject is most aware of and can readily control (such as smiling [440]) may be deliberately distorted by nonanxious speakers so as to convey the opposite impression to their actual felt emotions of discomfort or tension. However, anxious subjects, who are likely to feel the greatest discomfort while being deceitful, are less able to camouflage their feelings in this way.

Advertising and Political Campaigns

The superb effectiveness or blatant failure of an advertisement can often be understood in terms of the subservient role of explicit verbal contents to implicit behaviors. In any of a number of television commercials, a gas station attendant explains the advantages of a new gasoline product to a customer. In one such commercial, they face each other at a distance of only 6 inches to discuss the merits of the product. This is excessively close and is an extraordinary position for two strangers to be in [118; 154]. It leads one to wonder why it was used at all. It may be that such a position, because of its unexpected and unusual quality, was used deliberately by the advertiser to elicit arousal in the viewer. It was probably hoped that the added attention the advertisement would attract would increase its effectiveness.

Unfortunately, however, the advertiser paid a price in using this device. The 6-inch distance between two strangers is arousing, but also uncomfortable (unpleasant). Psychologists have shown that when a neutral event is repeatedly followed by a negative emotional response, a negative feeling becomes associated with parts of the event [198; 409]. The strong feelings aroused by the advertisement in this case are somewhat negative, so we expect some generalization of this negative affect to the product being advertised. To justify this advertisement, one would have to show that the beneficial contribution of increased arousal and attention far outweighs these negative effects. The same consideration applies to any other advertising that generates negative affect in the viewer during the course of the advertisement.

Television advertising is increasingly becoming a high-level art in which implicit behaviors within brief episodes can have a considerable impact on how pleasant and funny, or how unpleasant and ineffective the advertisement is. Sometimes a business manager may decide to deliver a short message himself, in an attempt to establish a more intimate relationship with the prospective customers. In this type of advertisement the facial expressions and the changes in tone of voice, postures, and gestures of the person delivering the message can be even more important than what he says (note our discussion of persuasion in the previous section). Unfortunately, most advertising of this sort featuring the business manager himself is poor and ineffective. One familiar example is a late-night advertisement by a man who owns the business being advertised. His speech is hesitant and halting, and his voice is flat. His face does show some expressiveness, but his posture is stationary and he uses no gestures. This kind of communication is particularly lacking in arousing quality and one can hardly expect such an impartial and bland message to be persuasive [1; 306; 329].

As an exercise, cut out a few full-page advertisements from different magazines and analyze the effectiveness of each by rating its emotional impact. If you find the emotional impact of an advertisement inadequate or inappropriate, describe how you would modify it so as to increase its effectiveness.

Incidentally, for reference, Robert Morley's and the late Zero Mostel's acting provide fine examples of the exact opposite—constantly mobile faces, tremendously subtle and expressive postures, and richly expressive voices.

The reason why blatant oversights occur in advertising is that most people are at best only vaguely aware of their own implicit styles over different communication media [266].

Notice how certain acquaintances or friends sound very different or even strange on the phone? Sometimes you can't even picture how a particular voice could possibly fit the person you know.

This happens because the characteristic level of pleasure, arousal, or dominance in a person's facial expressions, gestures, and postures can differ considerably from that conveyed by her manner of speech. It is possible, then, that a "different-sounding" friend has a very arousing and active face but her voice lacks expressiveness, thus giving a much less lively and more withdrawn impression of her on the phone. Chances are she is not even aware of this discrepancy. On the other hand, a person who has an inexpressive face and stiff postures may sound lively and vibrant on the phone if her voice effectively conveys different feelings.

Although it is easy to measure how arousing each individual is in terms of his facial, vocal, and gestural expressiveness, most people are unaware of these qualities in themselves. They may be unaware that they are adept at using only certain channels and thus may be unable to select the most appropriate channel to convey a specific message.

Consider the characteristic pleasantness, dominance-submissiveness, and arousing quality in your manner of speech, your facial expressions, your postures, and gestures. Rate each quality and each message source (for example, face) on a scale ranging from –3 to +3. Rate a close friend and ask him to rate you; then compare notes. You may find the exercise very revealing.

Romance

Implicit messages are also very important in the strategy and tactics of romance. In some of the predominantly orthodox Moslem areas of the Middle East, women are not permitted to be seen by men. But there is nothing to stop a veil from "accidentally" dropping, revealing a woman's face (and her interest). Similar "accidents" were used by women in the Victorian era. A woman could sneak a look from behind her fan and imply "I know I'm not supposed to look at strange men, but I can't help wanting to look at you." The convenience of being "clumsy" with handkerchiefs has long been universally recognized. In fact, ancient Chinese women found handkerchiefs so convenient that their costumes included "built-in" handkerchiefs in the form of elaborate and long sleeves which reached to the floor. As it was considered ill manners to look at men, they were taught to look down throughout an encounter. At a certain point during the conversation, a woman could raise her elaborate "sleeves" to cover her face in modesty. With this raising of her hand, it was convenient to steal an upward glance at the man. Blushing and covering her face, the woman appeared enticingly "modest," and with this charming gesture she also saw enough to be able to elaborate about the man during subsequent conversations with her confidantes.

Even today, people are discouraged from expressing personal feelings to strangers and so it becomes necessary to rely on implicit behavior to infer how another person feels and how to pursue a relationship further [343; 425]. A girl who has been on a first date can invite a second encounter by "accidentally" forgetting something in the boy's car. Or consider a boy who has met an attractive girl at a party and is wondering if he should ask her to "cut out." Having such a request turned down, just because it comes too soon or possibly because the girl simply is not interested, can be embarrassing and uncomfortable for both. Where the timing is wrong, the refusal of the request may have an abortive effect on the conversation. So, then, it becomes necessary to somehow find out just how much the girl is interested and when she will be willing to show it.

Social dancing affords one such opportunity. In the traditional dance forms, interest and liking could have been conveyed in terms of closeness and touching. With the newer dances, one needs to rely on other cues. If a person stays several feet from her partner, never smiles, and is constantly scanning the field, the disinterest is obvious. On the other hand, one who comes close to the partner, smiles, and welcomes eye contact is expressing positive interest and liking.

Such encounters can be understood in terms of the more positive connotations of looking at another, standing closer, touching, and sheer amount of conversation or attentiveness that represent the broad class of approach-avoidance behaviors.

Social Alienation

The fact that we have changed from dancing as partners to dancing more as individuals reflects the large-scale social alienation to which humans have had to adapt in moving from small rural communities to impersonal cities. Comedian Flip Wilson once said that people go to sensitivity groups to learn to touch each other. The increasing numbers of sensitivity groups, T-groups, group marathons, and even political demonstrations testify to the longing in this culture for close interpersonal contacts and for settings in which intimacy can be attained readily. The right to such an intimacy is bought through special agents (group leaders, psychotherapists) who define a space and spell out new rules that differ from those of the everyday world [22; 233]. The hope of such therapies is that the greater intimacy that people learn to attain and to tolerate with strangers over a short time will somehow equip them to express their feelings more openly in their everyday life.

With increasing social alienation, people seem to be relying more and more on implicit behavior to convey their own feelings and to understand the feelings of others. Until it becomes permissible to openly verbalize all feelings—an ideal that seems inherently impossible in social groups—it is possible to improve the communication process by taking note of the many feelings that actions can convey. Implicit messages are present all the time, whether we speak or not. They augment or contradict what we say and say what we are unable to put into words [230]. Therefore, actions can often have dramatic, though unintended, effects on others.

Clues to Another's Discomfort

Some of the examples we have considered illustrate how implicit cues are used to eliminate slight embarrassments and ease awkward moments in social situations. At other times, these cues may inadvertently lead to, or signal, discomfort and anxiety [81; 90; 377]. I remember watching a televised interview of a young man whose father was being held hostage by a revolutionary group in Uruguay. At the time of the interview, the chances of saving the father's life were very slim, and indeed he was killed on the following day. During the interview, his son did not reveal any obvious discomfort as he talked; and, considering the tremendous pressure of the situation, this was very puzzling. Then the astute cameraman, who had been focusing on the boy's head and shoulders, suddenly shifted the camera to focus on his hands. They were very tense and tightly clasped, revealing the strain under which he labored. This example shows how a person's verbal behavior, his facial expressions, or his tone of voice may reveal hardly any distress, while a great deal of discomfort and anxiety is conveyed in a less obvious way—extreme tension in the hands, blushing, or a throbbing jugular vein, for instance.

Actions that are part of obvious discomfort show up in more abbreviated forms in less strained situations. They can serve as important clues for understanding how another person feels, even when she says nothing about it. A young woman who is out with a man for the first time may exhibit the same uncomfortable motions when she stands close and faces him, contemplating a more intimate gesture. She may appear tense and avoid his eyes, without being able to reach for his hand. She would have less difficulty if she were to first take his hand in hers and then move closer and to a face-to-face position. This remedy is based on the rule that large and discontinuous changes in approach (or in avoidance) are more difficult to make than graduated ones [264]. Taking the man's hand while he walks alongside is less obviously a sexual advance than if she does so while facing him in close proximity.

Problem Implicit Styles

The preceding rule can also be applied to understanding why meeting strangers is such an ordeal for some people—there is suddenly a host of new things to cope with, and these people are overwhelmed (excessively aroused). One important element in this situation is not knowing how others feel toward them; this is much less the case with the people they already know [289]. Sometimes, then, the increased discomfort in someone you meet is not so much because they dislike you but rather because they experience arousal due to uncertainty about how you feel and will respond. The uneasiness at such times can be a considerable handicap.

We have all on occasion dealt with people who would not look us in the eye while talking or listening to us. I remember hiring a woman who throughout her first interview hardly even looked in my direction. Since, as we have seen, the amount of mutual gaze with another person can be a measure of liking, her avoidance of eye contact meant that she had some negative feelings and expectations about me, possibly as an authority figure. Also, I noted that she was uncomfortable and highly aroused and thus avoided eye contact to reduce arousal. Despite this, I hired her because of her qualifications. Indeed, she turned out to be an extremely good worker. I was also happy to observe that with time and increased familiarity, her predisposition to dislike and be uncomfortable was affected by her actual experiences and she began to have a normal degree of eye contact with me. However, in other work or social situations, her behavior could have had undesirable consequences. Another interviewer might have disqualified her simply because her behavior seemed odd. Socially, she was probably considered detached and uninterested.

This example is an extreme one; nevertheless, it shows how some people behave automatically and characteristically in ways that are considerably different from those of others. In fact, there are striking differences in the general pleasantness of different people's behavior. Dale Carnegie [57] noted these differences and recognized that the inadvertent tendency to be less pleasant is the underlying reason why some people have great difficulty in making friends or in simply having rewarding relationships. He suggested, for instance, that people should smile more if they want more friends. Although this was a gross oversimplification, we now have considerable evidence suggesting that pleasant and approaching cues are conducive to the initiation and maintenance of social exchanges [28; 127; 215; 294; 349; 414]. People differ in their use of these behaviors and thus in their success in social relationships. Those who are popular tend to have a pleasant and arousing manner, even when they meet a perfect stranger; lonely and unpopular persons, in contrast, tend to be less pleasant or unpleasant and aroused (uncomfortable, awkward, tense, or outright hostile) [263; 291; 293]. Although these findings may seem obvious to some, they are clearly not evident to all. Lonely people may abhor the fact that they do not have many friends or are unable to meet and make new ones. Yet, they are unaware of the ways in which their implicit style discourages others from getting close to them, enjoying them, and liking them.

The effects of pleasant-unpleasant implicit cues are especially pronounced among strangers. Even though verbal expressions of feelings and like-dislike toward a stranger are generally discouraged in this culture, subtle communication of these is all-important in determining whether an encounter will develop into a fruitful relationship or pass on as another insignificant event. A chance meeting is more likely to develop into a friendship when pleasant feelings are exchanged. Such feelings cannot be conveyed with words to a stranger because we would be judged too forward and presumptuous. It is thus necessary to use more subtle acts for this purpose. Thus, those who project neutral or negative feelings as part of their social style would be handicapped here, even though they may be very interested in the person they have just met [294].

Other difficulties arise when we cannot accurately interpret the pleasant and approaching quality of another's implicit behavior toward us or when we cannot convey disinterest to another or "read" it coming from another. Some of these problems arise when we must rely on implicit cues because it is impolite to be more explicit. We have all had the irritating experience of being with someone who did not understand the subtle cues of our desire to terminate the conversation or to be left alone. We can try to indicate that we are tired or have something else to do by talking and smiling less, turning slightly away, or even busying ourselves with other things and still fail to get the message across.

People who cannot "read" the implicit messages of disinterest from another often desperately need a relationship and find even slight rejection extremely threatening. Unfortunately, their inability to recognize someone's temporary disinterest due to circumstances can cause frustration and resentment and can ruin any chances of furthering a much needed relationship. This kind of unhappy experience increases such people's doubts about their self-worth. In despair, they cling even more in other encounters, only to experience more alienation and disappointment.

Some psychotherapeutic approaches have been developed in line with the idea that a person's implicit behavior is an important part of his effect on others and can strongly influence the reactions he receives. If a person walks around with a posture which silently cries out, "Please don't hurt me!" "You are beneath me," or "I don't need people," then he may be constantly confronted with unsatisfying situations or may find that people avoid him without any obvious reason. The problem here is the lack of awareness of one's own style and the emotional effect the style has on others. Some therapists start at this point in trying to produce change [40; 342]. The following approaches employ a similar scheme.

In sensitivity groups, people are encouraged to tell each other the feelings they get from one another [233]—this is more in line with the methods of verbal and insight-oriented therapies. The hope is that once a person recognizes the kind of effect she has, she will change her behavior for the better.

Other methods are even more direct in their approach to change. Wilhelm Reich [342] used relaxation exercises with his "stiff-charactered" obsessive-compulsive patients. He sought to loosen their unchanging ways and feelings by first modifying their characteristic postures and movements. According to him, this was the most effective means of dealing with these otherwise stubbornly incurable patients. The premise in his approach was that actions and feelings go hand in hand; and if feelings cannot be changed through discussion and insight, perhaps they can be modified by simply changing a person's characteristic implicit style, including postures, gestures, and facial and vocal expressions [40; 225; 339].

This premise has been elaborated extensively in the more recent action-oriented therapies, of which dance or body-awareness therapy is a good example. Here, instead of talking, the primary therapeutic activity is movement and the effort to express different kinds of emotions through movement. These in turn provide the background for a greater awareness of feelings and sensation (such as relaxation-tension or a desire for more activity) emanating from the body. With increased understanding of these muscular states, it becomes easier for patients to exercise control over them—to intensify a given sensation, decrease it, or replace it with another. For example, a person who is nervous and tense in the presence of others is taught to concentrate on his movements and try to relax. Once he has achieved this, he proceeds to master this state of physical relaxation while moving around with a partner who does the same thing. Further exercises carry him to a level where he can remain physically relaxed while also attending to others in a movement group. This provides the background for more comfortable interactions with members of the group outside the dance situation and for similar interactions with others who are not even in the group. The general theoretical basis for such an approach has been provided in discussions of systematic desensitization [409; 435].

In a different approach to dance therapy, the therapist begins by asking the client to move about on his own initiative; these movements can be particularly informative about the characteristic feelings that the client conveys in his movements. Analogous inferences were made from the stationary postures of schizophrenic patients [132]. Alternatively, the client may be asked specifically to express different emotions through movement. By observing these movements, the therapist, from his experience, is able to find out which emotions the client typically and easily conveys and which he has difficulty expressing. The latter are symptomatic of a more general difficulty and the client is encouraged to express these particular feelings in movements. The improved ability to express such feelings in actions can then directly gain expression in social situations or can provide the stimulus for a more explicit discussion of feelings. For instance, a client who learns to show a hurt feeling with postures and actions on the dance floor is better able to at least show this feeling in another person's presence, who might then ask, "What's the matter, did I hurt your feelings?"

Psychotherapy

Some of the most interesting uses of implicit messages occur in situations where the kind of impression one makes implicitly is different from that made verbally.

Psychoanalytically oriented therapists usually refuse to give direct answers or advice to clients. Questions like "What should I do, doctor?" do not receive specific answers. When a client repeatedly encounters this kind of reaction from her doctor, she begins to realize that her therapist is not going to tell her what to do. In fact, some therapists emphatically deny any attempt to influence what the client does. They contend that their primary aim is to provide an environment in which the client can explore and resolve her own thoughts and feelings about different matters that trouble her.

Despite such therapists' firm intention not to maneuver their clients, researchers who have viewed therapy sessions through one-way mirrors have found that these therapists do influence their clients, albeit in subtle ways. Such a therapist can readily convey interest or disinterest, pleasure, encouragement, or disappointment implicitly. He may lean back or turn away slightly instead of saying "I don't like what you just said" or "I don't like the kinds of things that you've been doing." Alternatively, if he likes what his client reports, he may convey more pleasure in his voice while speaking, address his client by first name, lean forward as he listens, have more eye contact, or ask for more elaboration [264, pp. 77–81].

As already mentioned, even the most adamant "nondirective" therapists do indeed influence their clients implicitly. Further, there is evidence that the changes that occur in the clients follow from these implicit messages of the therapists [408]. Some sophisticated therapists recognize the effectiveness of this method and act accordingly. However, many traditional psychotherapists still refuse to admit this inconsistency in their behavior. In view of such denials, it is puzzling why this two-sided approach to therapy ever developed. Why did Freud [129] find it undesirable to tell his clients what to do?

The answer is quite evident in our experiences with our friends and relatives. Someone might mention a problem that apparently is beyond his capacity to cope with and ask for advice. We give him the advice, and he ignores it without even giving it a try. Someone else may make a half-hearted attempt to apply the advice, only to come back and say, "See, it didn't work. Nothing works!"

This is the kind of situation that the therapist must avoid. He can't afford to tell his client what to do, have him try it in a half-hearted way, and then return to prove his therapist's incompetence. Also, he can't allow his authority to be questioned by having his client tell him, "No, that's no good. I can't do this. It won't work." Therapists have therefore learned to behave differently from their clients' friends and relatives. They firmly refuse to give any verbal and concrete advice, but they encourage their clients to talk about their problems and experiences. Such constant probing reveals the many examples of a problem area, and the therapist can implicitly show approval of or encouragement for even small changes that are in the right direction. Alternatively, he can assume a neutral or possibly negative attitude when a socially maladaptive way of coping with a problem is mentioned.

Similar interchanges occur between parents and their children and between married couples. A parent may find that a rebellious child systematically refuses to listen to her suggestions or demands. She therefore accidentally or deliberately resorts to using the same technique that therapists employ with their clients. She stops making any obvious suggestions to the child; but, when the child behaves in the way she wants, she gives him more attention or does small favors for him. Similarly, when a husband does something that upsets his wife and asks, "Are you upset?" the wife may respond with "No, I'm not upset," while implicitly communicating distress and aloofness. A sensitive husband understands and responds to some of these unverbalized feelings of his wife.

Summary

Understanding implicit communication helps provide effective tools for the analysis and improvement of the various processes of social influence. The use of pleasant and arousing implicit cues is helpful in selling, persuasion, advertising, and political campaigns; the presence of unpleasant and arousing cues can signal discomfort (as in the case of deceit) or can get in the way of establishing contact with strangers or of maintaining existing relationships. A number of the more progressive psychotherapies can be seen as attempting to create a greater awareness for clients of the impressions they inadvertently and implicitly convey. Such psychotherapies also apply specific massage, touch, relaxation, movement, dance, or play-acting techniques to force a client to bodily and implicitly express and experience feelings and attitudes that are not part of his or her regular repertoire.

Suggested Readings

The findings bearing on the processes of persuasion [1; 59; 68; 306; 312; 329] are broadly applicable to the understanding of most social influence processes, including selling, advertising, political campaigns, or even making and maintaining friendships. In contrast, findings obtained with studies of deceit [11; 206; 242; 267; 390] highlight avoidant (unpleasant and arousing) cues, which convey discomfort and which can generally hinder rewarding social exchanges and can lead to feelings of social alienation.

References

1. Addington, D.W. The effect of vocal variation on ratings of source credibility. *Speech Monographs*, 1971, *38*, 242–247.

2. Aiello, J.R., and Cooper, R.E. Use of personal space as a function of social affect. *Proceedings of the 80th Annual Convention of the American Psychological Association*, 1972, 7 (Pt. 1), 207–208.

3. Aiello, J.R., Epstein, Y.M., and Karlin, R.A. Effects of crowding on electrodermal activity. *Sociological Symposium*, 1975, *14*, 42–57.

4. Alexander, J.F. Defensive and supportive communications in family systems. *Journal of Marriage and the Family*, 1973, *35*, 613–617.

5. Allgeier, A.R., and Byrne, D. Attraction toward the opposite sex as a determinant of physical proximity. *Journal of Social Psychology*, 1973, *90*, 213–219.

6. Allport, F.H. *Social psychology*. Boston: Houghton Mifflin, 1924.

7. Allport, G.W., and Vernon, P.E. *Studies in expressive movement*. New York: Hafner, 1967.

8. Altman, I., and Haythorn, W. The ecology of isolated groups. *Behavioral Science*, 1967, *12*, 169–182.

9. Anastasi, A. *Differential psychology*. New York: Macmillan, 1958.

10. Andrew, R.J. The origins of facial expressions. *Scientific American*, 1965, *213*, 88–94.

11. Apple, W., Streeter, L.A., Krauss, R.M. Effects of pitch and speech rate on personal attributions. *Journal of Personality and Social Psychology*, 1979, *37*, 715–727.

12. Archer, D., and Akert, R.M. Words and everything else: Verbal and nonverbal cues in social interpretation. *Journal of Personality and Social Psychology*, 1977, *35*, 443–449.

13. Ardrey, R. *The territorial imperative*. New York: Atheneum, 1966.

14. Argyle, M. *Social interaction*. New York: Atherton, 1969.

15. Argyle, M., Alkema, F., and Gilmour, R. The communication of friendly and hostile attitudes by verbal and nonverbal signals. *European Journal of Social Psychology*, 1971, *1*, 385–402.

16. Argyle, M., and Dean, J. Eye contact, distance, and affiliation. *Sociometry*, 1965, *28*, 289–304.

17. Argyle, M., Ingham, R., Alkema, F., and McCallin, M. The different functions of gaze. *Semiotica*, 1973, *7*, 19–32.

18. Argyle, M., and Kendon, A. The experimental analysis of social performance. In L. Berkowitz (Ed.), *Advances in experimental social psychology*, Vol. 3. New York: Academic Press, 1967.

19. Argyle, M., Salter, V., Nicholson, H., Williams, M., and Burgess, P. The communication of inferior and superior attitudes by verbal and nonverbal signals. *British Journal of Social and Clinical Psychology*, 1970, *9*, 222–231.

20. Argyle, M., and Williams, M. Observer or observed? A reversible perspective in person perception. *Sociometry*, 1969, *32*, 396–412.

21. Ashcraft, N., and Scheflen, A.E. *People space*. Garden City, N.Y.: Anchor, 1976.

22. Bach, G.R., and Wyden, P. *The intimate enemy.* New York: William Morrow, 1968.

23. Bales, R.F. *Interaction process analysis*. Reading, Massachusetts: Addison-Wesley, 1950.

24. Barash, D.P. Human ethology: Personal space reiterated. *Environment and Behavior*, 1973, *5*, 67–72.

25. Barnlund, D.C. (Ed.), *Interpersonal communication: Survey and studies*. Boston: Houghton Mifflin, 1968.

26. Barnlund, D.C. Communicative styles in two cultures: Japan and the United States. In A. Kendon, R.M. Harris, and M.R. Key (Eds.), *Organization of behavior in face-to-face interaction*. The Hague: Mouton, 1975.

27. Baxter, J.C. Interpersonal spacing in natural settings. *Sociometry*, 1970, *33*, 444–456.

28. Bayes, M.A. Behavioral cues of interpersonal warmth. *Journal of Consulting and Clinical Psychology*, 1972, *39*, 333–339.

29. Beakel, N.G., and Mehrabian, A. Inconsistent communications and psychopathology. *Journal of Abnormal Psychology*, 1969, *74*, 126–130.

30. Berlyne, D.E. *Conflict, arousal, and curiosity.* New York: McGraw-Hill, 1960.

31. Berlyne, D.E. Arousal and reinforcement. In D. Levine (Ed.), *Nebraska Symposium on Motivation* (Vol. 15). Lincoln: University of Nebraska Press, 1967.

32. Berscheid, E., and Walster, E.H. *Interpersonal attraction.* Reading, Massachusetts: Addison-Wesley, 1969.

33. Birdwhistell, R.L. *Introduction to kinesics.* Louisville: University of Kentucky Press, 1952.

34. Birdwhistell, R.L. The kinesic level in the investigation of the emotions. In P.H. Knapp (Ed.), *Expression of the emotions in man.* New York: International Universities Press, 1963.

35. Birdwhistell, R.L. *Kinesics and context: Essays on body motion communication.* Philadelphia: University of Pennsylvania Press, 1970.

36. Boderman, A., Freed, D.W., and Kinnucan, M.J. "Touch me, like me": Testing an encounter group assumption. *Journal of Applied Behavioral Science,* 1972, *8,* 527–533.

37. Bond, M.H., and Komai, H. Targets of gazing and eye contact during interviews: Effects on Japanese nonverbal behavior. *Journal of Personality and Social Psychology,* 1976, *34,* 1276–1284.

38. Booraem, C.D., and Flowers, J.V. Reduction of anxiety and personal space as a function of assertion training with severely disturbed neuropsychiatric inpatients. *Psychological Reports,* 1972, *30,* 923–929.

39. Bourne, P.G. *Men, stress and Vietnam.* Boston: Little, Brown, 1970.

40. Braatoy, T.F. *Fundamentals of psychoanalytic technique.* New York: Wiley, 1954.

41. Braddock, J.C. Effect of prior residence on dominance in the fish platypoecilus maculatus. *Physiological Zoology,* 1949, *22,* 161–169.

42. Brannigan, C.R., and Humphries, D.A. Human non-verbal behaviour: A means of communication. In N.G. Blurton Jones (Ed.), *Ethological studies of child behaviour.* London: Cambridge University Press, 1972.

43. Breed, G.R. The effect of intimacy: Reciprocity or retreat? *British Journal of Social and Clinical Psychology,* 1972, *11,* 135–142.

44. Budd, R.W., Thorp, R.K., and Donohew, L. *Content analysis of communications.* New York: Macmillan, 1967.

45. Bugental, D.E. Interpretations of naturally occurring discrepancies between words and intonation: Modes of inconsistency resolution. *Journal of Personality and Social Psychology,* 1974, *30,* 125–133.

46. Bugental, D.E., Henker, B., and Whalen, C.K. Attributional antecedents of verbal and vocal assertiveness. *Journal of Personality and Social Psychology,* 1976, *34,* 405–411.

47. Bugental, D.C., Kaswan, J.W., and Love, L.R. Perception of contradictory meanings conveyed by verbal and nonverbal channels. *Journal of Personality and Social Psychology,* 1970, *16,* 647–655.

48. Bugental, D.E., Love, L.R., and Kaswan, J.W. Videotaped family interaction: Differences reflecting presence and type of child disturbance. *Journal of Abnormal Psychology,* 1972, *79,* 285–290.

49. Bugental, D.E., Love, L.R., Kaswan, J.W., and April, S. Verbal-conflict in parental messages to normal and disturbed children. *Journal of Abnormal Psychology,* 1971, *77,* 6–10.

50. Byrne, D. The influence of propinquity and opportunities for interaction on classroom relationships. *Human Relations,* 1961, *14,* 63–70.

51. Byrne, D. Attitudes and attraction. In L. Berkowitz (Ed.), *Advances in experimental social psychology* (Vol. 4). New York: Academic Press, 1969.

52. Byrne, D. *The attraction paradigm*. New York: Academic Press, 1971.

53. Byrne, D., Baskett, G.D., and Hodges, L. Behavioral indicators of interpersonal attraction. *Journal of Applied Social Psychology*, 1971, *1*, 137–149.

54. Byrne, D., and Buehler, J.A. A note on the influence of propinquity upon acquaintanceships. *Journal of Abnormal and Social Psychology*, 1955, *51*, 147–148.

55. Byrne, D., Ervin, C.R., and Lamberth, J. Continuity between the experimental study of attraction and real-life computer dating. *Journal of Personality and Social Psychology*, 1970, *16*, 157–165.

56. Calhoun, J.B. *The ecology and sociology of the Norway rat*. Bethesda, Maryland: Public Health Service, 1962.

57. Carnegie, D. *How to win friends and influence people*. New York: Simon and Schuster, 1936.

58. Cassirer, E. *The philosophy of symbolic forms*. New Haven: Yale University Press, 1953–57. 3 vols.

59. Chaiken, S. Communicator physical attractiveness and persuasion. *Journal of Personality and Social Psychology*, 1979, *37*, 1387–1397.

60. Charney, E.J. Postural configurations in psychotherapy. *Psychosomatic Medicine*, 1966, *28*, 305–315.

61. Chombart de Lauwe, P. *Famille et habitation*. Paris: Editions du Centre National de la Recherche Scientifique, 1959.

62. Christian, J. Phenomena associated with population density. *Proceedings of the National Academy of Science*, 1961, *47*, 428–449.

63. Clore, G.L., Wiggins, N.H., and Itkin, S. Judging attraction from nonverbal behavior: The gain phenomenon. *Journal of Consulting and Clinical Psychology*, 1975, *43*, 491–497.

64. Condon, J.C., and Yousef, F. (Eds.), *An introduction to intercultural communication*. New York: Bobbs-Merrill, 1975.

65. Condon, W.S., and Ogston, W.D. Sound film analysis of normal and pathological behavior patterns. *The Journal of Nervous and Mental Disease*, 1966, *143*, 338–347.

66. Condon, W.S., and Sander, L.W. Synchrony demonstrated between movements of the neonate and adult speech. *Child Development*, 1974, *45*, 456–462.

67. Conville, R.L., Linguistic nonimmediacy and communicators' anxiety. *Psychological Reports*, 1974, *35*, 1107–1114.

68. Cooper, J., Zanna, M.P., and Taves, P.A. Arousal as a necessary condition for attitude change following induced compliance. *Journal of Personality and Social Psychology*, 1978, *36*, 1101–1106.

69. Coutts, L.M., and Schneider, F.W. Visual behavior in an unfocused interaction as a function of sex and distance. *Journal of Experimental Social Psychology*, 1975, *11*, 64–77.

70. Craik, K.H. Environmental psychology. In K.H. Craik, B. Kleinmuntz, R.L. Rosnow, R. Rosenthal, J.A. Cheyne, and R.H. Walters (Eds.),

New directions in psychology 4. New York: Holt, Rinehart and Winston, 1970.

71. Crouse, B.B., and Mehrabian, A. Affiliation of opposite-sexed strangers. *Journal of Research in Personality*, 1977, *11*, 38–47.

72. Dabbs, J.M., Jr. Similarity of gestures and interpersonal influence. *Proceedings of the 77th Annual Convention of the American Psychological Association*, 1969, *4*, 337–338.

73. Darwin, C. *The expression of the emotions in man and animals.* London: Murray, 1872.

74. Davis, M. *Towards understanding the intrinsic in body movement.* New York: Arno, 1975.

75. Davitz, J.R. (Ed.), *The communication of emotional meaning.* New York: McGraw-Hill, 1964.

76. Davitz, J.R. *The language of emotion.* New York: Academic Press, 1969.

77. Dean, L.M., Willis, F.N., and Hewitt, J. Initial interaction distance among individuals equal and unequal in military rank. *Journal of Personality and Social Psychology*, 1975, *32*, 294–299.

78. DePaulo, B.M., Rosenthal, R., Eisenstat, R.A., Rogers, P.L., and Finkelstein, S. Decoding discrepant nonverbal cues. *Journal of Personality and Social Psychology*, 1978, *36*, 313–323.

79. Deutsch, F. Analysis of postural behavior. *Psychoanalytic Quarterly*, 1947, *16*, 195–213.

80. Deutsch, F. Analytic posturology. *Psychoanalytic Quarterly*, 1952, *21*, 196–214.

81. Deutsch, F., and Murphy, W.F. *The clinical interview.* New York: International Universities Press, 1955. 2 vols.

82. Dittmann, A.T. *Interpersonal messages of emotion.* New York: Springer, 1972.

83. Dittmann, A.T., and Llewellyn, L.G. Body movements and speech rhythm in social conversation. *Journal of Personality and Social Psychology*, 1969, *11*, 98–106.

84. Duffy, E. *Activation and behavior.* New York: Wiley, 1962.

85. Duke, M.P., and Nowicki, S., Jr. A new measure and social-learning model for interpersonal distance. *Journal of Experimental Research in Personality*, 1972, *6*, 119–132.

86. Duncan, S., Jr. Nonverbal communication. *Psychological Bulletin*, 1969, *72*, 118–137.

87. Duncan, S., Jr., and Fiske, D.W. *Face-to-face interaction: Research, methods, and theory.* Hillsdale, N.J.: Lawrence Erlbaum, 1977.

88. Efran, J.S. Looking for approval: Effects on visual behavior of approbation from person differing in importance. *Journal of Personality and Social Psychology*, 1968, *10*, 21–25.

89. Efran, J.S., and Broughton, A. Effect of expectancies for social approval on visual behavior. *Journal of Personality and Social Psychology*, 1966, *4*, 103–107.

90. Efron, D. *Gesture, race and culture.* The Hague: Mouton, 1972.

91. Eibl-Eibesfeldt, I. *Love and hate: The natural history of behavior patterns.* New York: Schocken, 1974. (*a*)

92. Eibl-Eibesfeldt, I. Similarities and differences between cultures in expressive movements. In S. Weitz (Ed.), *Nonverbal communication.* New York: Oxford University Press, 1974. (*b*)

93. Eibl-Eibesfeldt, I., and Haas, H. Film studies in human anthropology. *Current Anthropology,* 1967, *8,* 477–480.

94. Ekman, P., and Friesen, W.V. Head and body cues in the judgment of emotion: A reformulation. *Perceptual and Motor Skills,* 1967, *24,* 711–724.

95. Ekman, P., and Friesen, W.V. Nonverbal leakage and clues to deception. *Psychiatry,* 1969, *32,* 88–106. (*a*)

96. Ekman, P. and Friesen, W.V. The repertoire of nonverbal behavior: Categories, origins, usage, and coding. *Semiotica,* 1969, *1,* 49–98. (*b*)

97. Ekman, P., and Friesen, W.V. Constants across cultures in the face and emotion. *Journal of Personality and Social Psychology,* 1971, *17,* 124–129.

98. Ekman, P., and Friesen, W.V. *Unmasking the face.* Englewood Cliffs, New Jersey: Prentice-Hall, 1975.

99. Ekman, P., Sorenson, E.R., and Friesen, W.V. Pan-cultural elements in facial displays of emotion. *Science,* 1969, *164,* 86–88.

100. Ellsworth, P.C., and Carlsmith, J.M. Effects of eye contact and verbal content on affective response to a dyadic interaction. *Journal of Personality and Social Psychology,* 1968, *10,* 15–20.

101. Ellsworth, P.C., Carlsmith, J.M., and Henson, A. The stare as a stimulus to flight in human subjects: A series of field experiments. *Journal of Personality and Social Psychology,* 1972, *21,* 302–311.

102. Ellsworth, P.C., and Langer, E.J. Staring and approach: An interpretation of the stare as a nonspecific activator. *Journal of Personality and Social Psychology,* 1976, *33,* 117–122.

103. Ellsworth, P.C., and Ludwig, L.M. Visual behavior in social interaction. *Journal of Communication,* 1972, *22,* 375–403.

104. Engebretson, D.E., and Fullmer, D. Cross-cultural differences in territoriality: Interaction distances of native Japanese, Hawaii Japanese, and American Caucasians. *Journal of Cross-Cultural Psychology,* 1970, *1,* 261–269.

105. Evans, G.W., and Howard, R.B. Personal space. *Psychological Bulletin,* 1973, *80,* 334–344.

106. Ewer, R.F. *Ethology of mammals.* New York: Plenum, 1968.

107. Exline, R.V. Effects of need for affiliation, sex, and the sight of others upon initial communications in problem-solving groups. *Journal of Personality,* 1962, *30,* 541–556.

108. Exline, R.V. Explorations in the process of person perception: Visual

interaction in relation to competition, sex, and need for affiliation. *Journal of Personality*, 1963, *31*, 1–20.

109. Exline, R.V. Visual interaction: The glances of power and preference. In J.K. Cole (Ed.), *Nebraska Symposium on Motivation* (Vol. 19). Lincoln: University of Nebraska Press, 1972.

110. Exline, R.V., and Eldridge, C. Effects of two patterns of a speaker's visual behavior upon the perception of the authenticity of his verbal message. Paper presented at the meetings of the Eastern Psychological Association, Boston, Massachusetts, April 1967.

111. Exline, R.V., Ellyson, S.L., and Long, B. Visual behavior as an aspect of power role relationships. In P. Pliner, L. Krames, and T. Alloway (Eds.), *Nonverbal communication of aggression* (Vol. 2). New York: Plenum, 1975.

112. Exline, R.V., Gray, D., and Schuette, D. Visual behavior in a dyad as affected by interview content and sex of respondent. *Journal of Personality and Social Psychology*, 1965, *1*, 201–209.

113. Exline, R.V., and Winters, L.C. Affective relations and mutual glances in dyads. In S.S. Tomkins and C. Izard (Eds.), *Affect, cognition and personality*. New York: Springer, 1965.

114. Eysenck, H.J., and Eysenck, S.B. *Manual for the Eysenck Personality Inventory*. San Diego: Educational and Industrial Testing Service, 1963.

115. Falender, C.A., and Mehrabian, A. Environmental effects on parent–infant interaction. *Genetic Psychology Monographs*, 1978, *97*, 3–41.

116. Falender, C.A., and Mehrabian, A. The effects of day care on young children: An environmental psychology approach. *The Journal of Psychology*, 1979, *101*, 241–255.

117. Falender, C.A., and Mehrabian, A. The emotional climate for children as inferred from parental attitudes. *Educational and Psychological Measurement*, 1980.

118. Felipe, N.J., and Sommer, R. Invasions of personal space. *Social Problems*, 1966, *14*, 206–214.

119. Festinger, L. Architecture and group membership. *Journal of Social Issues*, 1951, *1*, 152–163.

120. Festinger, L. Group attraction and membership. In D. Cartwright and A. Zander (Eds.), *Group dynamics: Research and theory*. Evanston, Illinois: Row, Peterson, 1953.

121. Festinger, L., Schachter, S., and Back, K. *Social pressures in informal groups: A study of human factors in housing*. Stanford, California: Stanford University Press, 1963.

122. Fisher, J.D., Rytting, M., and Heslin, R. Hands touching hands: Affective and evaluative effects of an interpersonal touch. *Sociometry*, 1976, *39*, 416–421.

123. Fisher, R.L. Social schemas of normal and disturbed school children. *Journal of Educational Psychology*, 1967, *58*, 88–92.

124. Foa, U.G., and Foa, E.B. *Societal structures of the mind.* Springfield, Illinois: Thomas, 1974.

125. Freedman, J.L. *Crowding and behavior.* New York: Viking, 1975.

126. Freedman, N., and Hoffmann, S.P. Kinetic behavior in altered clinical states: Approach to objective analysis of motor behavior during clinical interviews. *Perceptual and Motor Skills,* 1967, *24,* 527–539.

127. Fretz, B.R. Postural movements in a counseling dyad. *Journal of Counseling Psychology,* 1966, *13,* 335–343.

128. Freud, S. The psychopathology of everyday life. In *The basic writings of Sigmund Freud.* New York: Random House, 1938 (first German edition, 1904).

129. Freud, S. *Therapy and technique.* New York: Collier, 1963.

130. Frijda, N.H. Recognition of emotions. In L. Berkowitz (Ed.), *Advances in experimental social psychology.* New York: Academic Press, 1969.

131. Fromme, D.K., and Beam, D.C. Dominance and sex differences in nonverbal responses to differential eye contact. *Journal of Research in Personality,* 1974, *8,* 76–87.

132. Fromm-Reichmann, F. *Principles of intensive psychotherapy.* Chicago: University of Chicago Press, 1950.

133. Gale, A., Lucas, B., Nissim, R., and Harpham, B. Some EEG correlates of face-to-face contact. *British Journal of Social and Clinical Psychology,* 1972, *11,* 326–332.

134. Galle, O.R., Gove, W.R., and McPherson, J.M. Population density and pathology: What are the relations for man? *Science,* 1972, *176,* 23–30.

135. Gans, H.J. *The urban villagers: Group and class in the life of Italian-Americans.* New York: Free Press of Glencoe, 1962.

136. Gans, H.J. *People and plans: Essays on urban problems and solutions.* New York: Basic Books. 1968.

137. Gitin, S.R. A dimensional analysis of manual expression. *Journal of Personality and Social Psychology,* 1970, *15,* 271–277.

138. Goffman, E. *Encounters: Two studies in the sociology of interaction.* Indianapolis: Bobbs-Merrill, 1961.

139. Goffman, E. *Interaction ritual: Essays on face-to-face behavior.* Garden City, N.Y.: Doubleday, 1967.

140. Goffman, E. *Relations in public: Microstudies of the public order.* New York: Basic Books, 1971.

141. Goldberg, G.N., Kiesler, C.A., and Collins, B.E. Visual behavior and face-to-face distance during interaction. *Sociometry,* 1969, *32,* 43–53.

142. Goldman-Eisler, F. *Psycholinguistics: Experiments in spontaneous speech.* New York: Academic Press, 1968.

143. Goldstein, M.A., Kilroy, C., and Van de Voort, D. Gaze as a function of conversation and degree of love. *Journal of Psychology,* 1976, *92,* 227–234.

144. Gottlieb, R., Wiener, M., and Mehrabian, A. Immediacy, discomfort-relief quotient, and content in verbalizations about positive and negative experiences. *Journal of Personality and Social Psychology*, 1967, *7*, 266–274.

145. Gottman, J.M. *Marital interaction*. New York: Academic Press, 1979.

146. Griffitt, W. Environmental effects on interpersonal affective behavior: Ambient effective temperature and attraction. *Journal of Personality and Social Psychology*, 1970, *15*, 240–244.

147. Griffitt, W., and Veitch, R. Hot and crowded: Influences of population density and temperature on interpersonal affective behavior. *Journal of Personality and Social Psychology*, 1971, *17*, 92–98.

148. Guardo, C.J. Personal space in children. *Child Development*, 1969, *40*, 143–151.

149. Gullahorn, J. Distance and friendship as factors in the gross interaction matrix. *Sociometry*, 1952, *15*, 123–134.

150. Haase, R.F. The relationship of sex and instructional set to the regulation of interpersonal interaction distance in a counseling analogue. *Journal of Counseling Psychology*, 1970, *17*, 233–236.

151. Haase, R.F., and Tepper, D.T., Jr. Nonverbal components of empathic communication. *Journal of Counseling Psychology*, 1972, *19*, 417–424.

152. Haggard, E.A., and Isaacs, K.S. Micro-momentary facial expressions as indicators of ego mechanisms in psychotherapy. In L.A. Gottschalk and A.H. Auerbach (Eds.), *Methods of research in psychotherapy*. New York: Appleton-Century-Crofts, 1966.

153. Haley, J. *Strategies of psychotherapy*. New York: Grune and Stratton, 1963.

154. Hall, E.T. *The silent language*. Garden City, New York: Doubleday, 1959.

155. Hall, E.T. A system for the notation of proxemic behavior. *American Anthropologist*, 1963, *65*, 1003–1026.

156. Hall, E.T., *The hidden dimension*. Garden City, New York: Doubleday, 1966.

157. Hall, E.T. *Handbook for proxemic research*. Washington, D.C.: Society for the Anthropology of Visual Communication, 1974.

158. Hall, K.R.L., and DeVore, I. Baboon social behavior. In I. DeVore (Ed.), *Primate behavior: Field studies of monkeys and apes*. New York: Holt, Rinehart and Winston, 1965.

159. Hare, A., and Bales, R. Seating position and small group interaction. *Sociometry*, 1963, *26*, 480–486.

160. Harper, R.G., Wiens, A.N., and Matarazzo, J.D. *Nonverbal communication*. New York: Wiley, 1978.

161. Harrison, R.P. *Beyond words: An introduction to nonverbal communication*. Englewood Cliffs, New Jersey: Prentice-Hall, 1974.

162. Hass, H. *The human animal*. New York: Putnam, 1970.

163. Hearn, G. Leadership and the spatial factor in small groups. *Journal of Abnormal and Social Psychology*, 1957, *54*, 269–272.

164. Heckel, R.V. Leadership and voluntary seating choice. *Psychological Reports*, 1973, *32*, 141–142.

165. Henley, N.M. Status and sex: Some touching observations. *Bulletin of the Psychonomic Society*, 1973, *2*, 91–93.

166. Henley, N.M. Power, sex, and nonverbal communication. *Berkeley Journal of Sociology*, 1974, *18*, 1–26.

167. Henley, N.M. *Body politics: Power, sex, and nonverbal communication.* Englewood Cliffs, N.J.: Prentice-Hall, 1977.

168. Heslin, R. Steps toward a taxonomy of touching. Paper presented at the meeting of the Western Psychological Association, Chicago, 1974.

169, Hess, E.H. *The tell-tale eye.* New York: Van Nostrand Reinhold, 1975.

170. Hildreth, A.M., Derogatis, L.R., and McCusker, K. Body buffer zone and violence: A reassessment and confirmation. *American Journal of Psychiatry*, 1971, *127*, 77–81.

171. Hines, M., and Mehrabian, A. Approach-avoidance behaviors as a function of pleasantness and arousing quality of settings and individual differences in stimulus screening. *Social Behavior and Personality*, 1979, *7*, 223–233.

172. Hobbs, N. Helping disturbed children: Psychological and ecological strategies. *American Psychologist*, 1966, *21*, 1105–1115.

173. Holstein, C.M., Goldstein, J.W., and Bem, D.J. The importance of expressive behavior, involvement, sex, and need-approval in inducing liking. *Journal of Experimental Social Psychology*, 1971, *7*, 534–544.

174. Hooff, J.A.R.A.M. van. The facial displays of catarrhive monkeys and apes. In D. Morris (Ed.), *Primate Ethology.* London: Weidenfeld and Nicholson, 1967.

175. Hooff, J.A.R.A.M. van. A comparative approach to the phylogeny of laughter and smiling. In R.A. Hinde (Ed.), *Non-verbal communication.* Cambridge, England: Cambridge University Press, 1972.

176. Horowitz, M.J., Duff, D.F., and Stratton, L.O. Personal space and the body buffer zone. In H.M. Proshansky, W.H. Ittelson, and L.G. Rivlin (Eds.), *Environmental psychology: Man and his physical setting.* New York: Holt, Rinehart and Winston, 1970.

177. Hutchinson, A. *Labanotation: The system for recording movement.* New York: Theatre Arts Books, 1970.

178. Huttar, G.L. *Some relations between emotions and the prosodic parameters of speech.* Santa Barbara, California: Speech Communications Research Laboratory, 1967.

179. Inbau, F.E., and Reid, J.E. *Criminal interrogation and confessions.* Toronto: Burns and MacEachern, 1963.

180. Insko, C.A., and Wilson, M. Interpersonal attraction as a function of social interaction. *Journal of Personality and Social Psychology*, 1977, *35*, 903–911.

181. Jackson, D.N. *Personality research form manual.* Goshen, New York: Research Psychologists Press, 1967.

182. Jaffe, J. Computer analysis of verbal behavior in psychiatric interviews. In D. Rioch (Ed.), *Disorders in communication: Proceedings of the Association for Research in Nervous and Mental Diseases* (Vol. 42). Baltimore: Williams & Wilkins, 1967.

183. Janis, I.L., Kaye, D., and Kirschner, P. Facilitating effects of "eating-while-reading" on responsiveness to persuasive communications. *Journal of Personality and Social Psychology*, 1965, *1*, 181–186.

184. Janisse, M.P. The relationship between pupil size and anxiety: A review. In I. Sarason & C. Spielberger (Eds.), *Stress and anxiety* (Vol. 3). Washington, D.C.: Hemisphere (Wiley), 1976.

185. Johnson, R.N. *Aggression in man and animals.* Philadelphia: Saunders, 1972.

186. Jones. E.E. *Ingratiation: A social psychological analysis.* New York: Appleton-Century-Crofts, 1964.

187. Jourard, S.M. *The transparent self.* Princeton: Van Nostrand, 1964.

188. Jourard, S.M. An exploratory study of body accessibility. *British Journal of Social and Clinical Psychology*, 1966, *5*, 221–231.

189. Jourard, S.M., and Friedman, R. Experimenter-subject "distance" and self-disclosure. *Journal of Personality and Social Psychology*, 1970, *15*, 278–282.

190. Jourard, S.M., and Rubin, J.E. Self-disclosure and touching: A study of two modes of interpersonal encounter and their interrelation. *Journal of Humanistic Psychology*, 1968, *8*, 39–48.

191. Jung, C.G. *Psychological types.* New York: Harcourt, Brace & World, 1933.

192. Kasl, S.V., and Mahl, G.F. The relationship of disturbances and hesitations in spontaneous speech to anxiety. *Journal of Personality and Social Psychology*, 1965, *1*, 425–433.

193. Kazdin, A.E., and Klock, J. The effect of nonverbal teacher approval on student attentive behavior. *Journal of Applied Behavioral Analysis*, 1973, *6*, 643–654.

194. Kelly, F.D. Communicational significance of therapist proxemic cues. *Journal of Consulting and Clinical Psychology*, 1972, *39*, 345.

195. Kendon, A. Some functions of gaze direction in social interaction. *Acta Psychologica*, 1967, *26*, 22–63.

196. Kendon, A. Movement coordination in social interaction: Some examples described. *Acta Psychologica*, 1970, *32*, 100–125.

197. Kendon, A., and Ferber, A. A description of some human greetings. In R.P. Michael and J.H. Crook (Eds.), *Comparative ecology and behavior of primates.* New York: Academic Press, 1973.

198. Kimble, G.A. *Hilgard and Marquis' conditioning and learning.* New York: Appleton-Century-Crofts, 1961.

199. Kinzel, A.F. Body-buffer zone in violent prisoners. *American Journal of Psychiatry*, 1970, *127*, 59–64.

200. Kipnis, D.M. Interaction between members of bomber crews as a determinant of sociometric choice. *Human Relations*, 1957, *10*, 263–270.

201. Kleck, R.E. Physical stigma and task-oriented interactions. *Human Relations*, 1969, *22*, 53–60.

202. Kleck, R.E., Buck, P.L., Goller, W.L., London, R.S., Pfeiffer, J.R., and Vukcevic, D.P. Effect of stigmatizing conditions on the use of personal space. *Psychological Reports*, 1968, *23*, 111–118.

203. Kleiman, D.G. The comparative social behavior of the Canidae. *American Zoology*, 1966, *6*, 335.

204. Kleinke, C.L., Meeker, F.B., and La Fong, C. Effects of gaze, touch, and use of name on evaluation of "engaged" couples. *Journal of Research in Personality*, 1974, *7*, 368–373.

205. Kleinke, C.L., and Pohlen, P.D. Affective and emotional responses as a function of other person's gaze and cooperativeness in a two-person game. *Journal of Personality and Social Psychology*, 1971, *17*, 308–313.

206. Knapp, M.L., Hart, R.P., and Dennis, H.S. An exploration of deception as a communication construct. *Human Communication Research*, 1974, *1*, 15–29.

207. Knowles, E.S. Boundaries around group interaction: The effect of group size and member status on boundary permeability. *Journal of Personality and Social Psychology*, 1973, *26*, 327–331.

208. Krasner, L. Studies of the conditioning of verbal behavior. *Psychological Bulletin*, 1958, *55*, 148–170.

209. Kraut, R.E., and Johnston, R.E. Social and emotional messages of smiling: An ethological approach. *Journal of Personality and Social Psychology*, 1979, *37*, 1539–1553.

210. Lacey, J.I. Somatic response patterning and stress: Some revisions of activation theory. In M.H. Appley & R. Trumbull (Eds.), *Psychological stress: Issues in research*. New York: Appleton-Century-Crofts, 1967.

211. LaFrance, M., and Broadbent, M. Group rapport: Posture sharing as a nonverbal indicator. *Group and Organizational Studies*, 1976, *1*, 328–333.

212. LaFrance, M., and Broadbent, M. *Nonverbal synchrony and rapport: Analysis by the cross-lag panel technique.* Paper presented at the meeting of the American Psychological Association, San Francisco, August 1977.

213. LaFrance, M., and Mayo, C. *Moving bodies.* Monterey: Brooks/Cole, 1978.

214. Lawick-Goodall, J. van. The behaviour of free-living chimpanzees in the Gombe Stream Reserve. *Animal Behaviour Monograph*, 1968, *1*(3), 161–311.

215. Lefebvre, L.M. Encoding and decoding of ingratiation in modes of

smiling and gaze. *British Journal of Social and Clinical Psychology*, 1975, *14*, 33–42.

216. Lett, E.E., Clark, W., and Altman, I. *A propositional inventory of research on interpersonal distance.* Research Report No. 1, Bethesda: Naval Medical Research Institute, 1969.

217. Lewin, K. *A dynamic theory of personality: Selected papers.* New York: McGraw-Hill, 1935.

218. Lindsley, D.B. Emotion. In S.S. Stevens (Ed.), *Handbook of experimental psychology.* New York: Wiley, 1951.

219. Little, K.B. Personal space. *Journal of Experimental Social Psychology*, 1965, *1*, 237–247.

220. Little, K.B. Cultural variations in social schemata. *Journal of Personality and Social Psychology*, 1968, *10*, 1–7.

221. Loeff, R.G. Differential discrimination of conflicting emotional messages by normal, delinquent, and schizophrenic adolescents. Unpublished doctoral dissertation, Indiana University, 1966.

222. Lomranz, J., Shapira, A., Choresh, N., and Gilat, Y. Children's personal space as a function of age and sex. *Developmental Psychology*, 1975, *11*, 541–545.

223. Lorenz, K. *On aggression.* Translated by M.K. Wilson. New York: Harcourt, Brace & World, 1966.

224. Lott, D.F., and Sommer, R. Seating arrangements and status. *Journal of Personality and Social Psychology*, 1967, *7*, 90–95.

225. Lowen, A. *Physical dynamics of character structure: Body form and movement in analytical therapy.* New York: Grune and Stratton, 1958.

226. Luft, J. On non-verbal interaction. *Journal of Psychology*, 1966, *63*, 261–268.

227. Maccoby, E., and Jacklin, C. *The psychology of sex differences.* Stanford, Calif.: Stanford University Press, 1974.

228. Mahl, G.F. Measuring the patient's anxiety during interviews from "expressive" aspects of his speech. *Transactions of the New York Academy of Sciences*, 1959, *21*, 249–257.

229. Mahl, G.F. Gestures and body movements in interviews. In J.M. Shlien, H.F. Hunt, J.D. Matarazzo, and C. Savage (Eds.), *Research in psychotherapy* (Vol. 3). Washington, D.C.: American Psychological Association, 1968.

230. Mahl, G.F., Danet, B., and Norton, N. Reflection of major personality characteristics in gestures and body movement. Paper presented at Annual Meeting, American Psychological Association, Cincinnati, Ohio, September 1959.

231. Mahl, G.F., and Schulze, G. Psychological research in the extralinguistic area. In T.A. Sebeok, A.S. Hayes, and M.C. Bateson (Eds.), *Approaches to semiotics.* The Hague: Mouton, 1964.

232. Maisonneuve, J., Palmade, G., and Fourment, C. Selective choices and propinquity. *Sociometry*, 1952, *15*, 135–140.

233. Malamud, D.I., and Machover, S. *Toward self-understanding: Group techniques in self-confrontation*. Springfield, Illinois: Thomas, 1965.

234. Maslow, A.H., and Mintz, N.L. Effects of esthetic surroundings: 1. Initial effects of three esthetic conditions upon perceiving "energy" and "well-being" in faces. *Journal of Psychology*, 1956, *41*, 247–254.

235. Mason, J.W. Psychological influences on the pituitary-adrenal cortical system. In G. Pincus (Ed.), *Recent progress in hormone research: Proceedings of the Laurentian hormone conference* (Vol. 15). New York: Academic Press, 1959, Pp. 345–389. (*a*)

236. Mason, J.W. Visceral functions of the nervous system. *Annual Review of Physiology*, 1959, *21*, 353–380. (*b*)

237. Matarazzo, J.D., Weitman, M., Saslow, G., and Wiens, A.N. Interviewer influence on duration of interviewee speech. *Journal of Verbal Learning and Verbal Behavior*, 1963, *1*, 451–458.

238. Matarazzo, J.D., and Wiens, A.N. *The interview*. Chicago: Aldine-Atherton, 1972.

239. McBride, G. *A general theory of social organization and behavior*. St. Lucia, Australia: University of Queensland Press, 1964.

240. McBride, G., King, M.G., and James, J.W. Social proximity effects of galvanic skin responses in adult humans. *Journal of Psychology*, 1965, *61*, 153–157.

241. McCauley, C., Coleman, G., and De Fusco, P. Commuters' eye contact with strangers in city and suburban train stations: Evidence of short-term adaptation to interpersonal overload in the city. *Environmental Psychology and Nonverbal Behavior*, 1978, *2*, 215–225.

242. McClintock, C.C., and Hunt, R.C. Nonverbal indicators of affect and deception in an interview setting. *Journal of Applied Social Psychology*, 1975, *5*, 54–67.

243. McDowall, J. Interactional synchrony: A reappraisal. *Journal of Personality and Social Psychology*, 1978, *36*, 963–975.

244. McGinley, H., LeFevre, R., and McGinley, P. The influence of a communicator's body position on opinion change in others. *Journal of Personality and Social Psychology*, 1975, *31*, 686–690.

245. Mehrabian, A. Communication length as an index of communicator attitude. *Psychological Reports*, 1965, *17*, 519–522.

246. Mehrabian, A. Attitudes in relation to the forms of communicator-object relationship in spoken communications. *Journal of Personality*, 1966, *34*, 80–93. (*a*)

247. Mehrabian, A. Immediacy: an indicator of attitudes in linguistic communication. *Journal of Personality*, 1966, *34*, 26–34. (*b*).

248. Mehrabian, A. Attitudes inferred from neutral verbal communications. *Journal of Consulting Psychology*, 1967, *31*, 414–417. (*a*).

249. Mehrabian, A. Attitudes inferred from non-immediacy of verbal communications. *Journal of Verbal Learning and Verbal Behavior*, 1967, 6, 294–295. (b)

250. Mehrabian, A. Orientation behaviors and nonverbal attitude communication. *Journal of Communication*, 1967, 17, 324–332. (c)

251. Mehrabian, A. Substitute for apology: manipulation of cognitions to reduce negative attitude toward self. *Psychological Reports*, 1967, 20, 687–692. (d)

252. Mehrabian, A. *An analysis of personality theories*. Englewood Cliffs, New Jersey: Prentice-Hall, 1968. (a)

253. Mehrabian, A. Communication without words. *Psychology Today*, 1968, 2, 52–55. (b)

254. Mehrabian, A. Inference of attitudes from the posture, orientation, and distance of a communicator. *Journal of Consulting and Clinical Psychology*, 1968, 32, 296–308. (c)

255. Mehrabian, A. Male and female scales of the tendency to achieve. *Educational and Psychological Measurement*, 1968, 28, 493–502. (d)

256. Mehrabian, A. Relationship of attitude to seated posture, orientation, and distance. *Journal of Personality and Social Psychology*, 1968, 10, 26–30. (e)

257. Mehrabian, A. The effect of context on judgments of speaker attitude *Journal of Personality*, 1968, 36, 21–32. (f)

258. Mehrabian, A. Measures of achieving tendency. *Educational and Psychological Measurement*, 1969, 29, 445–451. (a)

259. Mehrabian, A. Significance of posture and position in the communication of attitude and status relationships. *Psychological Bulletin*, 1969, 71, 359–372. (b)

260. Mehrabian, A. Some referents and measures of nonverbal behavior. *Behavior Research Methods and Instrumentation*, 1969, 1, 203–207. (c)

261. Mehrabian, A. A semantic space for nonverbal behavior. *Journal of Consulting and Clinical Psychology*, 1970, 35, 248–257. (a)

262. Mehrabian, A. Measures of vocabulary and grammatical skills for children up to age six. *Developmental Psychology*, 1970, 2, 439–446. (b)

263. Mehrabian, A. Some determinants of affiliation and conformity. *Psychological Reports*, 1970, 27, 19–29. (c)

264. Mehrabian, A. *Tactics of social influence*. Englewood Cliffs, New Jersey: Prentice-Hall, 1970. (d)

265. Mehrabian, A. The development and validation of measures of affiliative tendency and sensitivity to rejection. *Educational and Psychological Measurement*, 1970, 30, 417–428. (e)

266. Mehrabian, A. When are feelings communicated inconsistently? *Journal of Experimental Research in Personality*, 1970, 4, 198–212. (f)

267. Mehrabian, A. Nonverbal betrayal of feelings. *Journal of Experimental Research in Personality*, 1971, 5, 64–73. (a)

268. Mehrabian, A. Verbal and nonverbal interaction of strangers in a waiting situation. *Journal of Experimental Research in Personality*, 1971, *5*, 127–138. (*b*)

269. Mehrabian, A. *Nonverbal communication*. Chicago, Illinois: Aldine-Atherton, 1972. (*a*)

270. Mehrabian, A. Nonverbal communication. In J.K. Cole (Ed.), *Nebraska symposium on motivation, 1971* (Vol. 19). Lincoln: University of Nebraska Press, 1972. (*b*)

271. Mehrabian, A. Affiliation as a function of attitude discrepancy with another and arousal-seeking tendency. *Journal of Personality*, 1975, *43*, 582–590.

272. Mehrabian, A. *Manual for the questionnaire measure of stimulus screening and arousability*. Los Angeles: UCLA, 1976. (*a*)

273. Mehrabian, A. *Public places and private spaces: The psychology of work, play, and living environments*. New York: Basic Books, 1976. (*b*)

274. Mehrabian, A. Questionnaire measures of affiliative tendency and sensitivity to rejection. *Psychological Reports*, 1976, *38*, 199–209. (*c*)

275. Mehrabian, A. The three dimensions of emotional reaction. *Psychology Today*, 1976, *10* (3), 57–61. (*d*)

276. Mehrabian, A. A questionnaire measure of individual differences in stimulus screening and associated differences in arousability. *Environmental Psychology and Nonverbal Behavior*, 1977, *1*, 89–103. (*a*)

277. Mehrabian, A. Individual differences in stimulus screening and arousability. *Journal of Personality*, 1977, *45*, 237–250. (*b*)

278. Mehrabian, A. Characteristic individual reactions to preferred and unpreferred environments. *Journal of Personality*, 1978, *46*, 717–731. (*a*)

279. Mehrabian, A. Measures of individual differences in temperament. *Educational and Psychological Measurement*, 1978, *38*, 1105–1117. (*b*)

280. Mehrabian, A. *Basic dimensions for a general psychological theory: Implications for personality, social, environmental, and developmental studies*. Cambridge, Massachusetts: Oelgeschlager, Gunn & Hain, 1980.

281. Mehrabian, A., and Bank. L. A questionnaire measure of individual differences in achieving tendency. *Educational and Psychological Measurement*, 1978, *38*, 475–478.

282. Mehrabian, A., and Diamond, S.G. Seating arrangement and conversation. *Sociometry*, 1971, *34*, 281–289. (*a*)

283. Mehrabian, A., and Diamond, S.G. The effects of furniture arrangement, props, and personality on social interaction. *Journal of Personality and Social Psychology*, 1971, *20*, 18–30. (*b*)

284. Mehrabian, A., and Epstein, N. A measure of emotional empathy. *Journal of Personality*, 1972, *40*, 525–543.

285. Mehrabian, A., and Falender, C.A. A questionnaire measure of indi-

vidual differences in child stimulus screening. *Educational and Psychological Measurement*, 1978, *38*, 1119–1127.

286. Mehrabian, A., and Ferris, S.R. Inference of attitudes from nonverbal communication in two channels. *Journal of Consulting Psychology*, 1967, *31*, 248–252.

287. Mehrabian, A., and Friar, J.T. Encoding of attitude by a seated communicator via posture and position cues. *Journal of Consulting and Clinical Psychology*, 1969, *33*, 330–336.

288. Mehrabian, A., and Hines, M. A questionnaire measure of individual differences in dominance-submissiveness. *Educational and Psychological Measurement*, 1978, *38*, 479–484.

289. Mehrabian, A., and Ksionzky, S. Models for affiliative and conformity behavior. *Psychological Bulletin*, 1970, *74*, 110–126.

290. Mehrabian, A., and Ksionzky, S. Anticipated compatibility as a function of attitude or status similarity. *Journal of Personality*, 1971, *39*, 225–241. (*a*)

291. Mehrabian, A., and Ksionzky, S. Factors of interpersonal behavior and judgment in social groups. *Psychological Reports*, 1971, *28*, 483–492. (*b*)

292. Mehrabian, A., and Ksionzky, S. Categories of social behavior. *Comparative Group Studies*, 1972, *3*, 425–436. (*a*)

293. Mehrabian, A., and Ksionzky, S. Some determiners of social interaction. *Sociometry*, 1972, *35*, 588–609. (*b*)

294. Mehrabian, A., and Ksionzky, S. *A theory of affiliation*. Lexington, Massachusetts: D.C. Heath, 1974.

295. Mehrabian, A., and O'Reilly, E. Analysis of personality measures in terms of basic dimensions of temperament. *Journal of Personality and Social Psychology*, 1980, *38*, 492–503.

296. Mehrabian, A., and Reed, H. Some determiners of communication accuracy. *Psychological Bulletin*, 1968, *70*, 365–381.

297. Mehrabian, A., and Ross, M. Quality of life change and individual differences in stimulus screening in relation to incidence of illness. *Psychological Reports*, 1977, *41*, 267–278.

298. Mehrabian, A., and Ross, M. Illnesses, accidents, and alcohol use as functions of the arousing quality and pleasantness of life changes. *Psychological Reports*, 1979, *45*, 31–43.

299. Mehrabian, A., and Russell, J.A. *An approach to environmental psychology*. Cambridge, Massachusetts: M.I.T. Press, 1974. (*a*)

300. Mehrabian, A., and Russell, J.A. A verbal measure of information rate for studies in environmental psychology. *Environment and Behavior*, 1974, *6*, 233–252. (*b*)

301. Mehrabian, A., and Russell, J.A. The basic emotional impact of environments. *Perceptual and Motor Skills*, 1974, *38*, 283–301. (*c*)

302. Mehrabian, A., and Russell, J.A. Environmental effects on affiliation among strangers. *Humanitas*, 1975, *11*, 219–230.

303. Mehrabian, A., and West, S. Emotional impact of a task and its setting on work performance of screeners and nonscreeners. *Perceptual and Motor Skills*, 1977, *45*, 895–909.

304. Mehrabian, A., and Wiener, M. Non-immediacy between communicator and object of communication in a verbal message: Application to the inference of attitudes. *Journal of Consulting Psychology*, 1966, *30*, 420–425.

305. Mehrabian, A., and Wiener, M. Decoding of inconsistent communications. *Journal of Personality and Social Psychology*, 1967, *6*, 109–114.

306. Mehrabian, A., and Williams, M. Nonverbal concomitants of perceived and intended persuasiveness. *Journal of Personality and Social Psychology*, 1969, *13*, 37–58.

307. Mehrabian, A., and Williams, M. Piagetian measures of cognitive development for children up to age two. *Journal of Psycholinguistic Research*, 1971, *1*, 113–126.

308. Meisels, M., and Canter, F.M. Personal space and personality characteristics: A non-confirmation. *Psychological Reports*, 1970, *27*, 287–290.

309. Mendels, J. *The psychobiology of depression*. New York: Spectrum, 1975.

310. Middlemist, R.D., Knowles, E.S., and Matter, C.F. Personal space invasions in the lavatory: Suggestive evidence for arousal. *Journal of Personality and Social Psychology*, 1976, *33*, 541–546.

311. Miller, N.E. Some implications of modern behavior therapy for personality change and psychotherapy. In P. Worchel and D. Byrne (Eds.), *Personality change*. New York: Wiley, 1964.

312. Miller, N., Maruyama, G., Beaber, R.J., and Valone, K. Speed of speech and persuasion. *Journal of Personality and Social Psychology*, 1976, *34*, 615–624.

313. Minter, L.V. The effect of territory on dominance. Unpublished doctoral dissertation, UCLA, 1974.

314. Mita, T.H., Dermer, M., and Knight, J. Reversed facial images and the mere-exposure hypothesis. *Journal of Personality and Social Psychology*, 1977, *35*, 597–601.

315. Morris, D. *Intimate behavior*. New York: Random House, 1971.

316. Morsbach, H. Aspects of nonverbal communication in Japan. *Journal of Nervous and Mental Disease*, 1973, *157*, 262–277.

317. Moynihan, C., and Mehrabian, A. Measures of language skills for two- to seven-year-old children. *Genetic Psychology Monographs*, 1978, *98*, 3–49.

318. Moynihan, C., and Mehrabian, A. *Manual for the Child Language Ability Measures*. Los Angeles: UCLA, 1979.

319. Natale, M. Convergence of mean vocal intensity in dyadic communication as a function of social desirability. *Journal of Personality and Social Psychology*, 1975, *32*, 790–804.

320. Natale, M., Entin, E., and Jaffe, J. Vocal interruptions in dyadic communication as a function of speech and social anxiety. *Journal of Personality and Social Psychology*, 1979, *37*, 865–878.

321. Newcomb, T.M. *The acquaintance process.* New York: Holt, Rinehart and Winston, 1961.

322. Nichols, K.A., and Champness, B.G. Eye gaze and the GSR. *Journal of Experimental Social Psychology*, 1971, *7*, 623–626.

323. Osgood, C.E. The cross-cultural generality of visual-verbal synesthetic tendencies. *Behavioral Science*, 1960, *5*, 146–169.

324. Osgood, C.E. Dimensionality of the semantic space for communication via facial expressions. *Scandinavian Journal of Psychology*, 1966, *7*, 1–30.

325. Osgood, C.E., May, W.H., and Miron, M.S. *Cross-cultural universals of affective meaning.* Urbana: University of Illinois Press, 1975.

326. Osgood, C.E., Suci, G.J., and Tannenbaum, P.H. *The measurement of meaning.* Urbana: University of Illinois Press, 1957.

327. Osmond, H. Function as the basis of psychiatric ward design. *Mental Hospitals*, 1957, *8*, 23–32.

328. Osmond, H. The relationship between architect and psychiatrist. In C. Goshen (Ed.), *Psychiatric architecture.* Washington: American Psychiatric Association, 1959.

329. Packwood, W.T. Loudness as a variable in persuasion. *Journal of Counseling Psychology*, 1974, *21*, 1–2.

330. Patterson, M.L. Compensation in nonverbal immediacy behaviors: A review. *Sociometry*, 1973, *36*, 237–252.

331. Patterson, M.L., and Sechrest, L.B. Interpersonal distance and impression formation. *Journal of Personality*, 1970, *38*, 161–166.

332. Pattison, J.E. Effects of touch on self-exploration and the therapeutic relationship. *Journal of Consulting and Clinical Psychology*, 1973, *40*, 170–175.

333. Pellegrini, R.J., and Empey, J. Interpersonal spatial orientation in dyads. *Journal of Psychology*, 1970, *76*, 67–70.

334. Pellegrini, R.J., Hicks, R.A., and Gordon, L. The effects of approval-seeking induction on eye-contact in dyads. *British Journal of Social and Clinical Psychology*, 1970, *9*, 373–374.

335. Pepper, S.C. *World hypotheses.* Berkeley: University of California Press, 1942.

336. Piaget, J. *Psychology of intelligence.* Patterson, New Jersey: Littlefield, Adams, 1960.

337. Post, E. *Etiquette: The blue book of social usage.* New York: Funk and Wagnalls, 1960.

338. Proshansky, H.M., Ittelson, W.H., and Rivlin, L.G. (Eds.). *Environmental psychology.* New York: Holt, Rinehart and Winston, 1970.

339. Rappaport, B.S. Carnal knowledge: What the wisdom of the body has to offer psychotherapy. *Journal of Humanistic Psychology*, 1975, *15*, 49–70.

340. Razran, G.H.S. Conditioning away social bias by the luncheon technique. *Psychological Bulletin*, 1938, *35*, 693.

341. Razran, G.H.S. Conditional response changes in rating and appraising sociopolitical slogans. *Psychological Bulletin*, 1940, *37*, 481.

342. Reich, W. *Character analysis*. Translated by T.P. Wolfe. New York: Orgone Institute Press, 1945.

343. Riesman, D. *The lonely crowd*. New Haven: Yale University Press, 1950.

344. Riskin, J., and Faunce, E.E. An evaluative review of family interaction research. *Family Process*, 1972, *11*(4), 365–455.

345. Roger, D.B., and Schalekamp, E.E. Body-buffer zone and violence: A cross-cultural study. *The Journal of Social Psychology*, 1976, *98*, 153–158.

346. Rogers, C.R. A theory of therapy, personality, and interpersonal relationships, as developed in the client-centered framework. In S. Koch (Ed.), *Psychology: A study of a science* (Vol. 3). New York: McGraw-Hill, 1959.

347. Rosenfeld, H.M. Approval-seeking and approval-inducing functions of verbal and nonverbal responses in the dyad. *Journal of Personality and Social Psychology*, 1966, *4*, 597–605. (*a*)

348. Rosenfeld, H.M. Instrumental affiliative functions of facial and gestural expressions. *Journal of Personality and Social Psychology*, 1966, *4*, 65–72. (*b*)

349. Rosenfeld, H.M. The experimental analysis of interpersonal influence processes. *Journal of Communication*, 1972, *22*, 424–442.

350. Rosenfeld, H.M. Conversational control functions of nonverbal behavior. In A. Siegman and S. Feldstein (Eds.), *Nonverbal behavior and communication*. Hillsdale, N.J.: Lawrence Erlbaum, 1979.

351. Rubenstein, L., and Cameron, D.E. Electronic analysis of nonverbal communication. *Comprehensive Psychiatry*, 1968, *9*, 200–208.

352. Rubin, Z. Measurement of romantic love. *Journal of Personality and Social Psychology*, 1970, *16*, 265–273.

353. Ruesch, J., and Kees, W. *Nonverbal communication: Notes on the visual perception of human relations* (2d ed.). Berkeley: University of California Press, 1972.

354. Russell, J.A. Evidence of convergent validity on the dimensions of affect. *Journal of Personality and Social Psychology*, 1978, *36*, 1152–1168.

355. Russell, J.A., and Mehrabian, A. Distinguishing anger and anxiety in terms of emotional response factors. *Journal of Consulting and Clinical Psychology*, 1974, *42*, 79–83.

356. Russell, J.A., and Mehrabian, A. Task, setting, and personality variables affecting the desire to work. *Journal of Applied Psychology*, 1975, *60*, 518–520.

357. Russell, J.A., and Mehrabian, A. Some behavioral effects of the physical environment. In S. Wapner, S. Cohen, and B. Kaplan (Eds.), *Experiencing the environment*. New York: Plenum, 1976.

358. Russell, J.A., and Mehrabian, A. Evidence for a three-factor theory of emotions. *Journal of Research in Personality*, 1977, *11*, 273–294.

359. Russell, J.A., and Mehrabian, A. Approach-avoidance and affiliation as functions of the emotion-eliciting quality of an environment. *Environment and Behavior*, 1978, *10*, 355–387. (*a*)

360. Russell, J.A., and Mehrabian, A. Environmental, task, and temperamental effects on work performance. *Humanitas*, 1978, *14*, 75–95. (*b*)

361. Russo, N.F. Eye contact, interpersonal distance, and the equilibrium theory. *Journal of Personality and Social Psychology*, 1975, *31*, 497–502.

362. Sainsbury, P. Gestural movement during psychiatric interview. *Psychosomatic Medicine*, 1955, *17*, 458–469.

363. Schachter, S. *The psychology of affiliation*. Stanford, California: Stanford University Press, 1959.

364. Schaller, G.B. *The mountain gorilla: Ecology and behavior*. Chicago: University of Chicago Press, 1963.

365. Scheflen, A.E. The significance of posture in communication systems. *Psychiatry*, 1964, *27*, 316–331.

366. Scheflen, A.E. *Stream and structure of communicational behavior: Context analysis of a psychotherapy session*. Behavioral studies monograph No. 1. Philadelphia: Eastern Pennsylvania Psychiatric Institute, 1965.

367. Scheflen, A.E. Systems and psychosomatics. *Psychosomatic Medicine*, 1966, *28*, 297–304.

368. Scheflen, A.E. *How behavior means*. Garden City, N.Y.: Anchor, 1974.

369. Scherer, K.R. Acoustic concomitants of emotional dimensions: Judging affect from synthesized tone sequences. In S. Weitz (Ed.), *Nonverbal communication*. New York: Oxford University Press, 1974.

370. Scherer, K.R., London, H., and Wolf, J.J. The voice of confidence: Paralinguistic cues and audience evaluation. *Journal of Research in Personality*, 1973, *7*, 31–44.

371. Schiffenbauer, A., and Schiavo, R.S. Physical distance and attraction: An intensification effect. *Journal of Experimental Social Psychology*, 1976, *12*, 274–282.

372. Schlosberg, H. Three dimensions of emotion. *Psychological Review*, 1954, *61*, 81–88.

373. Schuham, A. The double-bind hypothesis a decade later. *Psychological Bulletin*, 1967, *68*, 409–416.

374. Seaton, R. (Ed.). *Miscellaneous undergraduate research on spatial behavior: A classified and annotated listing*. Berkeley: Department of Architecture, University of California, Berkeley, 1968.

375. Selye, H. *The stress of life.* New York: McGraw-Hill, 1956.

376. Sherif, M., Harvey, O.J., White, B.J., Hood, W.R., and Sherif, C.W. *Intergroup conflict and cooperation: The robbers' cave experiment.* Norman, Oklahoma: University Book Exchange, 1961.

377. Siegman, A.W., and Pope, B. (Eds.). *Studies in dyadic communication.* New York: Pergamon, 1972.

378. Silveira, J. Thoughts on the politics of touch. *Women's Press,* 1972, *1,* 13.

379. Silverthorne, C., Mickelwright, J., O'Donnell, M., and Gibson, R. Attribution of personal characteristics as a function of touch on initial contact. Paper presented at the meeting of the Western Psychological Association, Sacramento, 1975.

380. Simonds, P.E. The bonnet macaque in South India. In I. DeVore (Ed.), *Primate social behavior.* New York: Holt, Rinehart and Winston, 1965.

381. Snider, J.G., and Osgood, C.E. (Eds.). *Semantic differential technique.* Chicago: Aldine, 1969.

382. Solar, D., and Mehrabian, A. Impressions based on contradictory information as a function of affiliative tendency and cognitive style. *Journal of Experimental Research in Personality,* 1973, *6,* 339–346.

383. Sommer, R. Small group ecology. *Psychological Bulletin,* 1967, *67,* 145–151.

384. Sommer, R. *Personal space.* Englewood Cliffs, New Jersey: Prentice-Hall, 1969.

385. Sorrentino, R.M., and Boutillier, R.G. The effect of quantity and quality of verbal interaction on ratings of leadership ability. *Journal of Experimental Research in Personality,* 1975, *11,* 403–411.

386. Stang, D.J. Effect of interaction rate on ratings of leadership and liking. *Journal of Personality and Social Psychology,* 1973, *27,* 405–408.

387. Starkweather, J.A. Variations in vocal behavior. In D.M. Rioch (Ed.), *Disorders of communication.* Proceedings of ARNMD (Vol. 42). Baltimore: Williams & Wilkins, 1964.

388. Stephan, F.F. The relative rate of communication between members of small groups. *American Sociological Review,* 1952, *17,* 482–486.

389. Storms, M.D., and Thomas, G.C. Reactions to physical closeness. *Journal of Personality and Social Psychology,* 1977, *35,* 412–418.

390. Streeter, L.A., Krauss, R.M., Geller, V., Olson, C., and Apple, W. Pitch changes during attempted deception. *Journal of Personality and Social Psychology,* 1977, *35,* 345–350.

391. Strodtbeck, F.L., and Hook, L.H. The social dimensions of a twelve-man jury table. *Sociometry,* 1961, *24,* 397–415.

392. Strongman, K.T., and Champness, B.G. Dominance hierarchies and conflict in eye contact. *Acta Psychologica,* 1968, *28,* 376–386.

393. Stuart, R.B. Behavioral contracting within the families of delinquents.

Journal of Behavior Therapy and Experimental Psychiatry, 1971, *2,* 1–11.

394. Sundstrom, E., and Altman, I. Field study of territorial behavior and dominance. *Journal of Personality and Social Psychology,* 1974, *30,* 115–124.

395. Sundstrom, E., and Altman, I. Personal space and interpersonal relationships: Research review and theoretical model. *Human Ecology,* 1976, *4,* 47–67.

396. Taylor, D.A. and Altman, I. Intimacy-scaled stimuli for use in studies of interpersonal relations. *Psychological Reports,* 1966, *19,* 729–730.

397. Taylor, H.M. American and Japanese nonverbal communication. In J.V. Neustupny (Ed.), *Papers in Japanese Linguistics 3.* Melbourne: Monash University, 1974.

398. Tedesco, J.F., and Fromme, D.K. Cooperation, competition, and personal space. *Sociometry,* 1974, *37,* 116–121.

399. Thayer, S. The effect of interpersonal looking duration on dominace judgments. *Journal of Social Psychology,* 1969, *79,* 285–286.

400. Thayer, S., and Alban, L. A field experiment on the effect of political and cultural factors on the use of personal space. *Journal of Social Psychology,* 1972, *88,* 267–272.

401. Thayer, S., and Schiff, W. Observer judgment of social interactions: Eye contact and relationship inferences. *Journal of Personality and Social Psychology,* 1974, *30,* 110–114.

402. Tipton, R.M., Bailey, K.S., and Obenchain, J.P. Invasions of males' personal space by feminists and non-feminists. *Psychological Reports,* 1975, *37,* 99–102.

403. Tolor, A. Psychological distance in disturbed and normal children. *Psychological Reports,* 1968, *23,* 695–701.

404. Tomkins, S.S. *Affect, imagery, consciousness, Vol. 1: The positive affects.* New York: Springer, 1962.

405. Tomkins, S.S. *Affect, imagery, consciousness, Vol. 2: The negative affects.* New York: Springer, 1963.

406. Tomkins, S.S. Affect as the primary motivational system. In M.B. Arnold (Ed.), *Feelings and emotions.* New York: Academic Press, 1970.

407. Tomkins, S.S., and McCarter, R. What and where are the primary affects? Some evidence for a theory. *Perceptual and Motor Skills,* 1964, *18,* 119–158.

408. Truax, C.B. Reinforcement and nonreinforcement in Rogerian psychotherapy. *Journal of Abnormal Psychology,* 1966, *71,* 1–9.

409. Ullmann, L.P., and Krasner, L. *A psychological approach to abnormal behavior.* Englewood Cliffs, New Jersey: Prentice-Hall, 1969.

410. Van der Ryn, S., and Silverstein, M. *Dorms at Berkeley: An environmental analysis.* Berkeley: Center for Planning and Development Research, 1967.

411. Vine, I. The role of facial-visual signalling in early social development. In I. Vine and M. von Cranach (Eds.), *Social communication and movement*. New York: Academic Press, 1973.

412. Walker, J.W., and Borden, R.J. Sex, status, and the invasion of shared space. *Representative Research in Social Psychology*, 1976, 7, 28–34.

413. Watson, O.M., and Graves, T.D. Quantitative research in proxemic behavior. *American Anthropologist*, 1966, 68, 971–985.

414. Watzlawick, P., Beavin, J.H., and Jackson, D.D. *Pragmatics of human communication: A study of interactional patterns, pathologies, and paradoxes*. New York: Norton, 1967.

415. Weakland, J.H. The "double bind" hypothesis of schizophrenia and three-party interaction. In D.D. Jackson (Ed.), *The etiology of schizophrenia*. New York: Basic Books, 1961.

416. Webb, J.T. Interview synchrony: An investigation of two speech rate measures in an automated standardized interview. In A.W. Siegman and B. Pope (Eds.), *Studies in dyadic communication: Proceedings of a research conference on the interview*. New York: Pergamon, 1970.

417. Weinstein, L. Social schemata of emotionally disturbed boys. *Journal of Abnormal Psychology*, 1965, 70, 457–461.

418. Weinstein. L. Social experience and social schemata. *Journal of Personality and Social Psychology*, 1967, 6, 429–434.

419. Weiss, R.L., Hops, H., and Patterson, G.R. A framework for conceptualizing marital conflict: A technology for altering it, some data for evaluating it. In L.A. Hamerlynch, I.C. Handy, and E.J. Mash (Eds.), *Behavior change: The fourth Banff conference on behavior modification*. Champaign, Illinois: Research Press, 1973.

420. Werner, H., and Kaplan, B. *Symbol formation*. New York: Wiley, 1963.

421. Whitcher, S.J., and Fisher, J.D. Multidimensional reaction to therapeutic touch in a hospital setting. *Journal of Personality and Social Psychology*, 1979, 37, 87–96.

422. White, G.T. The mating game: Nonverbal interpersonal communication between dating and engaged college couples. Paper presented at the meeting of the Western Psychological Association, Sacramento, 1975.

423. White, R.W. Motivation reconsidered: The concept of competence. *Psychological Review*, 1959, 66, 297–333.

424. Wicker, A.W. Undermanning theory and research: Implications for the study of psychological and behavioral effects of excess populations. *Representative Research in Social Psychology*, 1973, 4, 185–206.

425. Wiener, M., and Mehrabian, A. *Language within language: Immediacy, a channel in verbal communication*. New York: Appleton-Century-Crofts, 1968.

426. Wiens, A.N., Saslow, G., and Matarazzo, J.D. Speech interruption behavior during interviews. *Psychotherapy: Theory, Research, and Practice*, 1966, 3, 153–158.

427. Willerman, B., and Swanson, L. An ecological determinant of differential amounts of sociometric choices within college sororities. *Sociometry*, 1952, *15*, 326–329.

428. Williams, E. Experimental comparisons of face-to-face and mediated communication: A review. *Psychological Bulletin*, 1977, *84*, 963–976.

429. Williams, F., and Sundene, B. Dimensions of recognition: Visual vs. vocal expression of emotion. *Audio Visual Communications Review*, 1965, *13*, 44–52.

430. Willis, F.N., Jr. Initial speaking distance as a function of the speakers' relationship. *Psychonomic Science*, 1966, *5*, 221–222.

431. Willis, F.N., Jr., and Hofmann, G. Development of tactile patterns in relation to age, sex, and race. *Developmental Psychology*, 1975, *11*, 866.

432. Wilner, D.M., Walkley, R.P., and Cook, S.W. *Human relations in interracial housing*. Minneapolis, Minnesota: University of Minnesota Press, 1955.

433. Winnick, C., and Holt, H. Seating position as nonverbal communication in group analysis. *Psychiatry*, 1961, *24*, 171–182.

434. Wohlwill, J.F. The emerging discipline of environmental psychology. *American Psychologist*, 1970, *25*, 303–312.

435. Wolpe, J. *The practice of behavior therapy*. New York: Pergamon, 1969.

436. Works. E. The prejudice-interaction hypothesis from the point of view of the Negro minority group. *American Journal of Sociology*, 1961, *67*, 47–52.

437. Wyler, A.R., Masuda, M., and Holmes, T. Magnitude of life events and seriousness of illness. *Psychosomatic Medicine*, 1971, *33*, 115–122.

438. Zahn, L.G. Cognitive integration of verbal and vocal information in spoken sentences. *Journal of Experimental Social Psychology*, 1973, *9*, 320–334.

439. Zahn, L.G. Verbal-vocal integration as a function of sex and methodology. *Journal of Research in Personality*, 1975, *9*, 226–239.

440. Zaidel, S.F., and Mehrabian, A. The ability to communicate and infer positive and negative attitudes facially and vocally. *Journal of Experimental Research in Personality*, 1969, *3*, 233–241.

441. Zajonc, R.B. Attitudinal effects of mere exposure. *Journal of Personality and Social Psychology Monograph Supplement*, 1968, *9*, 1–27.

442. Zander, A., and Havelin, A. Social comparison and interpersonal attraction. *Human Relations*, 1960, *13*, 21–32.

Index